Ghostly Figures

Contemporary North American Poetry Series

Series Editors | Alan Golding | Lynn Keller | Adalaide Morris

Ghostly Figures

MEMORY AND BELATEDNESS

IN POSTWAR AMERICAN POETRY

Ann Keniston

University of Iowa Press | Iowa City

University of Iowa Press, Iowa City 52242
www.uiowapress.org
Printed in the United States of America

Design by April Leidig

The University of Iowa Press is a member of Green Press
Initiative and is committed to preserving natural resources.

Printed on acid-free paper

Library of Congress Cataloging-in-Publication Data
Keniston, Ann, 1961–
Ghostly figures : memory and belatedness in postwar
American poetry / Ann Keniston.
pages   cm.— (Contemporary North American poetry series)
Includes bibliographical references and index.
ISBN 978-1-60938-353-4 (pbk), ISBN 978-1-60938-354-1 (ebk)
1. American poetry—20th century—History and criticism.
2. Memory in literature. 3. Literature and history—United
States—History—20th century. I. Title.
PS323.5.K46   2015
811'.509—dc23   2015005556

For Eric

Contents

Acknowledgments

The support, direct and indirect, of many colleagues and friends helped me write and complete this book. I am especially grateful to Bonnie Costello, Jeffrey Gray, and Jeanne Follansbee for their feedback on several chapters and to the anonymous readers of this book in manuscript form, whose insights and suggestions made it immeasurably better, as well as to Alan Golding, Dee Morris, and (especially) Lynn Keller for their faith in this project. Thanks too to the editorial and production team at the University of Iowa Press, including Elisabeth Chretien, Susan Hill-Newton, and my meticulous and generous copy editor, Rebecca Marsh. I am also grateful to the University of Nevada, Reno for a junior faculty research grant and to its College of Liberal Arts Scholarly and Creative Activities Grant Program and dean's office for several grants allowing travel to archives and conferences, as well as other support. This project also benefited from support from the UNR English department's summer research assistantship program and more specifically from the help of research assistants Brian Baaki and Mark Farnsworth for general research help; Becky Kogos and S. Laurel Griffiths for painstaking work on citations, notes, proofreading, and permissions; Jessica Rasmussen Bailey for much of the above plus invaluable help with permissions; and Lee Olsen for indexing. I am grateful to my graduate and undergraduate students at UNR for letting me try out my readings of several of these texts on them and for letting me to talk so much about memory; their commentary and ideas have deepened my own thinking. Thanks also to the audiences at the various conferences where I presented versions of these chapters. The encouragement with which my early ideas were received encouraged me to stick with and elaborate them. I am grateful too to Jo Gill and Anita Helle for publishing early versions of these chapters (respectively, a discussion of

Rich's *Dark Fields* of which only a few pages have survived intact in Gill's edited collection *Modern Confessional Writing* and a discussion of Plath's Holocaust poems in Helle's *The Unraveling Archive: Essays on Sylvia Plath*) and to Michael Davidson for publishing a version of the introduction. Thanks too to Routledge, University of Michigan Press, and *Contemporary Literature* for granting me permission to reprint these chapters.

Many friends and family members offered support, encouragement, and diversion of various kinds over the many years I was working on this book. I am especially grateful to Jen Hill and Jeanne Follansbee (again) for helping me work through my ideas and to both of them, plus many other friends, for diverting me when I needed to do something else. Thanks too to my colleagues in the UNR English department, especially department chairs Stacy Burton and Eric Rasmussen.

I am deeply grateful to the poets about whose work I write here. Their poems have inspired and consoled me over many years. I very much hope that the ideas and readings in this book express, if indirectly, this gratitude.

This book is in many ways a response to the aging of my parents and to my mother's death in 2006. I remain deeply grateful to them for teaching me to love literature and for supporting me in my wish to live a life in which I can read and talk about poetry every day. Thanks too to Suzanne Berger Keniston and to Brenda Steinberg for their support and love.

My husband, Eric Novak, and sons, Paul and Jeremy, made many sacrifices while I was writing and completing this book. I am especially grateful to Eric, who let me go off alone to write (and rewrite), who picked up the slack while I was away, who listened to my ideas when I was stuck, and who worked to adapt as our lives and marriage changed. This book is for him, in gratitude.

Permissions

Ghostly Figures

"Not needed except as meaning"

Memory and Belatedness in Postwar American Poetry

All the bells say: too late.
—John Berryman, "Dream Song 29"

We wanted to get
close, very close. But what
is the way in again? And is it

too late?
—Jorie Graham, "Act III, Sc. 2"

This was our ambition: to be small and clear and free.
Alas, the summer's energy wanes quickly,
A moment and it is gone. And no longer
May we make the necessary arrangements, simple as they are.
—John Ashbery, "Soonest Mended"

To adapt Berryman's assertion, the condition of being too late is everywhere in post–World War II American poetry. As my epigraphs, which I
have drawn from chronologically and formally diverse postwar American
poems, indicate, lateness is not simply a matter of temporal delay. Rather, as
all three of these excerpts reveal, postwar poems often depict speakers who
remember the past only partially, in ways that reveal that memory is itself

obstructed. Postwar poems often refer to events that are not represented directly. And they do not merely describe the condition of lateness: they also enact it through distortions of chronology, boundary, and syntax.

Such tendencies are evident in these passages, all three of which bind the condition of lateness to difficulties in verifying what has occurred. "Dream Song 29" ("There sat down, once") describes "a thing on Henry's heart / só heavy" but refuses to define or corroborate this thing, ending by revealing the inaccuracy of Henry's conviction that he has committed murder. Although lateness for Henry is affirmed by what "the bells say," it is unclear whether this saying preexists (and causes) Henry's sense of lateness or simply projects his existing feelings outward. Graham's "Act III, Sc. 2" (*Region* 66) identifies lateness only within a question and in a context that foregrounds the spatial over the temporal (the wish to "get / close" is obstructed; the speaker seeks "the way in again," implying similar earlier attempts). And while "Soonest Mended" does not name lateness, the poem in many ways typifies Ashbery's career-long concern with this topic, as when the passage slips from the retrospective "This was our ambition" to the present-tense "the summer's energy wanes quickly" to the negative subjunctive of "no longer / May we make the necessary arrangements."

All three excerpts also link the condition of lateness to the poem's construction, emphasizing performance, projection, and deflection. By imbuing the inanimate bells with the capacity for human speech, Berryman implies that they express Henry's thoughts (and by implication the poet's). Graham's failure to identify either her speaker or her addressee involves a related confusion of agency, as the poem's title suggests: the interplay of spatial and temporal distance chronicled by the excerpt seems occasioned by the performance of a theatrical play, and belatedness by implication seems devised for an audience. A similar artificiality is implied by Ashbery's use of an undefined and shifting "we," which is at once pretentious and intimate. To define one's "ambition" is possible, Ashbery implies, only in relation to this collective, for whom the poem's performance is at least partly anachronistic, as is evident in expressions like "Alas."

This book contends that the rhetoric of belatedness evident in the passages above, along with the way it is bound to questions of poetic making, is emblematic; belatedness is a central, if seldom noticed, concern in post-war American poetry. Postwar poems often indicate that they are too late by chronicling impossible and distorted chronologies, refusing closure or resolution, and insisting on repetition or prolepsis, the last of which creates artificial situations of remembering. Such tendencies reveal the difficulty of remembering, and so it is perhaps unsurprising that many postwar poems also manifest their belatedness by manipulating, at times violently, their own formal structures, employing tropes and figures in ways that inter-rogate equivalence, proximity, and intimacy.[1] In the process, they reveal belatedness to be not only a temporal condition but a rhetorical strategy.

The term *belatedness* conflates a physical condition characterized by its relation to the present with a psychological state that presupposes an act of recollection. According to the *OED*, belatedness involves being "detained beyond the usual time," a particular condition that assumes a bodily state of delay defined in relation to a norm ("the usual time"). But it also refers to being "out of date, behind date," a more general, even existential, and interior condition, which requires that the present state be compared to an earlier, remembered one. Psychoanalytic theory, to which the concept of belatedness is central, also defines the term as connecting an actual, lived experience to something more abstract; the term often describes the physical enactment of a past trauma, which reveals the trauma's psycho-logical persistence. But rather than laying the original trauma to rest, this reenactment confirms that the original event can be expressed only in a dis-guised form that both repeats and further obscures what actually occurred. Here, too, belatedness links immediate with existential conditions of delay and in the process implies a connection similar to the one I will explore throughout this book. The term, I will argue, conflates the literal condition of belatedness—the lived experience of chronological disruption, often evi-dent in scenes of disturbed or partial memory and of arriving too late to in-tervene or understand—with what I will call figurative belatedness, or the manifestations of this condition through linguistic and symbolic structures, especially tropes and figures.

Poems from the outset foreground similar tensions; they often originate in, respond to, and incorporate lived, "real" sensations, emotions, and ideas but remain, as linguistic constructions, unable fully to convey this subject matter. In fact, the traces of literal belatedness in poems—evident, for example, in descriptions of externally verifiable but temporally remote recalled events, chronological delays, descriptions of remembering past events, and the like—are inseparable from the language that expresses them. The opposition between the literal and the figurative is essential both to poems and to how they are discussed, but at times the distinction also collapses: the literal cannot always be readily distinguished from the figurative, or one may be manifest through the other, as several critics have argued.[2]

This entanglement of the literal and the figurative is central to my reading of postwar belatedness. Like my epigraphs, the poems I discuss in the following chapters—by Sylvia Plath, Adrienne Rich, several poets writing about AIDS, Jorie Graham, and Susan Howe—repeatedly render the literal condition of belatedness figurative. They emphasize the temporal condition of coming after, often focusing on events familiar to their readers or, in the case of elegy, the universal situation of bereaved survival. They also impel this condition to stand—often metaphorically—for ideas and things that have nothing to do with time. But these poems also reveal the difficulty of the metaphoric equivalences on which they rely by employing tropes and figures that challenge analogy and connection. According to Mary Kinzie, tropes are always precarious in that they only partly excise the differences between the entities compared (155–56). For example, John Donne's analogy between compasses and separated lovers in "A Valediction: Forbidding Mourning" must deny the obvious differences between them, including the fact that compasses are made of metal and have sharp points, unlike lovers. (In bad similes and metaphors, Kinzie claims, the differences overwhelm the similarities [164].) Many of the tropes and figures in the postwar poems I consider reveal something of this precariousness. When metaphor and simile are deployed, for example, the analogies they create are often implausible or forced. In other cases, synecdoche, asyndeton, and metonymy emphasize relations that are even more partial or random.[3] And the figure of apostrophe repeatedly expresses not faith in but doubt about the possibility of being heard.

In another context, James Berger has claimed that "in literary studies, trauma theories . . . offer a poetics" ("There's No" 52).[4] Elements of trauma theory, he implies, can be separated from the actual situations to which they refer and used to define a mode of reading. My aim is similar: I wish to read belatedness in postwar poems not only as a thematics but as a poetics. As I have been implying, such a reading both relies and puts pressure on the notion of equivalence and in particular on the poem's figurative capacity to bind distinct entities. The condition of coming too late, that is, does not merely imply an analogy in which lateness stands for or crystallizes the poetic predicament. Nor does it necessarily imply a chronology, either one in which the lived experience of lateness precedes the poem's figurative representation of it or one in which the poem as a formal construct preexists its subject matter. Instead, the often impacted tropes and figures in postwar poems reveal their inextricability from the difficulties of belatedness. The lived condition of belatedness is by definition difficult to identify as such; it is also often hard to determine the particular events to which poems refer or to verify whether their authors actually experienced such events. But these difficulties are not (merely) problems in postwar poems. They also enable them, like all poems but perhaps more emphatically, to comment on their status *as* poems and thus by implication on the social and cultural function *of* poems.

In a sense, my claim here echoes the common critical precept that in poems, theme cannot be divorced from form. This precept has often been disregarded, especially in relation to "political" or "public" poems, which tend to be evaluated in terms of the accuracy with which they convey actual material or political events in ways that disregard their status as figurative constructs. But postwar poems concerning public events also exist as words and syntax and so expose the gap between fact and language. Poems on public topics in particular emphasize the problem of verisimilitude even when they disavow it. In the poems I examine, a tension often exists between the need for clarity and the impulse to obscure or even eradicate actual events. The effect is that these poems are neither wholly transparent (as an aesthetic often associated with "political" poetry sometimes assumes) nor wholly opaque (as in an aesthetic often associated with experimental poetry).[5] Nor, despite what several readers including Paul de Man have implied, is their figuration primarily self-referential.[6] Instead, the figures in postwar poems emphasize both the actual, physical world and its inaccessibility. But these poems also complicate the distinction between literal and figurative modes of belatedness by insisting on inexpressibility, often manifest both through linguistic disruption and through obscure (or deliberately obscured) subject matter.

The most detailed earlier discussion of belatedness in poetry remains Harold Bloom's 1970s consideration of its exclusively literary function. Bloom's famous and controversial central claim is that the "strong poet" engages in misreading or "misprision" of precursor works in order to define his own place in the canon. He does so through a series of strategies of venerating and also displacing the work of earlier poets that range from "swerv[ing]" away to "completion" and "breaking" (*Anxiety* 14–16).[7] Although Bloom's analysis focuses on the relations between poets of different eras, belatedness is for him, according to one gloss, inextricable from "an anxiety about being modern, specifically, about being too late to be able to say something that will renew grief" (Spargo, *Ethics* 136).

Bloom's analysis of belatedness does not consider the relation of poems to extraliterary modes of remembering. More recently, several readers, including R. Clifton Spargo, Walter Kalaidjian, and others, have begun to construct an alternative notion of belatedness, especially in postwar poetry.[8] Such readings often define belatedness in relation to Freud's notion of *Nachträglichkeit* or deferred action, a term also central to trauma theory, and stress the difficulties associated with representing distinctively late-twentieth-century subject matter, especially the Holocaust. In this context, several readers have attempted to define the relation between poetry's literal and figurative elements. In discussions that have informed my own thinking, focusing respectively on modern poetry and the poetry of Sylvia Plath, Walter Kalaidjian and Jacqueline Rose both note the recurrence of Freudian *Nachträglichkeit* in postwar poetry.[9] They also attempt to define the effect of extreme subject matter on poetic figuration and the reverse—the effect of poetic figuration on extreme subject matter. Strikingly, both do so in indirect and figurative language, perhaps reflecting the difficulty of clearly explaining this connection. Kalaidjian's claim is that "the formal resources of the poet's craft," including "its figurative language, . . . forge a salutary medium for staging [modern] traumatic histories in ways that resist . . . banal spectacle" (11). Here multiple and perhaps conflicting metaphors are implied: "formal resources" are created or "forged," a process that yields a "medium" or material on and with which the artist works as well as a "stage" on which he performs. Such images insist that craft does not passively contain the "traumatic histories" it conveys. Nor does poetic form alter these "histories." Rather, the aim of poetic craft seems to be to represent these histories in a way that protects them from being co-opted or reduced to mere "spectacle."

In describing the relation between traumatic subject matter and figuration, Rose uses different terms, calling the Holocaust "the event which puts under greatest pressure—or is most readily available to put under such pressure—the concept of linguistic figuration" (207). While Kalaidjian emphasizes the stability of the histories he describes, Rose's image of pressure foregrounds not the integrity of events but the transformational potential of "figuration" (a notion roughly analogous to Kalaidjian's "formal resources," which, he indicates, include "figurative language"): figuration, it seems, actually changes the Holocaust.

In many of the postwar poems I examine in this book, the tension between what poems say and the figuration through which they say it is implicit. But Robert Pinsky's "The Anniversary" (*Gulf* 19–21), commissioned for the first anniversary of the September 11, 2001, attacks on the Twin Towers and Pentagon, directly considers the relation of the literal to the figurative and of events to language. As such, the poem proposes a more explicit and perhaps more useful poetics of belatedness than do Kalaidjian and Rose. Pinsky's concern is not with how the figurative shapes or compresses the literal or how the literal affects the figurative. Instead, a situation identified as belated impels the figurative to emerge from the *failure* of the literal.

Pinsky asserts midway through the poem that the blood "donated" following the attacks was "not needed, except as meaning." The actual blood contributed by Americans on 9/11 and the days following, as Pinsky notes, was superfluous; it arrived too late to be used for transfusions because the victims were already dead, although those making the donations didn't know it at the time. This failure to be literally "needed" enables the blood to take on "meaning" or figurative significance. Pinsky never specifies what this meaning is; in fact, meaning seems to be an undefinable and unquantifiable effect of the temporal failures (to anticipate and respond in helpful ways) that "The Anniversary" associates with the attacks. Thus, the phrase "except as meaning" is appended onto and only partly qualifies the negation of "not needed." Pinsky's claim is to some extent cautionary: the poem warns its readers not to embrace meaning as intrinsic or true but instead to recognize that it can be affixed to events only after the fact. It is this failure, though, that seems to enable interpretation and figuration, as well as the belated composition of poems such as Pinsky's.

||||||||||||||||

Belatedness is not, of course, limited to postwar poems. In fact, memory is arguably among lyric poetry's most important subjects. When William Wordsworth claimed in the Preface to *Lyrical Ballads* that poetry originates in "emotion recollected in tranquillity," he was setting forth a less impacted version of the kind of belatedness that persists in postwar poetry. (Wordsworth also asserted that this recollection leads to a new emotion distinct from but also "kindred to that which was before the subject of contemplation," apparently linking one act of remembering to earlier ones.) Assertions of lateness echo through English-language poetry in ways that support Sharon Cameron's claim that poetry is centrally concerned with "anxieties of temporal sequence" (24).[10] Lyric poems are perhaps uniquely positioned to explore such anxieties, as I have already begun to suggest: by definition, they acknowledge but distinguish themselves from narrative.[11] Belatedness is especially evident in modernism's insistence both on the past's incursions into the present and on the obstacles to representing this past, as well as in its more general emphasis on the unrepresentability of past traumatic events. (The poems of Thomas Hardy and T. S. Eliot, for example, enact these dynamics in quite different ways.[12])

While my focus is not on the relation between postwar and earlier poetry, the postwar emphasis on belatedness clearly evokes precursors, especially modernist ones. Postwar poetry's tendency to define itself in terms of and in reaction to modernist poetry has been often discussed.[13] This tendency is especially important in the context of belatedness, which itself looks back in time. Moreover, modernism has often been characterized as deeply concerned with time; it enacts, in Fredric Jameson's terms, "the great . . . thematics of time and temporality, the elegiac mysteries of *durée* and memory" (16).[14] The postwar poems I examine below are similarly concerned with the difficulties of chronicling the past and perhaps particularly with what Jameson calls "the waning of our historicity" (21). But, in ways consistent with several theorizations of postmodernism, postwar poems seem to have abandoned the longing for coherence that informs much modernist poetry. Instead, these poems begin—and here I differ from most discussions of postmodernism—with the assumption of irrevocable belatedness.[15]

||||||||||||||||||

Although belatedness can be located in poetry written during different time periods, a particularly acute consciousness of coming after is fundamental to postwar American culture, which, as the term *postwar* indicates (along with the terms *postmodern* and *post-1945*), tends to be defined in terms of its position after earlier events.[16] (Modernism, it could be generalized, was in contrast concerned with its own avant-garde status.) But the condition of being "post" is not only chronological (we are now in the period after these events) but ideological (this period is defined by the condition of coming after, in a way that recalls the *OED*'s definition of belatedness as being "out of time, behind time"). One symptom of this double meaning is evident in frequent descriptions of postwar American culture as informed by not only retrospection but derivativeness. The (famously postmodern) recurrence of simulacra in contemporary culture cogently expresses both the burden and potential of this position: the only things that now can be made, it seems, are versions of already-existing things and of the already-existing and still-proliferating representations of them. But simulacra can also, as postmodern theorists sometimes claim, subvert their own redundancy by wholly replacing "real" originals. They therefore both affirm and undermine the anxieties often associated with earlier, especially modern, modes of appropriation.[17]

Unlike the purely chronological terms *postmodern* and *post-1945*, the term *postwar* associates this period with World War II. The events associated with this war—including Hitler's annexation of European countries, the Nazi extermination camps, Japan's invasion of several countries, and Allied interventions in both Europe and Japan, which culminated in the 1945 American use of atomic bombs in Hiroshima and Nagasaki—are often identified with significant changes in how national identity and human nature more generally were understood. The German concentration camps are often identified with a new, highly systematic method of destroying an entire people, an act that horrifically amplified the scale of the violence of which humans had been hitherto capable. This new era of mass violence was confirmed by the world's entry, with the U.S. attacks on Japan, into the "atomic age." Such events were both intensified and complicated by those of subsequent decades, including the Cold War (a conceptual "war" focusing on the threat of future attacks), the Vietnam War (in which U.S. involvement was not a response to a direct threat to its interests), and the more recent "War on Terror" (an often clandestine series of attacks waged against a mostly invisible and ill-defined enemy not limited to a single nationality). Similarly, the concept of genocide—the term, introduced to the lexicon in 1944 in relation to the Holocaust, remains controversial—has come to seem less an anomaly than a feature of late twentieth- and early twenty-first-century existence.[18] The simultaneous urgency and instability of such events have also drawn attention to questions of nomenclature—what *is* a genocide? who defines terror and terrorists?—and thus to the unreliability and contingency of language more generally.[19]

The Holocaust is often seen as particularly uncontainable. In relation to the Holocaust, moreover, the idea of aftermath is unstable in ways that evoke the double sense of the *post* in *postwar*. To come "after" the Holocaust signals, as Jean-François Lyotard has noted, both "a periodization" (88) and something quite different and far more difficult to define.[20] As

Dominick LaCapra has claimed, the "after" in "after Auschwitz," "does not have a merely chronological meaning" but rather refers both forward and backward in time: "even events that occurred before [the Shoah] . . . could not be understood or 'read' in the same way" afterward (6). Central to this period, then, is the inextricability of a temporal position—related to what I have been calling literal belatedness—from an epistemological and onto-logical one that both expresses and destabilizes chronology.

It is often argued that the Holocaust undermined the possibility of direct representation, perhaps especially artistic representation, as is evident in Theodor Adorno's famous assertion that to "write poetry after Auschwitz is barbaric" (34). (Here too, "after" refers both to a chronological and an epis-temological predicament.) LaCapra asserts that the Holocaust "unsettled" "the standard opposition between uniqueness and comparability" in a way that undermined the possibility of analogy itself (7). In contrast, James Young has argued that although many have attempted to find a mode of speaking about the Holocaust directly (*Writing* 89–92), it cannot be un-derstood or represented "without recourse to metaphor" (*Writing* 89) and thus "can never lie outside of literature, or understanding, or telling" (98).[21] The link between the Holocaust and the tropological, Young implies, de-rives from a double meaning that recalls the one located by Adorno and Lyotard in the term *after*: the Holocaust, Young claims, is both a meta-phoric tenor—which can be described only via other, often fragmentary images—and a vehicle, to which other events can, or perhaps must, be compared.

It is unsurprising, then, that concerns with history and memory have been central to the postwar period, as has been especially evident in the "memory boom" of the past fifty or so years.[22] But this emphasis on remem-bering is in many cases itself belated. To cite a well-known example, intense discussion of the Holocaust began only in the 1960s (Huyssen 12–14). And while memory is frequently discussed in contemporary American culture, questions recur about what it entails. On the one hand, memory is often viewed as politically and ethically necessary. It is argued, for example, that to prevent the Holocaust from being repeated, it must be never be forgotten, a warning both echoed and undermined by a kind of metaphoric proliferation, in which subsequent traumatic events are defined in relation to the Holocaust.[23] On the other is the recognition that memory is not simple or in many cases even possible. Thus, many critics have argued that the Holocaust cannot in fact be remembered because it undermined the very concepts of event and memory. The Holocaust, in Dori Laub's terms, *produced no witnesses*" (80). Maurice Blanchot implies something similar when he claims that disaster is manifest through its repudiation of verifiability and chronology.[24]

As I suggested above, the term *belatedness* has often been used in reference to the experiences of victims and survivors of traumatic events, especially the Holocaust. Trauma theory derives from the same cultural and historical context as postwar poetry, and it considers related problems of accuracy and verisimilitude.[25] Here too, the relation of the literal to the figurative is central and vexed. Trauma theory is thus useful in situating and, to some extent, explaining postwar poetic belatedness. Yet there are also crucial differences between actual traumatic experiences and poems. Poems are not merely or wholly expressions of trauma theory's ideas, partly because they are so obviously distinct from the lived experiences on which trauma theory focuses. Perhaps most crucially, belatedness in poems is not an unwilled symptom but rather an aesthetic (and also at times political) strategy.

Trauma theory's emphasis on belatedness results from an itself belated rereading of Freud. Freud used the term *Nachträglichkeit* ("belatedness" or "deferred action") in passing, and it has been subsequently renovated and elaborated by Jacques Lacan, among others.[26] For Freud, according to one gloss, *Nachträglichkeit* occurs at times of rupture or incongruity, in relation to "whatever it has been impossible in the first instance to incorporate fully into a meaningful context" (Laplanche and Pontalis 112); "only the occurrence of the second scene can endow the first one with pathogenic force," giving the original memory a meaning that paradoxically impels its subsequent repression (113). According to another summary, neither the first nor the second scene is "necessarily traumatic"; instead, the trauma derives from the fact that the "second event . . . triggered a memory of the first event that only then was given traumatic meaning and hence repressed" (Leys 20). Trauma is thus defined by deferral or belatedness, a "temporal delay or latency" that renders "the past . . . available only by a deferred act of understanding and interpretation" (20).

Similar notions of concealment are central to Freud's claim that in all memories "what is important is suppressed and what is indifferent retained" ("Screen" 306). The creation of memories thus involves a process of "substitut[ion]" by which "the inessential elements" of an experience replace its "essential elements" (307). This process of substitution evokes literary trope insofar as it often reveals, Freud claims, either relations of "continuity" (something like metaphor) or the protometonymic "substitution of something in the neighbourhood (whether in space or time)" (308). Thus, Freud suggests, the literal accuracy of memories is undermined in favor of a more radically metonymic model: "it may indeed be questioned whether we have any memories at all *from* our childhood: memories *relating to* our childhood may be all that we possess" (322).

Trauma theory builds on and extends these ideas, often with a focus on Freud's later writings about pathological manifestations of this delay in processing trauma, especially for the patient who "does not *remember*" the past but "*acts* it out" ("Remembering" 150) and in the experiences of shell-shocked World War I soldiers ("On Transience"). Emphasizing the experience of Holocaust witnesses (as I will elaborate in chapter 2, the term refers both to survivors and bystanders), trauma theory focuses not on the individual pathology that Freud stresses but rather on large-scale, collective disaster. Trauma theory is thus less concerned with therapeutic cures for traumatic experiences than with elaborating what theorist Cathy Caruth identifies as Freud's "central . . . insight into trauma"—that "the impact of the traumatic event lies precisely in its belatedness" (Introduction 9).[27] More specifically, post-traumatic stress disorder, in Caruth's terms, always involves a common "*structure*" to which belatedness is central (italics in original); "the [traumatic] event is not assimilated or experienced fully at the time, but only belatedly, in its repeated *possession* of the one who experiences it" (4, italics in original). It is therefore "fully evident only in connection with another place, and in another time" (8).

That these claims are relevant to the relation between the literal and the figurative is evident in Caruth's claim that the "dreams, hallucinations and thoughts" that characterize PTSD are "absolutely literal, unassimilable to associative chains of meaning" (Introduction 5) even though they also produce "a deep uncertainty as to [their] very truth" (6). The belated repetition of trauma, that is, exposes trauma's indirectness or figurativeness even as it retains the trauma's literal outlines.[28] The claims of several recent theorists have further complicated the notion that traumatic experience is "tru[e]" or authentic. Holocaust testimony is, after all, a genre with particular and recurrent conventions (Whitehead 33–34), and traumatic events more generally are often invoked and "script[ed]" "as emergencies, or even, indeed, as traumatic" to particular political ends (Edkins 5). A series of high-profile controversies about erroneous and faked memoirs describing traumatic experiences have further confused the question of veracity: is it necessary to depict the literal and historical facts of past events? Or is it acceptable, or even necessary, to distort such facts?[29]

It might thus be argued that postwar culture's concern with memory is overdetermined, as is postwar poetry's concern with figuration. Belatedness's recurrence in poetry, to which figuration is central, is thus a logical, even expected development. Certainly, the postwar poems I discuss reveal several tendencies that trauma theory attributes to the experiences of actual survivors: they rely on repetition, flashback, and prolepsis; they undermine linear or simple chronology; they define past events through subsequent moments that only partly resemble them; they draw attention to the figurativity and indirectness of their own language; and they invoke particular addressees in ways that reveal skepticism about witness and audience. But, despite what several readers have claimed, the postwar American poems I consider do not directly express experiences of trauma or witness.[30] The Holocaust poems of Sylvia Plath, Adrienne Rich, and Jorie Graham, for example, emphasize their speakers' temporal and physical distance from this event. Nor do these or other poems express the helplessness typical of trauma survivors. Instead, they exploit the condition of belatedness, often by converting the survivor's unwilled psychological response into something not only conscious but exaggerated. Recurrent scenes of performance imply that these poems in fact enact belatedness rather than expressing a helpless subjection to it.

This sense of distance derives, in many of the poems I examine, from the fact that they were written long after the events they chronicle. This situation in some ways recalls what Marianne Hirsch has called "postmemory," a condition affecting the children of trauma survivors (77), who acutely feel, Hirsch claims, their "unbridgeable distance" from participants (76). Postmemory relies not on lived experience (referred to by Hirsch as "*repetition* or *reenactment*") but on "previous *representations*" (76) of the traumatic event. (James Young has made a similar argument about a "post-Holocaust generation of artists" with no blood relation to survivors [*At Memory's* 1]).[31] While these ideas help explain the emphasis in many postwar poems on what Hirsch identifies as the "mediat[ed]" (76) and Young calls the "hyper-mediated" (1), postwar poems do not, as Young does, depict the failure of immediacy as a "problem" (3). Instead, they tend to insist on a position of nonwitness, and when they do adopt the persona of a witness or victim, they often do so ironically. As belated nonwitnesses, the speakers of these poems are perhaps freer than actual survivors to redefine and manipulate what Pinsky calls "meaning."

The postwar poems I consider can in this context be read as extensions of a movement throughout twentieth-century American poetry toward increasing doubt about the possibility of depicting historical events. In 1930, Ezra Pound affirmed that a poem that "included history" (46) could be written and that he could do just this. But in 1940, the much younger W. H. Auden made a famously negative comment not about what poems could include but about whether they could alter the world they conveyed, something that Pound seems to have assumed was possible. "Poetry," he asserted, "*makes* nothing happen: it survives / . . . / A way of happening, a mouth" (italics added). Auden here qualifies his initial claim that poetry cannot effect change in the world. In 1962, toward the end of his life, William

Carlos Williams offered a somewhat more positive but similarly qualified pronouncement, emphasizing poetry's capacity not to influence the world but to represent it:

It is difficult
to *get* the news *from poems*
yet men die miserably every day
for lack
of what is found there.
(2:318, italics added)

By 1977, Robert Lowell had turned away from such grand pronouncements about poetry to a narrower concern with the aesthetic merits of a poetry of reportage. The speaker of "Epilogue" views his own poems as "snapshot[s], / lurid, rapid, garish, grouped, / heightened from life, / yet paralyzed by fact." But soon after, he seems to espouse something like this aesthetic of verisimilitude, asking himself, "Yet why not say what happened?"

These increasingly curtailed depictions of poetry's capacity to affect its readers or even convey lived experience have many possible sources. Particularly compelling in the postwar period is the decline in poetry's cultural significance, which if anything has become more acute, or at least more often discussed, in the last decade.[32] I will return to this idea, as well as to other ways of understanding the emphasis on belatedness in postwar poetry. My reading does not, however, emphasize the accuracy of this poetry's depiction of literal events or the ways these events affected their authors. Instead, I will emphasize how often-familiar events are both represented and manipulated through figurative strategies that emphasize but also interrogate what Lowell called "what happened."[33]

|||||||||||||||||

I have entitled this book *Ghostly Figures* partly because ghosts clearly dramatize the more general issues I have been associating with a poetics of belatedness. Ghosts of different kinds are evident in the poems I discuss, although my focus is not exclusively on poems about haunting. This recurrence is perhaps unsurprising given that imagery of haunting and possession seems central to several discussions of belatedness. Caruth, for example, defines belatedness as a process by which a traumatic event repeatedly takes *"possession"* (Introduction 4, italics in original) of the one remembering it: "to be traumatized is precisely to be possessed by an image or event" (5). The dynamics of possession thus, Caruth implies, articulate or give form to the condition of belatedness. In a quite different discussion of recent American ethnic fiction, Kathleen Brogan associates haunting with "the dangerous incorporation of the dead" (9). Postwar poetic ghosts function similarly, offering, as Brogan claims of "stories of cultural haunting," "a go-between, an enigmatic transitional figure moving between past and present, death and life, one culture and another" (6).[34] As liminal and transgressive entities, ghostly figures in poems deny death's closure because they are by definition posthumous. Straddling the life-death divide, they destabilize it, gesturing back to deaths that have already occurred as they proleptically signal the poet's future death. In the process, ghosts reveal the paradoxical features of elegy, a subgenre to which I will often refer in the chapters that follow; elegies also confirm the finality of death, but by dwelling on and at times re-performing death, they challenge this finality.

Ghosts also concisely join the literal with the figurative. Ghosts are generally manifest physically—they can be heard, seen, or felt—but they are not wholly human. More crucially, they do not, most people agree, in fact exist. Ghosts in postwar poems exemplify these tensions. Unlike their modernist precursors, postwar ghosts mostly do not speak, cannot be touched, and appear only in dreams or when summoned.[35] And because they often seem anachronistic, they tend to be more awkward than threatening. Even as these ghosts keep appearing, they reveal that they have no existence beyond the poem. They thus reveal their figurativeness, making it clear that they embody not a real person returning from death but the survivor's feelings or wishes. In this way, even as they refuse to be reduced to mere symbols, they evoke the psychoanalytic notion that ghosts are metaphors for what is feared or desired or (perhaps more exactly) for what is feared because it is desired. Literary ghosts have often been understood as metaphors for poetic vocation and power, as Harold Bloom and Susan Stewart have in different ways argued and as I will explore in more detail in subsequent chapters.[36] To summon a ghost in a poem is thus to draw attention to the poem's artifice.

I have been elaborating the ways that ghosts in postwar poems are physically present as almost-living figures or personae. But I also intend my title *Ghostly Figures* to gesture in another direction. Insofar as they are figurative, poetic ghosts reveal the ghostliness of poetic figures themselves. That is, tropes and figures in postwar poems are often provisional or artificial, and they tend to draw attention to themselves in ways that facilitate their dismantling.

The relation of ghosts to simultaneously literal and figurative positions is central to Frank Bidart's 2009 poem "Like," which I will discuss in more detail in chapter 3. The poem reveals the ways the condition of ghostliness —and, by implication, of belated survival—embodies concerns about poetic representation and figuration, especially simile. The poem early on describes the attempt of the bereaved, whom the poem addresses, to convert the dead into or "imagine" them in ghostly or "spectr[al]" form:

> secretly you imagine then
> refuse to imagine
>
> a spectre
>
> so like what you watched die . . .
> 　　　　　(*Metaphysical* 11–12)

While the speaker depicts the specter as both "imagine[d]" and "refuse[d]," this specter remains distinct from the actual person who has "die[d]." Here the term *like* introduces a simile that establishes a partial equivalence between the "spectre" and what "you watched die"; the word functions as a preposition. But several lines later, the speaker implies that the dead have in fact been made into specters by means of analogy or "*like*," which is presented as a noun. "The dead hate *like*," the speaker omnisciently asserts, because that term allows "the living" to "replace" the dead by converting the actual dead into figurative specters. Although the dead resist this process of conversion, the speaker affirms that such acts of replacement are necessary, since "we live by symbolic // substitution." The poem thus shifts, to recall my title, from making a claim about the figurativeness of ghosts to making one about the ghostliness of the figures that describe them. In the process, the actual, if "imagine[d]," specters in the poem are converted into poetic figures.

||||||||||||||||

Exploring the relation of the literal to the figurative through a mostly occluded act of remembering the dead, "Like" reveals the entanglement of the temporal condition of belatedness with the poem's awareness of its status as a linguistic and tropological construct. Two poems written after and about the September 11, 2001, attacks, one of them also by Bidart, more clearly reveal the double function of belatedness as a temporal condition and a poetics and thus as what I have been calling both literal and figurative.

Belatedness is particularly overdetermined in relation to the 9/11 attacks, perhaps because they seemed incommensurable even as they strongly evoked previous events, especially the 1945 Japanese attack on Pearl Harbor. The attacks also seemed to bring traumatic events—often seen by Americans as geographically or temporally remote—"home," as the title of one book on the attacks indicates (Greenberg). But the frequent allusion to the traumatic nature of the attacks also by implication evoked earlier traumas, even in cases where such analogies were denied.[37] This sense of temporal and geographical echoing was intensified insofar as the attacks also seemed to repeat similar, earlier scenes in (fictional) movies, as has also often been noted.[38] Certainly, poems about 9/11 often depict the attacks as repetitive and emphasize the impossibility of gaining perspective on them.

Before they were even written about, then, the attacks challenged the distinction between the "real" and the "virtual" and between the literal and the figurative, as Jeanne Follansbee Quinn and I have argued at greater length elsewhere. On the one hand, they were often seen as dramatically inserting the real (or at least a Lacanian Real associated with what Slavoj Žižek calls "violent transgression" [6]) into postmodern virtuality; they have several times been characterized as defining the endpoint of postmodernism. But on the other hand, they were not, for most Americans, entirely real. Because they were watched on television both as they were occurring

Memory and Belatedness in Postwar American Poetry | 19

and after the fact, the attacks seemed simultaneously immediate and distant, unique and infinitely repeated. They thus created a condition of what Marc Redfield has called "virtual trauma," or, more exactly, they virtualized traumatic experience. In this context, poems that explore the connection between the literal and the figurative and the attacks are expanding on features inherent in the attacks.

Robert Pinsky's "The Anniversary," to which I alluded briefly above, emphasizes the condition of temporal or literal belatedness.[39] Whereas the poem's first published version was entitled "9/11," the final title establishes a chronological remove from the attacks, which reveals, the poem makes clear, the ways what actually occurred changed over time.[40] "We adore images," the poem begins, favoring the first-person plural that recurs throughout, along with "the spectacle / Of speed and size" and "the working of prodigious / Systems." And so

on television we watched

The terrible spectacle, repetitiously gazing
Until we were sick not only of the sight
Of our prodigious systems turned against us

But of the very systems of our watching.
(*Gulf* 19)

As the poem displaces "repetitio[n]" from the witnessed "spectacle" to the act of "gazing," it enacts these repetitions linguistically, emphasizing how the attacks both reiterated and changed the "adore[d] images": the formerly beloved spectacles become "terrible" and "our prodigious systems [turn] against us." In this way, Pinsky binds repetition to distortion and visual to linguistic repetition.

This mode of repetition is partly explained by references later in the poem to partial and failed remembering. In contrast to earlier prose writings in which Pinsky claimed that Americans are "defined by memory, not by blood" ("Commencement"), the poem insists on the inevitability of forgetting things, from Donald Duck to the origin of the images on the dollar bill.[41] Doubt about what occurred also informs the central description of the 9/11 firefighters:

> Some say the doomed firefighters
> Before they hurried into the doomed towers wrote
> Their Social Security numbers on their forearms.

Here Pinsky describes an actual, verifiable event—the firefighters did enter the burning towers—but raises doubt about its details. The poet relies first on hearsay ("Some say") and then "imagine[s]"—in keeping with the initial reference to "images"—the details of the scene. The description also overlays multiple time frames: the firefighters write their numbers on their arms in anticipation of the later moment when their corpses will be found and identified, but they fail to imagine the actual, worse outcome, in which almost no remains were found. This outcome, however, is proleptically known by the poem's readers and the poet, who look back at that moment and also ahead to what later occurs. The repetition of "doomed" signals and multiplies the poem's foreknowledge, as the opening did with "repetitious," applying it to both the firefighters and the towers.

Pinsky links the temporal, literal condition of belatedness of such scenes to the process of figuration in ways that exemplify the process of what Bidart's "Like" calls "symbolic // substitution." The slippage between these concepts is evident in the poem's recurrent references to representation and figuration, especially the terms "images" and "meaning." Central to the poem is the question of "what holds us together" as well as of whether wholeness can be synecdochically created from scattered parts.

"Americans," Pinsky claims in the poem, echoing earlier prose statements, are "not / A people by blood or religion." They are instead defined by fragmentary and metonymic connections between the birth and death years of Will Rogers, Frederick Douglass, Emily Dickinson. These diverse characters did not know one another or do the same work. Instead, they are bound because the years they were alive overlapped.[42] In the absence of other modes of making meaning, such superficial connections offer the only *system* by which Americanness can be defined. The poem's repeated images and language, including the "spectacle[s]" and "systems" of the opening and the conversion of donated blood into "meaning" discussed above, enact the disrupted processes of memory. They also offer fractured and repetitive replacements for a mode of remembering that has become, the poem makes clear, inadequate.[43] Thus, the figurative ("meaning") derives from the literal ("blood") as well as from its failure to be "needed."

Bidart's very different representation of the attacks in his 2002 "Curse" explores a similar sense of repetition and recursiveness in far more violent terms. Unlike Pinsky, Bidart refuses to discuss meaning and interpretation. Instead, he relies on a literalizing rhetoric of revenge that precludes the possibility of figurative transformation in ways that anticipate the ambivalence of "Like" about such transformation. The poem's literalism is ultimately complicated, though, by the implication that the poem itself is the utterance of an unreliable speaker.

Here too, temporal belatedness is central to the poem's premise. "Curse" comprises a multipart curse that attempts to exact belated revenge, as Bidart's note explains, on those who have already "brought down the World Trade Center towers" (*Star Dust* 83).[44] It does so by commanding the attackers to go back in time so the towers' collapse can be recreated in a way that extends its effects to them: in this counterfactual and belated account, their death reenacts that of their real-life victims.

The poem depicts this situation not in abstract language but through descriptions of a series of physical acts of ingestion and regurgitation:

May the listening ears of your victims   their eyes   their

breath

enter you, and eat like acid
the bubble of rectitude that allowed you breath.

Here Bidart mixes literally possible and impossible acts: eyes and ears cannot actually enter someone else, but breath can; rectitude is invisible, but bubbles are not. By literalizing retribution, the speaker achieves his anachronistic goal of impelling the victims' breath belatedly—despite the fact that the actual victims of the 9/11 attacks cannot in fact now breathe—to destroy the perpetrators'.

A related dynamic of recycling and "spit[ting] out" is evident in the poem's language. Here is the first sentence (stanza breaks and italics in original):

May breath for a dead moment cease as jerking your

head upward you hear as if in slow motion floor

collapse evenly upon floor as one hundred and ten

floors descend upon you.

The poem phonemically recycles words and sounds: "breath," "dead," "cease," "head," "hear," and "floor" echo and remake one another. More generally, the poem does not proceed; rather, each line cannibalizes the last.[45] As such, the similarity between bodies and words affirms the curse's logic; progress and escape, along with remembering and healing, are now impossible. The poem instead enacts a repetitive logic of retribution that insists on bodily presence and functions.

Yet this position is itself a stance and therefore figurative. Curses are always performative in the sense defined by J. L. Austin: they can alter actual events only in the subjunctive mood and within the provisional space of their own utterance (6). The actual 9/11 victims cannot be converted into perpetrators because they are already dead; and because the attackers are also already dead (or because those the poem punishes are not the actual attackers but those who planned the attacks from afar), the poem can never adequately punish them. Here, as in all curses, language stands in for action.[46] In this way, the literalism in "Curse" is revealed to be mere rhetoric, a purely symbolic utterance that cannot alter actual events.

"Curse" exposes this figurativity most clearly in the last two lines by introducing a first-person speaker apparently distinct from the narrator of the rest of the poem. This shift implies that the poem has been until then the performance of a particular character rather than a more universal utterance.[47] As the speaker enters as "I," he acknowledges his role as curse-maker: "Out of the great secret of morals, *the imagination to enter / the skin of another*, what I have made is a curse." The speaker has, he reveals, corrupted or, in the terms of the poem's note, "reduced" an excerpt from Percy Shelley's *Defense of Poetry*, turning "the great secret of morals" into "a curse" that undermines the "sympathetic identification, [the] identification with others" essential to Shelley's assertion about imagination (*Star Dust* 83). Yet in separating himself from the attackers, the speaker also reveals his "identification" with them: his act of having "made . . . a curse" links him to the attackers, whom he identifies as makers when he exhorts them, "May what you have *made* descend upon you" (italics added). The poem's act of cursing thus requires an act of identification that literalizes Shelley's metaphorical reference to "*enter*[ed] . . . / *skin*," transforming the figurative into the literal in ways that expose the mechanics of the transformation.

"Curse" in this way links the chronological condition of belatedness to figuration, meaning, and representation in ways quite different from "The Anniversary." But both poems reveal the inextricability of these elements, linking time to figuration or Pinsky's "meaning" to "what holds us together." It is significant that "Curse," like Bidart's "Like," ends by foregrounding the role of making. Language and the compulsion to make, are, it seems, what persist, often in ways that obscure the need to come to terms with or remake the actual past.

||||||||||||||||

My intention here and in the chapters that follow is not to make a claim applicable to all post-9/11 or postwar poems nor to offer a survey of them. Rather, I mean through close readings of a diverse group of poems published throughout the postwar period (the poems I consider were published in the early 1960s, the 1990s, and the early 2000s) to draw attention to the recurrence of belatedness as both a thematics and a poetics. In the process, I hope to exemplify the continued relevance of the method of close reading I here practice, especially in poems about recognizable historical events. I have chosen these particular poets—and these volumes and poems by them—because they offer especially clear examples of the ways literal and figurative belatedness coincide and connect. Similar concerns are evident, perhaps less explicitly, in other poems and volumes by these poets. Similar patterns are also evident in the work of other postwar poets, as I will begin to suggest in the coda. Belatedness therefore offers an interpretive model that links the thematics and poetics of diverse poems, one methodologically consistent with several other recent studies of postwar poetry.[48] My reading also implies a strategy for healing some of the critical divisions in how postwar poems have often been understood. The poets whose work I discuss have been associated with aesthetics and literary movements that are often contrasted, including both the confessional and the experimental (exemplified respectively by Plath and Howe) and both the personal and the political (exemplified by Merrill and Graham on the one hand and Rich and Paul Monette on the other). That members of these apparently distinct, even aesthetically antithetical groups share a preoccupation with memory and its obstruction suggests that this poetry—highly heterodox though it clearly is—is more unified than is sometimes thought.

This book is structured partly as a taxonomy of belatedness and its figurative manifestations. Each chapter focuses on a recurrent set of tropes and figures evident in the work of the poet or poets I consider, ranging from synecdoche to simile, metaphor to metonymy, and apostrophe to prosopopoeia. As these figures are both deployed and interrogated, they themselves become ghostly, revealing their own provisionality. Juxtaposing them thus reveals the pervasiveness of postwar poetry's tendency to interrogate the figures on which it relies. In fact, it can be generalized that postwar poets are especially interested in this kind of interrogation in relation to situations of partial or occluded retrospection.

But, as I have begun to suggest, I also mean to imply a tentative narrative of dismantling and diffusion. Although the poets I discuss are not necessarily representative of their historical or poetic moments (nor are they evenly spaced throughout the roughly sixty-five-year period I consider), a development is evident through my (mostly chronological) chapters: over time, belatedness becomes more diffused or ghostly as well as more explicitly figurative and self-referential, reflecting increasingly on poetry's purpose and function. Analogy becomes more radically destabilized; metaphor is replaced by metonymic and other contingent modes of connection in a process that culminates, in Susan Howe's 2003 *The Midnight*, in a repudiation of the very separation of literal from figurative.

This narrative resembles that of postmodernism, which, as I implied above, is often described in terms of fragmentation, simulacra, self-referentiality, and performance. Often, though, postmodernism is associated with the excision (or all but excision) of the literal, historical, and real; only layers of virtuality or textuality persist. Certainly the poems I explore foreground such elements. Yet they also retain traces of the literal both as the poem's trigger and in some cases as its endpoint. The poem itself, especially in Howe's sequence, is increasingly a material object as well as a linguistic construct. In this way, poetry seems to have at least partly anticipated recent critiques of postmodernism's refusal of the real.[49] As this book demonstrates, postwar poems embrace artifice while refusing to disregard actual events.

My consideration of the ways in which four poets, plus a cluster of poets writing about AIDS, depict belatedness also reveals that belatedness is a generative precondition for poetry. If belatedness as a concept remains hard to identify when it is implied and unstable when it is explicit, this is part of my point. Belatedness is itself a kind of ghost in postwar poems, perhaps most evident when the figures through which it is represented collapse or implode, revealing that they have been ghostly all along.

Chapter 1, "The Holocaust Again: Literal and Figurative Fragmentation in Sylvia Plath's *Ariel*," begins by examining the ubiquity of belatedness in the reception of Plath's late poems. The 2004 publication of Plath's *Ariel: The Restored Edition* in particular purported to "restore" the authentic, original version of this volume, but I argue that it in fact perpetuated the compulsion to read Plath's late poems through her subsequent suicide in ways that reiterate the poems' rhetoric of anticipation and belatedness. I then consider how Plath's two most iconic (and most commented on) poems about the Holocaust, "Daddy" and "Lady Lazarus," exploit a similar rhetoric of belatedness. While earlier critics often condemn Plath's distorted representation of the Holocaust, I claim that this distortion expresses her speakers' belatedness: the Holocaust is accessible only in partial and fragmentary ways or, in Plath's recurrent term, "bit[s]." As Plath insists on temporal distance and instability (or literal belatedness), these poems also express belatedness figuratively by systematically fragmenting their own poetic figures and tropes. In "Daddy" Plath insists on partial and contingent analogies, especially similes. The speaker of "Lady Lazarus" is herself fractured yet compelled to perform for an audience she both requires and reviles. Such tendencies challenge the assumptions of sympathy and kinship that generally underlie both apostrophe and reader address, while also challenging the synecdochic assumption that parts refer to wholeness. I turn at the chapter's end to a reading of other poems in Plath's *Ariel* that extend this belated poetics of fragmentation.

Chapter 2, "'To feel with a human stranger': Address and Asymmetrical Witness in Adrienne Rich's *Dark Fields of the Republic*," considers this 1995 volume's treatment of related issues, including the disruption of memory in the aftermath of the Holocaust and other scenes of political violence. But rather than renarrating past events as Plath does, Rich interrogates the structure and possibility of witness and identification, concepts central to trauma theory's notion of belatedness. Rich's poems are nearly always read as statements of political commitment that espouse the necessity of bearing witness to the suffering of others and conveying that suffering directly to the reader. But a number of poems in *Dark Fields* directly question the notion of sympathetic witness through scenes of what I call asymmetrical witness, in which two observers see radically different things. In ways that evoke chapter 1's discussion of the address of "Lady Lazarus," I explore the inconsistency of Rich's address: the volume's poems repeatedly blur apostrophe, or the address of others within the poem, with reader address, which exposes the poem as a construct. By exposing their own acts of what Judith Butler has called "fram[ing]" (*Frames*), the poems of *Dark Fields* impel their readers to consider what Butler (and others) call poetry's ethical function, its capacity to speak to and for others.

The elegies discussed in chapter 3, "'I am the ghost who haunts us': Prosopopoeia and the Poetics of Infection in AIDS Poetry," foreground imagery of posthumousness and haunting that are also present in poems by both Plath and Rich that refer to historical events. But these elegies—by Frank Bidart, Thom Gunn, D. A. Powell, Paul Monette, Mark Doty, and James

Merrill—tend to be emotionally and temporally closer to their subjects than the poems discussed in chapters 1 and 2. As these elegies mediate between the demands of private grief and political consciousness-raising, they refer repeatedly to ghosts and ghostliness. The dead often appear in ghostly form in these poems, but ghostliness is also rendered figurative. These poems, like Plath's, interrogate metaphor; they also, like Rich's, reconsider address. But more often, AIDS poems rely on a fragile prosopopoeia that enables the dead to speak in limited and partial ways. These poems tend to explore this capacity for speech in one of two ways, each with distinct political implications. One group of poems embraces what I call a poetics of infection, refusing to distinguish living from dead and self from other through figures that emphasize proximity and asymmetry. Here, temporal boundaries are dismantled, distance is refused, and prosopopoeia is embraced. The poetics of immunity, in contrast, insists on separation and boundary, often using metaphors as barriers against a dangerous sense of engulfment. Yet the recurrent ghosts in these elegies work to undermine distinction in ways that ultimately affirm loss despite and through the attempt to deny it.

Chapter 4, "'Deep into the lateness now': Likeness and Lateness in Jorie Graham's *Region of Unlikeness*," turns from the mostly implied thematics of belatedness in earlier chapters to a volume that makes lateness and delay explicit. Graham's 1991 collection, I argue, directly poses a question implied by my previous chapters: what does it mean to join private with political narratives and personal memory with public history in a situation of belatedness? Graham asserts directly that what she calls "lateness" can be described only by means of "likeness." These poems, more strenuously than those I examine in earlier chapters, explore figures of likeness, especially simile, as a way of linking the private, present-day life of their speakers with public, recollected, and often traumatic scenes. But Graham also exposes the artificial nature of such analogies, proposing an alternative predicated on "unlikeness" or contingent, metonymic relations. Graham's poems thus directly bind temporal disruptions to the often inadequate figures with which the belated poet depicts them.

Chapter 5, "'Spectral scraps': Displacement, Metonymy, and the Elegiac in Susan Howe's *The Midnight*," locates in Howe's 2003 sequence an extension of Graham's tentative exploration of a metonymic mode that conveys the ruptures essential to belatedness. Howe's sequence does not emphasize temporality or metaphor, as do earlier chapters. Instead, it focuses nearly entirely on spatialized and metonymic relations, juxtaposing excerpts of prose, photographs, and poems in ways that create a series of places of joining. Such juxtapositions undermine the distinction between the literal and the figurative that recurs in my earlier chapters: these poems embrace a wholly spatial poetics. Yet the condition of belatedness is also central to the volume. Traces of the temporal, that is, persist in ways that recall Jameson's characterization of the postmodern as a "displacement of the temporal" (156). Howe never allows her dead mother to speak; nor does she represent her in ghostly form, as AIDS elegies might. Instead, she displaces ghostliness onto the text itself, describing her sequence as a series of "spectral scraps," visible and speaking entities that do not eradicate but conceal the need for elegy. In this way, Howe makes clear that her metonymic poetics enables her to evade but also express the grief inherent in the condition of belated survivorship.

While belatedness often expresses an occluded and indirect mode of memory, I conclude by turning to moments in several postwar poems that reveal an apparently contradictory concern with waiting and forgetting. In the coda, "'To begin the forgetting': Belatedness beyond Memory," I argue through rereadings of poems discussed in earlier chapters as well as discussion of several others that belatedness in postwar poems is not concerned only with memory or the past. It also imagines what will come afterward, an act that converts grief to what Judith Butler has called grievability, the potential of *future* grief. I look closely at moments in several poems that situate performance, especially the public reading of poems, within belatedness. In Robert Pinsky's "The Forgetting," for example, performance facilitates forgetting, which in turn allows the poet indirectly to imagine his own poem's future receipt by its readers. Such scenes suggest that belatedness can, and perhaps must, break free from the past, the literal, and even, at times, from the confinement of its own figurativeness.

Chapter One

The Holocaust Again

Literal and Figurative Fragmentation in Sylvia Plath's *Ariel*

To read Plath is to engage from the outset with belatedness. I am, to begin with, focusing in this chapter on what are perhaps Sylvia Plath's most anthologized and most discussed poems. And by considering, as many have before me, how "Daddy" (*Ariel Restored* 74–76) and "Lady Lazarus" (14–17) depict the Holocaust, I am returning to a topic about which it may seem that everything has already been said.[1] I am in this way reading Plath's Holocaust poems *again*. I begin by acknowledging this situation because the pressures associated with it are fundamental to belatedness. Being conscious of one's belatedness can create a sense of exhaustion, even paralysis, originating in the awareness that it is impossible to devise a new or wholly original way of understanding an already familiar topic. But this situation can also impel the belated reader—recklessly, cautiously, or with a sense of urgency—to attempt to do something new, however modest, with these familiar materials. Belatedness in fact often seems to engage both these impulses.

Certainly a similar mixture of exhaustion and urgency informs Plath's belated relation to the Holocaust. Rather than depicting the Holocaust as a literal or actual event, Plath's poems make it available only in fragments or what Plath several times calls "bit[s]." The poems thus present a doubly belated relation to the Holocaust, imposing distance on an event that, while it remains relevant for the poet, is already temporally and physically inaccessible. Plath's Holocaust poems manipulate and deface this already disrupted event by further fracturing the pieces that remain. In this way, Plath reveals that belatedness is not simply an effect of temporal distance from the Holocaust but rather a stance adopted and also performed by the poems written about it.

Plath's late Holocaust poems thus offer an especially clear model of the poetics of belatedness as defined in the introduction, a model also evident, if less explicitly, in Plath's late poems on other subjects, as I will argue in the final section of this chapter. In particular, Plath's treatment of what I have called literal belatedness—prompted by Plath's actual, lived situation after and apart from the Holocaust—is enacted thematically through her manipulations of chronology within the poems. In ways that cannot be separated from these temporal effects, belatedness is also evident figuratively, through Plath's repeated and often violent interrogations of metaphor, simile, metonymy, synecdoche, and apostrophe. These effects intensify the poems' belatedness; because the Holocaust is already inaccessible, the poems' figurative disruptions reiterate and intensify what has already occurred.

By juxtaposing my position as a belated reader of Plath's poems with what is already present in the poems, I am engaging in an act of repetition that recalls another recurrent feature of Plath criticism: critical discussion of and debate about Plath's poems and life have often uncannily mimicked conflicts within the poems, as several readers have noted.[2] Although Plath's belatedness has been mentioned only in passing, it deeply informs the experience of reading Plath's late poems.[3] The poems that end the original published version of *Ariel*, edited by Ted Hughes and published posthumously in 1965, were composed just five days before Plath's death. Many of these late poems refer to death, including suicide, and thus seem to look proleptically ahead to Plath's actual suicide.[4] It is in fact difficult to read *Ariel* without being aware of this future event; many readers have noted the poems' suicidal rhetoric, and even readers who attempt to avoid doing so tend to reinscribe it.[5] The poems in this way invite readings that resist chronology; their imagery, generally seen as part of a poem's figurative apparatus, seems to predict what will literally occur to its author. Arguing that the speakers of these poems do not necessarily know about their author's imminent suicide tends to be ineffectual as well, since the poems themselves seem anticipatory. Related problems arise when the poems' author is distinguished from their speaker. As readers, we cannot avoid the knowledge that comes with hindsight; we can (and in some ways must) look back on the suicide that Plath herself could not ascertain would occur.

This condition is not identical to belatedness, which involves a consciousness of being too late and thus impelled toward the past, but it is related. Prolepsis jumps forward in time so it can look back; it establishes a kind of artificial situation of memory and thus of belatedness. Reading Plath's late poems through her subsequent death makes the poems themselves seem posthumous, although of course they are not. This situation also impels a feeling of powerlessness in the reader—we wish to stop the inevitable from occurring, but cannot—that recalls the flashbacks that trauma theory associates with traumatic belatedness. Because we are too late to intervene, we reexperience the story of Plath's suicide whenever we read the poems. To read late Plath thus affirms the irrevocability of chronology (insofar as Plath must die after writing these poems) and also reveals how deeply informed that chronology is by both anticipation and remembering.

A related interplay of anticipation and remembering is even more apparent in the 2004 publication of *Ariel: The Restored Edition,* edited by Plath's daughter, Frieda Hughes, following the death of her father, Ted Hughes.[6] As the title indicates, this edition restores Plath's selection and ordering of the poems included in her final volume, replacing Hughes's posthumous alterations to the order and contents with a "restored" original that had until that point been lost or concealed.[7] Much of this edition's power thus comes from its challenge to the proleptic narrative of Plath's suicide foregrounded by Hughes's edition. But this restoration is also in some ways too late: it exists alongside the originally published edition, which remains in print and better known. Several features of the restored *Ariel* highlight this belatedness. The book's cover image, a facsimile of a typed and hand-annotated earlier cover page by Plath, includes a series of crossed-out, handwritten titles, none of which is "Ariel," implying that Plath's final ordering and title were provisional. The foreword by Frieda Hughes also offers rationales for and affirms the superiority of her father's ordering of the volume.[8] That such issues are related to the problem of how to remember Plath is apparent in the foreword's juxtaposition of contradictory versions of Plath's life and composition process, including hearsay about Plath, Frieda's personal recollections, Ted's accounts, and attempts to imagine Plath's experiences from Plath's own perspective.[9]

I begin with these issues, which have been inadequately examined in discussions of the restored *Ariel,* because they reveal the centrality of dynamics of belatedness and anticipation in Plath studies.[10] Questions of truth are often implicit in discussions of the two versions of *Ariel*: is the version that Plath compiled truer to her intention, or is it fair to assume that, had she lived, she would have amended the book's contents, including, as Hughes did, poems composed later? Related questions have long been central to critical evaluation of Plath's Holocaust poems. With few exceptions, scholars have based their assessments of Plath's Holocaust poems on the accuracy of the poems' depiction of the Holocaust itself. This tendency is surprising; it seems to ignore the persistent difficulty of determining what is literally true both of Plath's life and of her poems. It also mostly disregards the general critical consensus that distorted, ironic, or parodic representations of past events are not only morally acceptable but often aesthetically necessary.[11]

Critical approaches to Plath's Holocaust poems, though, have changed quite dramatically over time. Early readers often condemned the poems for their unethical and appropriative treatment of the Holocaust.[12] These readers generally claimed that Plath used the Holocaust to describe fundamentally personal issues, but more recent readings focus on the ways Plath's writing, in Robin Peel's terms, "relat[es] to the *public,* often *political* discourses from which it emerged" (18, italics added). Many readings from the 1980s and 1990s focused on the ways Plath's Holocaust references signaled her ambivalence about gender roles; more recent readers have considered how Plath's representation of the Holocaust reflected her attitudes toward Cold War politics.[13]

These diverse readings, though, share a common assumption: they view Plath's poems as fundamentally metaphorical and thus assume that the Holocaust in the poems stands for something else, although the tenor of this metaphor has changed over time. Thus, Irving Howe's 1972 condemnation of "Daddy" for the "monstrous, utterly disproportionate" (12) nature of its analogy between private suffering and the Holocaust rests on the claim that "Sylvia Plath *identifies* the father . . . with the Nazis" (11, italics added), a notion echoed by George Steiner's assertion that Plath's "last, greatest poems culminate in an act of *identification*, of total communion with those tortured and massacred" (300–01, italics added). James Young includes his quite different reading of Plath's Holocaust imagery in a larger discussion entitled "Interpreting Holocaust Metaphor" (*Writing* 117–33).[14] An implicitly metaphorical framework is also evoked by Robin Peel's general claim that "Plath's poetry and prose" should be read "as reconstructed *barometers* of"—that is, as ways of accurately measuring and representing—"their time" (19, italics added). It is also evident in Susan Gubar's revisionary attempt to transform what others have viewed as the "mere figure" of her poems into their literal subject (or their vehicle into their tenor); for Gubar, the poems are "'really' about the psychological repercussions of Auschwitz on literature and Jewish identity" ("Prosopopoeia" 194).

A quite different critical trend has only occasionally informed readings of Plath's representation of the Holocaust. As Susan Van Dyne was among the first to note, Plath's poems reveal a persistent interest in performance and artifice, one that recalls Judith Butler's well-known claims about the performativity of gender.[15] Jacqueline Rose's reading of Plath's writing in terms of fantasy draws on similar assumptions.[16] Such readings imply that Plath in fact destabilizes identification and verisimilitude, as well as metaphor, revealing what one critic has called a "postmodern conception of historical understanding" (Boswell 58).[17]

Several statements Plath made about her poems, although they are often read in different terms, reveal her aversion to metaphoric readings of her poems.[18] In an essay published in October 1962, the month she wrote "Daddy" and "Lady Lazarus," Plath resists the idea that what she called "Hiroshima" stands for the personal. Instead, she describes her reliance on "deflection," claiming, "My poems *do not* turn out to be about Hiroshima, *but* about a child forming itself finger by finger in the dark" ("Context" 64, italics added). Here Plath refuses analogy altogether. In an interview the same month, she also links public to personal events, and here too, she avoids equating the two, instead claiming only that "personal experience . . . should be relevant, and relevant to the larger things, the bigger things such as Hiroshima and Dachau and so on" (Orr 169–70). This "relevan[ce]" assumes discrepancies, including that in size (for example, between the apparently small "personal" and something "bigger") and thus implies an act of juxtaposition rather than equivalence. ("Hiroshima" similarly functions as a synecdoche for human cruelty and violence more generally in both statements.) Insofar as Hiroshima and the Holocaust were often seen as predictors of a coming nuclear apocalypse (Strangeways 373–74), Plath's references to them may also link the past with an anticipated future.

My claims about Plath's Holocaust poems build on the resistance to metaphoric equivalence implicit in these statements. They also evoke Paul Ricoeur's general assertion that metaphor reveals not a static and fixed equivalence between two unlike entities but the limits of that equivalence: "instead of giving the name of the species to the genus, of the genus to the species, or of the species to another species, metaphor . . . blurs the conceptual boundaries of the terms considered" and thus "confus[es] . . . established logical boundaries" (81). This confusion is perhaps especially apparent in relation to the Holocaust, which—as Young has suggested—"literaliz[ed] metaphor" (*Writing* 93).[19]

As I will argue in the remainder of this chapter, Plath's late poems systematically disrupt the structure and assumptions of metaphor. "Daddy" and "Lady Lazarus," Plath's most developed and successful poems about the Holocaust, reveal features that recur in many of the poems of Plath's *Ariel*. These poems do not report on or recall actual past events, although it has been credibly argued that Plath's poems about the Holocaust were at least partly reactions to the Eichmann trials, which were going on at the time and about which Plath almost certainly read in the newspaper (Peel 38–41). Instead, Plath makes her literally belated relation to the Holocaust evident by repeatedly disrupting chronology and adopting a stance of posthumousness through which past events continue to contaminate the present. At the same time, belatedness is apparent in figures that emphasize discrepancy and contingency. Metaphors and similes are frequently disrupted by metonymy, as Rose has pointed out in relation to "Daddy" (228), as well as by a provisional synecdoche. Plath's apostrophe disrupts the possibility of genuine, intimate speech addressed to a sympathetic listener, instead emphasizing the staged and parodic. I will elaborate these points throughout this chapter, first through close readings of "Daddy" and "Lady Lazarus" and then through a discussion of the different dynamics evident in poems included only in Ted Hughes's *Ariel* and in Plath's own version of the volume.

|||||||||||||||||||

In the introduction, I referred to the difficulty of directly defining the relation of the literal to the figurative in the context of writing about trauma. As the at times inconsistent metaphors by Walter Kalaidjian and Jacqueline Rose make clear, it is nearly impossible to describe this relation without recourse to figurative language, a tendency that reveals the entanglement of the figurative with the literal (as well as the theoretical). In two essays focusing on the figures employed by the critic Paul de Man, Neil Hertz offers a mode of reading that attempts to acknowledge the influence of literal events on figuration without reducing the latter to the former. Hertz first identifies a series of recurrent and "lurid" figures in de Man's writings, including images of dismemberment, mutilation, and disfigurement ("Lurid"). He later associates these figures with de Man's lived experience, especially the likelihood that he witnessed his mother's suicide by hanging ("More" 8). While Hertz acknowledges the presence in de Man's writings of recurrent "obsessions" (10), he also resists that idea, claiming instead that de Man's figures express "veiled autobiography" (10). The implication is that factual or biographical knowledge helps situate the figurative but does not eradicate its strangeness *as* figure.

Something similar is evident in Plath's Holocaust imagery. Here too the figurative (broadly construed as the trope, the word, the image, the phrase) does not merely or wholly express the literal (the outside world, the object, the event, the recollection). Instead, the poems insist that the Holocaust, which from the outset is not depicted as intact or real, can be depicted only via the poems' fractured figures.

Plath was clearly interested in the Holocaust and became more interested in late 1961 and 1962.[20] Yet the Holocaust was both physically and temporally remote from her own life. According to one reader, she learned about the Holocaust in school and studied it in college (Strangeways 371). Her lived relation to the Holocaust thus recalls trauma theory's discussion of the response of "the second generation," whose members, as Marianne Hirsch has claimed, experience not "identification" with the trauma of past events but a sense of "unbridgeable distance" from them (76). Yet the poems also differ dramatically from the ways Hirsch and others describe the response of the children of actual survivors. Plath's speakers are not helpless or guilty. Instead, they manipulate the Holocaust savagely and at times gleefully. Because the poems contain descriptions of performances, they provide especially clear examples of my general point about the difference between poems and trauma theory. If Plath's critique of trauma theory is proleptic, since the theory postdates her death, this asynchronicity evokes related asynchronicities evident within the poems as well as in how they have been read.

||||||||||||||||

What I have been calling literal belatedness—the depiction of a situation of aftermath—is, unsurprisingly, apparent in the ways "Daddy" and "Lady Lazarus" represent time and narrative. Both poems explore ruptured time frames, and both take place following deaths, in "Daddy" that of the speaker's father and in "Lady Lazarus" that of the speaker herself. Elegy traditionally mourns a death that has already occurred, positioning the speaker as a survivor. It thus affirms a belatedness that derives from a chronological process that generally culminates in the survivor taking leave of the dead. But "Daddy" and "Lady Lazarus" complicate this narrative structure by undermining conventional temporal and spatial distinctions between the living and the dead. Lady Lazarus speaks posthumously, and a similar sense of the unnatural and uncanny is apparent in the repeated but ineffectual acts of murder and attempted murder in "Daddy." Both poems thus complicate what might be called the ordinary or literal belatedness of survival. Their speakers are drawn back and forth across the line of mortality, at once asserting their similarity to and difference from the dead. Both also extend and even parody the belatedness of elegy in ways that draw attention to their manipulations of temporality: these protagonists are belated not because they chronicle bereavement but because they refuse it.

"Daddy" is structured chronologically. The poem depicts the speaker's repeated attempts to gain access to and kill Daddy even as he becomes, paradoxically, imbued by her with increasing power, as expressed through the changing metaphors and similes through which she describes him: early on, he is compared to a "statue" and "black shoe," then animated as "a Frisco seal," then compared to a "German" and a "swastika"; finally, he becomes an apparently immortal "devil" and "vampire."

Yet the poem also refuses this narrative at several key moments, especially when it turns from the chronicle of Daddy's increasingly powerful metamorphoses to a different and more "literal" acknowledgment that Daddy is actually dead. The speaker juxtaposes two distinct accounts of Daddy's previous death, one in which the daughter is responsible for the death ("Daddy, I have had to kill you") and another in which he has already died without the speaker's intervention ("You died before I had time," the next line reads, and toward the end of the poem, the speaker asserts, "I was ten when they buried you"). The speaker thus experiences Daddy's death as an event both within and exceeding her control. That Daddy, while dead, remains alive further complicates the situation; the poem both recollects and anticipates his death. "Daddy" thus juxtaposes an ongoing narrative of revenge, a retrospective view of his past death, and a proleptic anticipation of the future time when Daddy will be killed by the "villagers." This juxtaposition is partly ironic: the speaker's vindictiveness comes too late, as the ambiguous line "you died before I had time" (to love you fully? to murder you myself?) makes especially clear.

The poem's insistent repetitions (beginning with the first line, "You do not do, you do not do") and rhymes (the entire poem rhymes on the *oo* sound) intensify the obstruction of forward motion. So does Plath's reliance (typical of the *Ariel* poems) on the present and present perfect tenses. The first half of the poem in particular does not flash back to discrete events that occurred in the past. Instead, past events are represented as ongoing, interrupted by what occurs in the present moment. Thus, the speaker asserts not "Daddy, I *had* to kill you" or "Daddy, I *killed* you," but "Daddy, I *have had to* kill you," impelling this event into the present. (Significantly, this line is followed by the simple past of "You died before I had time," which interrupts the poem's fantasized narrative.)

The connection between these inconsistencies and the larger question of how literal events relate to their figurative representation is revealed by several moments in the poem that directly consider just this question. The poem alternates between a tone of straightforward, historical reportage ("You died before I had time") and a clearly figurative interpretation of these events (the next line is "Marble-heavy, a bag full of God"). This tension is especially apparent when the speaker uses the figurative to undermine the literal just following a description of Daddy "at the blackboard" in an apparently real, ordinary "picture." The speaker contradicts his apparent professorial mildness by insisting that he is nevertheless "a devil" despite, or even because of, his apparent innocuousness.

The poem's representation of the Holocaust reveals a similar sense of disruption. Drafts of the poem included the terms *Nazis* and *Hitler*, but Plath excised them in the revision process.[21] In the final version, the Holocaust is still present, but not as a coherent or intact event. Instead, it has been broken into pieces (through references to "Jew," "fascist," "swastika, "barb wire," "Meinkampf," and the like, all of which gesture, but incompletely, toward an event that the poem never names or explains. A related sense of fragmentation is apparent in the relation of the Holocaust imagery to the poem as a whole. Although the poem is often read as being "about" the Holocaust, imagery drawn from it—and references to Polish, Austrian, and German place names—appear only in seven of its sixteen stanzas. The poem elsewhere incorporates a range of settings from the opening "Frisco" to the final unspecified village and analogies for Daddy ranging from seals to vampires.

The temporal disruptions and resulting depiction of literal belatedness in "Daddy" are intensified in "Lady Lazarus," which Plath wrote about two weeks later. Although here the Holocaust is, if anything, more central than in "Daddy," "Lady Lazarus" excises much of the narrative and conflict of "Daddy." Along with a range of references to elements drawn from the Holocaust and a recurrent (if inconsistent) tension between past and present,

"Daddy" includes an underlying sense of antagonism between Jews and Nazis. "Lady Lazarus" includes few of these features. It does not depict the Holocaust as a conflict or even an event. Instead, the poem takes place in a present moment defined by repetition: this is resurrection "Number Three" of Lady Lazarus's nine (or rather, she "like the cat . . . [has] nine times to die"). The poem thus takes place in a liminal state between one death and the next and between the first rebirth and the final death. This state challenges the poem's final assertion of victorious resurrection, since the poem's logic implies that each rebirth must be followed by another death. While "Daddy" represents its speaker's attempt to reimagine an actual past-tense death, "Lady Lazarus" contains very few references to the past. Not surprisingly, the Holocaust is also more radically fractured. It appears not as a recognizable event but instead as the precondition of the poem's speech act. The powerful figure of Daddy (and his various avatars) becomes in "Lady Lazarus" an undefined "Herr Doktor. / . . . Herr Enemy," who never appears or acts in the poem. Nor is it clear whether the phrase refers to a single addressee or two different characters.

In the place of the basically narrative framework of "Daddy," "Lady Lazarus" conflates several distinct time frames. The Biblical era of Lazarus, the time of the Holocaust, and an apparently more recent scene of a carnival sideshow coexist, but the relation between them (does one follow the other? is one a metaphor for the other?) is unclear. While "Daddy" contains repeated words and phrases (including the speaker's stuttered "Ich, ich, ich, ich" and the words "Daddy" and "you"), Lady Lazarus's literal, lived situation is defined by repetition. Not only must she continually die and be resurrected, but she must keep performing her own bodily dismantling and reassembly, as the scene of the "big strip tease" makes especially clear. The speaker is all that remains of a Holocaust that is otherwise absent.

"Lady Lazarus" in these ways extends the sense of literal or chronological belatedness of "Daddy," as is especially clear in what seems to be the poem's most straightforwardly autobiographical moment, which reiterates a similar moment in "Daddy." In "Daddy," the speaker juxtaposes two chronologically distinct events: "I was ten when they buried you. / At twenty I tried to die / And get back, back, back to you." But "Lady Lazarus" unmakes the distinction between these events; the distinction between Daddy's death and the speaker's own is also eradicated, and the attempt at suicide depicted in "Daddy" here becomes something achieved and therefore recollected. Lady Lazarus recalls her own deaths at both ten and twenty, which have been disconnected from any cause and rendered equivalent, as is indicated by the parallel phrases "The first time [I died]" and "The second time."

In the introduction I noted Jacqueline Rose's description, in a discussion of Plath's poems, of the "pressure" put by the Holocaust on "the concept of linguistic figuration" (207). Certainly both poems manipulate figures of equivalence and intimacy in ways that enact and extend the belatedness apparent in their representations of temporality in the past. In the process, Plath implies that the Holocaust itself is a product of language rather than an autonomous historical event; it is available and expressible only through the unstable figures with which Plath conveys it.

In this context, it is significant that both poems use the term "bit" in reference to the speaker. In "Daddy," the speaker describes herself as "a bit of a Jew," fracturing a concept (Jewishness) that is generally seen as coherent. (The poem may here evoke the Nazi formula for determining whether partly Jewish people were classed as Jews.) In "Lady Lazarus," a similar quantification of something generally seen as indivisible is apparent in the speaker's reference to the "bit of blood" she displays to her audience and for which she receives a perhaps disproportionate "large charge." Here, in contrast to "Daddy," the speaker chooses self-division; breaking herself into pieces lets her receive both compensation and a thrill.

This repeated term gestures toward a larger pattern of fracturing and division in these and other poems in *Ariel*, one that evokes but contradicts the emphasis in comments by both Ted and Frieda Hughes on Plath's poetic commitment to preserving what both call "piece[s]" of her work and life.[22] Jacques Lacan associates the concept of the "*corps morcelé*" or "fragmented body" (sometimes translated as the "body in bits") with the estrangement from the bodily inherent in child development during the mirror stage (6). But in "Daddy," "Lady Lazarus," and other late poems, descriptions of breaking and rupture refer not only to the speaker's body or even to the poem's subject matter but also to the poem's formal and figurative resistance to cohesiveness.

"Daddy," as I indicated above, is structured around a series of metaphors and other analogies and thus around the notion of equivalence. But Plath also demonstrates the randomness and fluidity of metaphoric equivalence: each analogy, found to be inadequate or perhaps too mild, is quickly abandoned for another. Daddy's power is also inconsistent. He is at times deanimated (as "shoe," "statue," and "swastika") and at times not only alive but supernaturally powerful (as "devil" and "vampire"). Moreover, many of the poem's comparisons reveal that the speaker is also capable of bodily transformation. When Daddy is a "black shoe," she must inhabit him "like a foot" that is also personified insofar as it "Barely [dares] to breathe or Achoo"; when he is a Nazi, the speaker becomes a "gypsy ancestress."

As Rose notes, many of poem's analogies are not truly metaphorical. Rather than affirming a permanent or complete resemblance between Daddy and some other entity, the poem relies on simile, metonymy, and synecdoche. Simile, by inserting an intermediate "like" or "as" between the two objects compared, is generally seen as more contingent and less permanent than metaphor; metonymy too is in Rose's terms "partial, hesitant, and speculative" and reveals the "instability [of] any identity thereby produced" (228). Synecdoche also tends to deanimate as well as to reduce what is described, as when the poem represents Nazis via their attributes, including "Luftwaffe," "moustache," "Aryan eye," "swastika," and "boot."

The speaker's description of herself in relation to the Nazi-like Daddy reveals this analogy's instability:

I *thought* every German was you.
And the language obscene

An engine, an engine
Chuffing me off *like a Jew.*
. . . .
I began *to talk like a Jew.*
I think I may well be a Jew.

. . . .
With my gypsy ancestress and my weird luck
. . . .
I may be a bit of a Jew. (italics added)

As this passage progresses, the identification of speaker with Jew, already partial, is repeated and also reduced. At first her Jewish identity is the vehicle of a simile describing the German language. Then it is more directly associated with attributes of the speaker, but the identification is further qualified; she resembles a Jew only in the way that she talks. Then Plath omits the "like" of simile but intensifies the tentativeness of the analogy: a Jew is what "I think I may" be. The most direct analogy between self and Jew, "I may be a bit of a Jew," is also the most tentative and partial, and it is aligned with the earlier reference to a series of objects possessed by and synecdochically associated not with Jews but with gypsies, another class of Nazi victims.

Just as the speaker's identity as Jew is dismantled while being asserted, Daddy is never directly or wholly identified as a Nazi. The passage cited above begins with a synecdoche in which the speaker associates the singular Daddy with the collective "every German." The relationship here is tentative (the speaker "*thought* every German was you") but stable. But then Plath sets forth an analogy between the German language and an engine, which undoes the ordinary tropological distinction between the literally present tenor and the vehicle to which it is compared. "Language" is initially the vehicle; it is the actual entity to which the "engine" is compared. But the engine then becomes the vehicle of a second analogy. The term *engine* metonymically evokes the trains carrying Jews to concentration camps, which also transport the speaker, confirming her transformation into a Jew.

In this passage, the Holocaust is evoked as a vehicle to which the German language is compared. Elsewhere, the Holocaust is presented as an actual event or tenor. At times it is located

In the German tongue, *in the Polish town*
Scraped flat by the roller
Of wars, wars, wars. (italics added)

Elsewhere, references to the Holocaust—synecdochically evoked via the fascist, boot, and heart—are also described as actual. As the vehicle of the simile, they pre-exist Daddy, who exemplifies them:

> Every woman adores *a Fascist*,
> The boot in the face, the brute
> Brute heart of *a brute like you*. (italics added)

The late assertion "I made a *model of you,* / A man in black with a Meinkampf look" (italics added), though, positions the Holocaust differently: Daddy is the original version, later mimicked by the Hitler-like "model" in black.

The emphasis here, as in the analogy of speaker to Jew, is not on fixed or stable analogies but rather on the process of tropological conversion. The poem fails to define either Daddy or the Holocaust as its "real" subject or to grant either priority. In this way, Plath's fragmentation of the Holocaust's coherence is inseparable from her use of the figures of simile, metaphor, and synecdoche. The figurative strategies on which Plath relies enact the same failures of identification and analogy that mark Plath's temporal relation to the Holocaust.

Puns, which recur throughout Plath's late poems, intensify this sense of instability. The doubled or punning meaning of the poem's final word "through" ("Daddy, daddy, you bastard, I'm through") has often been noted. Earlier in the poem, it suggests both access (in that the voices on the phone try to "worm through") and separation (in that the speaker claims she is "finally through" with Daddy). The last line thus binds two contradictory claims: the speaker is gaining proximity to Daddy by asserting that she has finally vanquished him. The importance of other puns (or words with double or multiple meanings) is less frequently noted in Plath's late poems, although her awareness of them is evident in her dictionary underlinings of the contradictory definitions of words in her poems. For example, Plath underlined the etymology of *swastika* in her dictionary, which implies a sense of beneficence and care at odds with its Nazi associations: "*svastika,* fr. *svasti* <u>welfare</u>, fr. *su* <u>well</u> + *asti* <u>being, prop</u>." (*Webster's*). This etymology ironizes the reference to the swastika in "Daddy," suggesting that Daddy's identification with a swastika, like the Nazis' cooption of it as emblem, recalls his parental role as caregiver, a role eradicated from the poem.

Plath uses the word *tongue* twice in "Daddy," first in relation to the speaker, whose attempts to speak to Daddy are obstructed because "the tongue stuck in my jaw," and the second in relation to "the German tongue" or language, which becomes the engine that transports the speaker into a Jewish identity associated with an actual concentration camp. The term joins a body part with a language, something internal and private with something external and shared, and a part of the speaker with a quality associated with Daddy. In the process, it undermines the poem's oppositions between victimized speaker and aggressive Daddy in ways that draw attention to the speaker's troubling tendency through the poem to embrace the very attributes she reviles in Daddy, especially his violence.

The doubled use of *tongue* also exposes the paradox of the poem as a speech act, since the speaker's previous inability to speak (she says directly, "I could hardly speak") is evident in the poem's halting and stuttering language, challenging its rhetoric of victory and revenge. Although the speaker chronicles in the past tense a series of increasingly ferocious acts of defiance against Daddy ("I thought every German was you," "I made a model of you"), she more often insists on Daddy's continuing presence and power ("I have had to kill you," "I never could tell," "Daddy, you can lie back now"). This inconsistency emphasizes the poem's double function. As it chronicles what its speaker has already done, "Daddy" performs (or re-performs) these acts, boasting of them in ways that imply an attempt to ensure future liberation rather than (only) an account of an already completed act. Like the two references to the tongue, this doubling reveals the poet's awareness that the poem cannot create a reality beyond its own ritualized and debased speech act. The sense of artifice and performance is intensified by the literal uselessness of the poem's vindictiveness: as in Bidart's "Curse," which I discussed, Daddy does not need to be murdered because he is already dead.

The repeated references to the difficulty of speech—"The tongue stuck in my jaw," "I could hardly speak"—emphasize something similar, as does the poem's repeated reversion to a debased babytalk that implies an infantile speaker distinct from the poet. The poem is caught, as Plath makes clear, between authentic rage and histrionic utterance, which may explain Plath's identification of the poem as "light verse" (Stevenson 270) and the fact that she and a friend apparently "f[e]ll about with laughter" when Plath read the poem aloud (Stevenson 277).[23] Both serious and comic, poignant and parodic, in the end the poem is, like any poem, a construct of language and imagery. As a belated utterance, it cannot represent or comment on the extrinsic or literal reality of either the Holocaust or Daddy.

The address in "Daddy" does something similar, as I have argued at more length elsewhere (*Overheard* 29–36). The poem is insistent, even exaggerated, in its address; the term "Daddy" recurs five times in the poem and the pronoun "you" in reference to Daddy sixteen times. The poem, as I have indicated, is preoccupied both with Daddy's current state of being dead and with the (redundant and illogical) wish to kill him, a double focus that evokes the similar inconsistency of poetic address. Elegiac apostrophe by definition addresses someone known to be dead and thus denies the psychological reality of this death for the bereaved speaker. Plath's address concisely expresses this paradox, but Plath extends its temporal implications: like all apostrophe to the dead, Plath's address of Daddy denies the literal fact of his death, but the speaker also advocates for and justifies his future death. This impossible double position ultimately reveals the poem's address, like its tone of vengeance, to be a stance, one that derives from the speaker's actual belated survival.

I have been arguing that belatedness is evident in "Daddy" not only in the speaker's description of chronology and remembering but also in the figures through which she depicts the Holocaust. This fact is especially significant since the speaker remains separate from Daddy and the "personal" situation in the poem remains unreconciled with the "public" situation of the Holocaust. Plath has been criticized for this discrepancy, yet my reading suggests that the discrepancy is the point. As it repeatedly refuses to convey the Holocaust as a historical event, the poem reveals that the Holocaust's power lies *in* its fracturing, a sense of atrocity that floats free from its source.

The figurative belatedness of "Lady Lazarus," a poem Rose does not discuss, is more extreme than in Daddy. Here, Plath unequivocally abandons the possibility of analogy and thus measurement, partly by abandoning the earlier poem's tropes of balance and equivalence. I discussed above the chronological disruptions of "Lady Lazarus," especially its conflation of different time frames, its excision of the sense of conflict and plot of "Daddy," and its refusal to depict the Holocaust as a conflict or even a historical event. While "Daddy" breaks the Holocaust into pieces, in "Lady Lazarus," the Holocaust is already in pieces, and the speaker embodies this fragmentation. But the poem also, more radically than "Daddy," refuses the possibility of deriving wholeness or meaning from its fragments. It undermines the possibility of a fixed or stable identity by presenting instead a scene of performance before a hostile audience.

By depicting the speaker's broken body, "Lady Lazarus" intensifies and literalizes the synecdoche of "Daddy." In "Daddy," the logic of synecdoche, by which part stands for whole, is unquestioned: "engine" and "swastika" refer to the Holocaust. But in "Lady Lazarus," the relation of part to whole is represented inconsistently. The speaker at times asserts that her body's broken bits can be reassembled (partly through the revival of her corpse), as when she claims, "I may be skin and bone, // Nevertheless, I am *the same, identical* woman" (italics added). Elsewhere, though, especially toward the poem's end, her description of the details of her dismemberment complicates this possibility:

Ash, ash—
You poke and stir.
Flesh, bone, there is nothing there—

A cake of soap,
A wedding ring,
A gold filling.

The dash after "there" elides a series of conflicting ways of linking the vanished flesh to the soap, ring, and filling that persist after the body's obliteration. The Nazi soap (purportedly made from the ash of burned bodies) suggests physical transformation: it literally derives, like the ash, from the flesh and bone. The ring and filling, though, suggest something quite different.

As former possessions of the speaker, they metonymically (and also synecdochically) represent her, as the crown represents the king.

The passage also suggests another, more disturbing alternative—that the body has been transformed into a commodity. Commodities participate in a system of valuation quite different from that of poetic images. Images can be freely transformed and altered; they can be nonmathematically made to represent each other, so that something insignificant can represent something important and the reverse. But the value of commodities is by definition quantifiable. Because they are exchanged, they can be exploited for private gain. That Plath was interested in the ways that gold can function both as commodity and as something else is apparent from her dictionary underlinings, which emphasize gold's physical qualities (it is "very heavy" and is marked by "yellow color," its metaphoric capacity to signify "riches," and its significance as a means of exchange (*Webster's*). The poem's late image of "The pure gold baby // That melts to a shriek" combines these different aspects, along with the commodification implicit in the Nazis' extraction of gold fillings from those they killed. But unlike the Nazis, who melted down the gold fillings taken from the mouths of their victims so as more easily to quantify and reuse the gold, Plath uses "melt[ing]" as a synonym for dissolution, converting gold's apparent solidity, value, and permanence into a temporary, intangible human cry.

The implications of considering the broken body not in terms of its inherent worth but as a commodity are explored earlier in the poem:

There is a charge

For the eyeing of my scars, there is a charge
For the hearing of my heart—

. . . .

And there is a charge, a very large charge,
For a word or a touch
Or a bit of blood

Or a piece of my hair or my clothes.

In one sense, the speaker's ability to bestow a word or touch reveals that she has anachronistically survived her own destruction. Yet the bits of blood, hair, and clothes suggest a different, synecdochic model, one that evokes the Catholic relics worshipped as a representation of the intact saint. Here, then, the passage presents the speaker as both intact and broken, an incongruity heightened by the blood's division into discrete "bits." But the passage also links the speaker's fragmentation with commodification; it leads to the exaction of a "charge" or fee. As with the description of the ring and filling, this economic reading undermines the synecdochic one. The speaker's willingness to be paid to reveal her scars and bestow her blood implies that the pieces she displays are valuable not because they allude to or represent the now-burned body but because of what they can be exchanged for.

Yet this reading, too, is unstable. The word *charge* signals something quantifiable and external (the fee paid by the crowd eager to witness this spectacle) but also something internal (the speaker's and also the audience's thrill at her self-revelation). (Plath's dictionary underlinings highlight these and other meanings of the word, including the sense of unjust accusation.[24]) The instability is crucial to both the passage and the poem as a whole. "Lady Lazarus" thus affirms and challenges its synecdochic logic in ways that interrogate the value of human life and the integrity of the human body as well as the memory of the Holocaust. Commodification, this passage suggests, has challenged what might otherwise be a more benign tropological mode. The speaker here flaunts her capacity to convert the horrors of the Holocaust not only into a spectacle but into a money-making venture. And the presence of the jostling, eager audience suggests that both the speaker and her readers see the Holocaust in the same way.

As the passage I just cited makes clear, "Lady Lazarus" emphasizes the speaker's need to transmit her experiences to an audience. The impersonal construction "There is" in relation to the "charge" elides the speaker's experiences with those who witness her. While the savage description of the "peanut-crunching crowd" recalls the hostile address of "Daddy," the scene of performance is different. While the performance of revenge in "Daddy" had no real audience (insofar as Daddy was already dead), "Lady Lazarus" describes a doubled scene of performance reliant on apostrophe and address. (This scene is even more complex in the poem's earlier drafts.[25]) At the beginning of the poem, the speaker addresses the singular "my enemy" using the elevated and artificial "O" of apostrophe, and toward the end, she addresses him again (as "Herr Enemy"). This addressee in the last stanzas is equivalent or perhaps transformed to "Herr Doktor," "Herr God," and "Herr Lucifer." (The "O," though, is replaced with the less formal, less archaic, more evaluative "So.") Moreover, midway through, the speaker abandons the imagery of the Holocaust for a very different scene of a circus sideshow that is also a "big strip tease," whose spectators she also addresses.

These shifting addressees recall the psychoanalytic model of repetition central to trauma theory's notion of belatedness. The speaker's performance before the crowd seems partly a belated attempt to gain mastery or possession of her earlier victimization by the Nazi doctor.

> The peanut-crunching crowd
> Shoves in to see
>
> . . . .
>
> Gentlemen, ladies
>
> These are my hands
> My knees.

But, in contrast to what psychoanalysis might predict, this reenactment of injury is not restorative or therapeutic. Instead, it reveals the separation of the speaker from her witnesses, as well as the failure of narrative development in the poem more generally. What Lady Lazarus articulates is not her connection with but her separation from and contempt for her spectators. This sense of disdain challenges the intimacy implied by the shift to addressing the gentlemen and ladies: the speaker does not alter the contempt she has expressed all along about her reincarnation. Nor, when the poem addresses "Herr Doktor. / . . . Herr Enemy" in stanza 22, is its tone substantially different from that to the gentlemen and ladies in stanza 10.

This performance thus seems to be a theatricalized and perhaps parodic version of the speaker's earlier victimization by the Doktor; it reveals that she has all along been performing her victimization. This section also vividly exposes the dismantling or corruption of the Holocaust as a "real" event: all that is left of the Holocaust is the performance of victimization. Yet the passage is also ambivalent about the extent to which Lady Lazarus retains control of her body: although she is unwrapped by an unidentified "them," she identifies her revealed parts as her own ("my hands / My knees"). Plath also implies that Lady Lazarus's performance shields her against vulnerability. Her description of the performance follows her straightforward acknowledgment of vulnerability ("I am only thirty") and precedes her similarly straightforward account of her past deaths ("The first time it happened . . . / The second time . . .").

Plath's hostile address to the gentlemen and ladies has often been read as an articulation of Plath's relation to the actual readers of her self-exposing or "confessional" poems.[26] This reading recalls trauma theory's discussion of the risk of "'contagion'" evident in "the traumatization of the ones who listen" (Caruth, Introduction 10). It also intensifies the belatedness inherent in the poem's premise of posthumous speech; the drama within the poem can be linked to the drama of the poem's reception only when the poem is read proleptically, in terms of acts of readership that will occur later on. Plath here seems to have anticipated her readers' subsequent response to her poems in much the same way that she seems to have anticipated her suicide. Thus, the poem functions both as a belated and an anticipatory performance. Because Plath has already depicted her readers' responses to her poems, when these readers later respond ravenously or contemptuously to her self-revelations, they are merely enacting a role Plath scripted for them. Indeed, poems like "Lady Lazarus" seem designed to incite just these reactions in readers.

In this way, in contrast to much writing about the Holocaust, which seeks *either* to keep it alive or bring it back to life, "Lady Lazarus" asserts the *simultaneous* presence of death and resurrection, deanimation and animation, and fragmentation and wholeness.[27] Despite Lady Lazarus's insistence that what she describes is "real," the figures on which the poem relies put these notions under what Rose calls, in reference to the Holocaust itself, intense "pressure" (207). In the process, the poem offers an extreme argument about belatedness: in a multiply belated situation, poetic figuration fails, and must fail, to transform or reanimate the images it manipulates. It is from this failure, to recall Pinsky's "The Anniversary," which I discussed in the introduction, that poetic "meaning"—here a meaning all but evacuated of meaning or, as Pinsky later in that poem asserts, an always deferred "meaning . . . beyond / Meaning"—becomes possible.

|||||||||||||||||

Many of the dynamics related to belatedness that I have been examining in these two poems are, as I suggested above, evident in other poems in *Ariel*, although "Lady Lazarus" and "Daddy" are somewhat atypical in that they refer explicitly to public events. This similarity is unsurprising, given the short period in which many of these poems were written; many of Plath's late poems use similar terms and a similar tercet form, and they treat similar topics. Many deal in different ways with literal or chronological belatedness, often evident in manipulations of time frame that refuse the possibility of narrative or change. They also repeatedly confuse the literal with the figurative and undermine their own analogies.

Certainly, a number of the poems in Plath's *Ariel* consider the past and acts of memory in ways that draw attention to their speakers' condition of literal belatedness, although for the most part their references to past events are less explicit than in the poems I have been discussing or in Plath's earlier poems, as Uta Gosmann has argued.[28] Several directly treat historical events and characters, including, for example, the Napoleon-like figure who narrates "Getting There" (*Ariel Restored* 57–59).[29] Others consider the possibility of reconstructing a fragmentary past. For example, "The Detective" asks questions about a series of clues and ends by commanding Watson to "Make notes" [31–32]). Others update earlier stories: "Magi" juxtaposes "angels" from the Biblical scene with "laundry" and "the multiplication table" (37), while "Gulliver" addresses the fictional character and elaborates his physical situation in the present tense (56). Others, including "Poppies in October" (44), refer directly to the condition of lateness.[30]

Related dynamics are also evident in *Ariel*'s recurrent narratives of often violent escape. "Purdah" (62–64) first characterizes its speaker as a viewed object, defined by her "visibilities" and her capacity to be possessed ("I am his"), then moves to a future scene in which the speaker gains autonomy, evident in her capacity to "unloose" a range of dubious weapons, including "One feather" and "One note" (63–64). Similar scenes of escape appear in a number of other poems, including "Fever 103°" (78–80), "Ariel" (33–34), and "Stings" (86–88). Yet these poems repeatedly compromise their own narratives of liberation by implying, as do both "Daddy" and "Lady Lazarus," that the future will not in fact be very different from the past or that escaping will lead to the speaker's destruction. I noted above that the use of the present perfect in "Daddy" affirms the past's continuing incursion into the present. This verb tense recurs in other poems, undermining their speakers' attempts to vanquish the past. Repeated images of smoke, veils, and mirrors also undermine the sense of closure that might otherwise be associated with fire's capacity to impel rupture or rebirth.[31]

Such scenes of chronological instability are often expressed, as in "Daddy" and "Lady Lazarus," through a figurative mode that destabilizes equivalence by focusing on shifting and often unexplained images, at times in relation to the self-consciously poetic term "image" itself. "Thalidomide" (9–10), for example, both personifies the image and associates it with the termination of life; it "Flees and aborts." Other poems are structured as lists of images or similes: "Cut" (25–26) converts a cut finger into a series of other objects and situations, while in "Elm" (27–28), the speaker's revelation of her self-dissolution ("I break up in pieces") follows a list of ambiguously placed objects (including "the sea," "hooves," "rain," and "sunsets"). Such poems ("Fever 103°" is another) draw attention to the often unexplained relation between static, literal things and symbolic processes of change or metamorphosis. Another group of poems exemplifies the difficulty of identifying the relation between highly opaque and decontextualized images.[32]

Other poems interrogate their own figurative capacity to transform objects. Several draw attention to this process by using similes and improbable analogies, as when the speaker of "The Bee Meeting" (81–83) hopes that the bees will mistake her for "cow parsley." Others, including "Berck-Plage" (51, 53) and "The Courage of Shutting Up" (45–46), punningly shift, as does "Daddy," between the physical and metaphoric significance of the tongue.[33] While such references tend to challenge the stability of objects or nouns,

Plath's use of adjectives or verbs as nouns (including "those pale irretrievables" [28] and a "strangle of branches" [28] in "Elm"; "The abstracts" [37] in "Magi"; and a "Sheath of impossibles" [62–63] in "Purdah") reveals a quite different impulse to fix ordinarily transient qualities.

The simultaneous existence in print of Plath's and Ted Hughes's versions of *Ariel* intensifies the recurrent temporal and figurative displacements within the poems: the same poems can be read in different settings. Several poems included only in Hughes's edition emphasize scenes of temporal discontinuity more extreme than in "Daddy" and "Lady Lazarus." "The Swarm" (*Ariel* 72–74) associates "Somebody . . . in our town" currently shooting at swarming bees (a character whom several critics identify with Hughes himself) with Napoleon.[34] Here—in contrast to the depiction of Napoleon in "Getting There," which emphasizes bodily fragmentation—the focus is on historical juxtaposition. Napoleon's early invasions of "Russia, Poland, and Germany!" and smug sense of being "pleased, . . . pleased with everything" are here opposed to his subsequent defeat at Waterloo and exile to Elba; the speaker's foreknowledge of what Napoleon was ignorant of is then extended to the bee shooter, whose arrogance seems similarly destined for humiliation. "Mary's Song" (*Ariel* 52), a poem also omitted from Plath's ordering, resembles "Lady Lazarus," which Plath wrote less than a month earlier, in its juxtaposition of the Holocaust with a Biblical character; here too, Plath emphasizes their incongruity.

These poems reveal Plath's interest in responding to "public" events in ways that involve different time frames. Plath's Holocaust poem "Little Fugue" (*Ariel* 78–80), written six months before "Daddy" and included only in Hughes's *Ariel*—Plath likely rejected it from the volume because she did not think highly of it—focuses more directly on the Holocaust and memory than Plath's later poems, asserting "I am lame in the memory," listing a series of recalled fragments prefaced by "I remember," and including specific memories of the speaker's father. It might thus be inferred that Plath became in subsequent months able to consider memory and survivorship less directly, partly by compressing and, to recall Rose's phrase again, "put[ting] pressure on" the poem's figuration, making *it* articulate the condition of belatedness that is more baldly identified in "Little Fugue."

Other, very late poems excluded from Plath's *Ariel* but included in Hughes's reveal an even more explicit concern with memory and the passage of time. Several of these poems also juxtapose different time frames, contrasting a present defined by movement and change with an eternity associated with stillness and paralysis. These dynamics are central to "Years" (*Ariel* 81), which was composed, like "Mary's Song," in November 1962. "Years" claims "Eternity bores me, / I never wanted it" and then contrasts the death of the speaker's soul with a "great Stasis," which the speaker then belittles, prophesying instead a future associated with the "merciless churn" of horse hooves. While the poems in Plath's *Ariel* sometimes end by gesturing toward a provisional future act of liberation or destruction, many of the very late poems not included in her version of *Ariel* directly imagine such a future. "Totem" (84) is told nearly entirely in the future tense, while "Sheep in Fog" (3) ends with a look toward a future heaven that is "Starless and fatherless, a dark water."

Several of Plath's late poems also extend the posthumous gaze of "Lady Lazarus," looking not only ahead to but back from death. "Words" (*Ariel* 95), for example, takes place "years later," while "Edge" (*Ariel* 93), one of Plath's two final poems (the other is the more playful "Balloons" [88–89]) looks back from the state of being dead, emphasizing what is "perfected," "accomplish[ed]," and "over." (This prolepsis has been central to readings of the poem as a harbinger of Plath's imminent suicide.) Plath's *Ariel*, in contrast, moves, as others have noted, toward reconciliation; its last word, as Plath herself noted, is "spring."

The discrepancy between the volumes raises, as I indicated above, questions about Plath's intention and that of those who published *Ariel*: is it more accurate (or ethical or aesthetically important) to convey Plath's wishes or to offer a full chronology of her work? But it also reveals belatedness's political function. Belatedness here enables, among other things, a strategy of reading; as has been several times argued, Hughes's changes to Plath's volume were motivated at least partly by self-interest.[35] By emphasizing the inevitability of Plath's suicide, Hughes's version shields him from responsibility for her death by perpetuating the notion that Plath was ill and unstable, a conviction also evident in his own poems about Plath in *Birthday Letters*. Accentuating Plath's rhetoric of belatedness and prolepsis thus seems to have served Hughes personally (by absolving him of responsibility for Plath's death and therefore of guilt), as well as both publicly (they preserved his reputation, arguably to the detriment of Plath's) and financially (insofar as the mystique associated with her suicide caused increased sales of her books, with royalties paid to Hughes).

|||||||||||||||||||

I have been focusing throughout this chapter on Plath's consideration of the relation between belatedness and remembering. Though this relation is often obstructed, it is also direct. But at least one poem included only in Plath's *Ariel* explores belatedness from a different perspective, by considering forgetting. "Amnesiac" (*Ariel Restored* 71–72), like "Paralytic" (included in both versions) and several other poems, uses its title to identify an otherwise unnamed protagonist afflicted with a condition involving extreme limitations. The poem also resembles a number of poems in Plath's version (including "Barren Woman" [*Ariel Restored* 13], "The Jailor" [23–24], and "Elm" [27–28]) in its adoption of an unstable authorial position. Mostly narrated by the characters named in the titles, these poems also look *at* these characters. "Amnesiac" contains a similarly multiple perspective: beginning by addressing a male amnesiac, it is narrated midway through by a detached observer and ends by giving voice to the amnesiac.

This inconsistency illuminates the narrative challenges of writing about amnesia, which can generally be described only from the outside. The poem begins with this paradox, describing the "beautiful blank" of having forgotten, then implausibly enumerating the various things that have been "Erased." The image of erasure deanimates the amnesiac, a situation literalized and extended by the third-person narrator's description of his forgetting as a process in which "Old happenings // Peel from his skin." Yet, as this image suggests, amnesia also offers the protagonist freedom. The amnesiac later confirms this sense of escape and possibility by refusing to return "home" and associating forgetting with both sweetness and identity: "Sweet Lethe is my life."

The poem thus presents forgetting as a way to replace a tired reality (defined both by the compulsion to remember and the physical confinement of the hospital) with brighter, at times titillating fantasies.[36] It associates the failure of memory with potential and agency rather than fear and disorientation. That this position is difficult to maintain is clear from the poem's struggles to keep control of its own fragments. But "Amnesiac" also illuminates the concern with the transformative potential of forgetting in many of the other poems in *Ariel*. Certainly a number of its terms, including "sweet[ness]," "Lethe," and "peel[ing]," recur elsewhere.[37]

The poem's extreme repudiation of memory reveals a more general, if occluded, feature of Plath's *Ariel*: here, forgetting enables access to processes of stripping, peeling (or unpeeling), and erasure to which Plath refers throughout the volume and that are both liberating and dangerous. To forget is poetically useful; it creates opportunities for breaking and rupture, disrupting what might otherwise rely too heavily on facts. Reading "Amnesiac" alongside "Daddy" and "Lady Lazarus" reveals that these better-known poems do not so much chronicle ruptures in memory as repudiate memory itself. Beginning in the aftermath of an event from which many details have already been, in the terms of "Amnesiac," "Erased," they explore the liberating possibilities of dream, performance, and what Rose calls fantasy.

More exactly, "Daddy" and "Lady Lazarus" explore the possibilities of transformation. The nurses "rise on either side of [the amnesiac] like stars"; here the simile imports something unexpected and improbable into the hospital scene. Plath's similes, as I have suggested, tend to pull back from full identification. They emphasize a fracturing often linked to destruction, as the partial analogies between Daddy and Nazi reveal. Yet "Amnesiac" reveals that destructiveness occurs *through* a rhetoric of transformation; in Plath's late poems, the two impulses are always paired. Dispensing with memory, "Amnesiac" implies, is the precondition for transformation. Without needing to remember what actually happened, the belated poet is free to construct an alternative present, and even a future, from the pieces that remain. In Plath's late poems, as I have already indicated, motion—especially self-destructive flight and uprising—often prefigures stillness. But "Amnesiac" tells a story that ends with a stillness that signals not destruction but escape, just as forgetting enables fantasy. Recalling this potential for liberation reveals an alternative to the critical narrative that moves inexorably toward (and then looks back from) Plath's suicide. To recall the utility of forgetting also releases Plath's poems from readings that evaluate them based on their verisimilitude (or lack thereof). This alternative reading instead emphasizes invention and liberating performance.

The amnesiac is, in the end, a liminal figure, poised between immobility and liberation and between passivity and agency. The Holocaust in Plath's poems is similar: it exists in the poems as a specter, neither totally alive nor totally dead. Plath's *Ariel* poems make clear that if the Holocaust cannot be possessed, it also cannot be vanquished. Its images of smoke, corpses, and burning are present even in poems that do not allude directly to the Holocaust. Like smoke itself, they pervade Plath's late poems, only partly visible but nearly omnipresent. Something similar is true for Plath's belated readers. The fractured presence of the Holocaust makes us aware of our own condition of aftermath, even if we do not ordinarily identify ourselves as coming after the Holocaust. This sense of transmission confirms the Holocaust's evasive power. Or, more exactly, the power of Plath's poems lies for contemporary readers not only in their allusions to the Holocaust but more crucially in their experience of talking about it again, in the context of an overload of talk about the Holocaust. It is the multiplicity of these modes of belatedness—literal, figurative, and readerly—that enable Plath's late poems to keep speaking to us, awkwardly, illogically, but with an authority that signals Plath's particularly negative lyric mastery.

Chapter Two

"To feel with a human stranger"

Address and Asymmetrical Witness in Adrienne Rich's
Dark Fields of the Republic

I ended the previous chapter by considering the overlaying of different modes of belatedness in Plath's late poems. The temporal condition of belatedness is figuratively evident, I argued, in the inconsistent address of "Lady Lazarus" (*Ariel Restored* 14–17). Lady Lazarus moves from description to address, first of the "Gentlemen, ladies" observing her, then of "Herr Doktor. / . . . Herr Enemy," and finally of "Herr God, Herr Lucifer." In the process, she shifts from something like reader address to apostrophe (address to those absent or dead). This interest in the reader's reaction is more generally evident in the ways Plath's *Ariel* poems interrogate witness. Repeatedly, these poems ask, or impel their readers to ask, whether their speakers are reliable witnesses and by implication whether we, as readers, are obligated to accept their claims. The poems themselves thus seem proleptically to pose questions about their own reception. To cite an obvious example, does the fact that Plath manipulates and defaces the Holocaust make these poems, in Irving Howe's terms, "monstrous, utterly disproportionate" (12) or, in the stronger language of George Steiner, a "larceny" (301)?[1] And if so, should or must we as readers condemn this work? Such questions here and elsewhere often have moral implications; they encourage us to determine not only how we want to respond to the poems but how we should.

Witness is clearly involved in such questions, but it is worth noting that two different notions of witness are often conflated in discussions such as Howe's and Steiner's. The first involves immediacy: to witness something is to see it at first hand. But the second, more detached mode of witness generally requires temporal distance. When a witness describes a crime in court, for example, she is reconstructing what she previously saw (the common term is "*eye*witness"), converting it into a narrative or testimony with the power to condemn or free a suspect. The *OED* acknowledges these two different ideas: to witness is first of all "to be a witness, spectator, or auditor of (something of interest, importance, or special concern)" and "to see with one's own eyes," that is, to observe actual (often traumatic) events (to bear witness *to* them). But *to witness* is also "to testify to" and "to furnish oral or written evidence of" such events or to recount them later to people not originally present (to bear witness *before* or *for* others). Belatedness is thus essential to witness, and when the thing described has not been experienced personally, this belatedness is increased. In such cases, what might be called the immediate phase of witness is excised, leaving only what has variously been called "vicarious," "secondary," or "belated witness."[2] (The term *testimony* is sometimes used to signal the subsequent description of what was witnessed beforehand.[3]) The gap between these two modes of witnessing evokes the partly analogous distinction I have been establishing between literal belatedness (which is immediate and experiential) and figurative belatedness (evident indirectly, through language).

In this context, it becomes clear that behind several condemnations of Plath's Holocaust poems lies the assumption that those who did not witness the Holocaust firsthand (that is, experience it personally) have no authority to describe it as if they had. Instead, these readers imply, nonwitnesses should adopt terms that acknowledge their distance. Plath's error—and indeed her moral failing—is thus in depicting herself (via her poems' speakers) not as a detached observer of (a secondary witness to) the Holocaust but as a participant in it (a primary witness). Although I argued in chapter 1 that Plath's speakers depict the Holocaust in terms that emphasize belatedness, this belatedness has not always been evident to readers. In fact, complaints about these poems often imply that poetic (as opposed to oral) witness requires a double allegiance, both to the truth of what occurred and to the poem's readers, whose understanding of past events is shaped partly by the poems. Plath clearly reveals neither kind of allegiance: her Holocaust poems disregard the truth of the events she describes and often express contempt for their readers. It can be argued, though, that these poems also expose the fundamental asymmetry of witness itself, the gap between how events are seen and how they are (later) conveyed to others.

Plath's poems thus illuminate the problematic relation between witness and poetry. Yet these ideas have been often linked, at least over the past twenty or so years. Carolyn Forché was among the first to define such a poetry in her influential 1993 anthology *Against Forgetting*, in which she identified and collected what the book's subtitle calls an international "Twentieth-Century Poetry of Witness." Such poetry, as Forché claims in the anthology's introduction, derives from "conditions of historical and so-cial extremity" experienced personally by the poets and evident in their biographies (30), including "exile, state censorship, political persecution, house arrest, [and] torture" (29). Forché calls the volume as a whole "a po-etic memorial to those who have suffered and resisted through poetry itself" (31) and associates this poetry not only with "trauma" (33) but with "claims against the political order . . . made in the name of justice" (31). Yet she also associates the anthology's poems with "paradox and difficult equivocation" (40) and claims that because it is not always possible to ascertain whether "a given text . . . [is] 'objectively' true" (31), it is difficult to read poems "in purely evidentiary terms" (33).

In a 2011 essay, Forché extends these ideas in ways that qualify her ear-lier emphasis on lived experience. She also acknowledges, if briefly, the importance of "*aftermath*" to poems about traumatic events ("Reading").[4] Forché here redefines *witness,* in terms adapted from Emmanuel Levinas, as "a call to the *other,*" and asserts, citing Philippe Lacoue-Labarthe, that the poem's act of bearing witness is "not simply an act of memory" but "the out-line of once infinite responsibility for *the other one*" ("Reading").[5] Forché's emphasis on responsibility evokes her earlier assertion about the relation of poetry to "resist[ance]" and "justice." It also recalls, at least indirectly, related assumptions about ethics implicit in some condemnations of Plath's Holocaust poems, as I indicated above.

Despite Forché's revision of her earlier views, the concept of the "poetry of witness" has remained influential in readings of postwar poetry; here too "witness" tends to be associated with personal and direct experience, generally of traumatic events.[6] And Adrienne Rich's poems have often been read as examples of this kind of poetry, perhaps partly because Rich herself has indicated her interest in the topic.[7] This concern is evident throughout Rich's career, especially in her early volumes, published around the time of *Ariel*, which tend to speak—often autobiographically—from the position of someone coming to speech. This tendency reveals, as have sometimes been noted, thematic similarities between Plath and Rich's poems, perhaps unsurprisingly, given that they were contemporaries and sometime rivals. Yet Rich outlived Plath by some fifty years, and her later poems often interrogate the assumptions that underlie witness and testimony. In particular, Rich's 1995 volume *Dark Fields of the Republic*, on which I will focus in this chapter, presents an extended meditation on and interrogation of the tensions inherent in the project of bearing witness, especially to past events of which the speaker has no firsthand experience. By emphasizing the condition of belatedness (as well as physical distance), the poems in *Dark Fields* critically reassess the notion of witness and the possibility of an effective and politically mobilizing poetry of witness by exploring its dangers, especially of too easily appropriating the (often past) experiences of others. As Rich commented in 1994, a year before the publication of *Dark Fields*, questioning the utility of the poetry of witness is "really at the very core of who I am" (Rothschild).[8]

Plath figuratively conveys the thematics of belatedness by interrogating analogy and, in "Lady Lazarus," undermining the sympathy generally associated with poetic address. The poems of *Dark Fields* frequently describe the experiences of others, often depicting their speaker as an observer. Like "Lady Lazarus," they also directly consider and at times address their readers. Lady Lazarus both reviles and admits to pandering to her audience. Rich's speakers enact a related ambivalence: they at once attempt to interest or convince their readers and express despair at their inability to do so. The figure of address recurs in the volume; approximately two-thirds of its forty-two poems and numbered sections include an often undefined or shifting "you."[9] By using this figure inconsistently, in a way that emphasizes slippages and asymmetry, Rich figuratively expresses the temporal problems intrinsic to bearing belated witness. More exactly, Rich's address exposes the gap between the first, passive phase of witness and the belated transmission of this material to others, especially future readers. Rich repeatedly conveys scenes of what I here call asymmetrical witness, often by slipping between apostrophe—address of those once present but currently absent—and address to an undefined group of future readers. Such tensions often foreground the poems' multiple time frames; they are caught between the wish to comprehend past events and (belatedly) to convey them to a future audience.

Such issues are central to "Comrade" (*Dark Fields* 59–60), the first poem in the volume's six-poem final sequence "Inscriptions." "Comrade" explores the asymmetry of witness with particular economy: it reveals the discrepancy between looking back at those who have suffered and forward to the reader's reception of the poem. The poem presents an explicit and doubled scene of testimony; the poem describes (and so gives testimony to) a scene of "testimony" within the poem.

Toward the end of the first stanza, not-quite-parallel syntax concisely expresses the problem of how to connect watching someone else with telling about the experience:

My testimony: yours: Trying to keep faith
not with each other exactly yet it's the one known and unknown
who stands for, imagines the other   with whom faith could be
    kept. (59)

Both "I" and "you," the first three words reveal, are engaged in acts of testimony, and the first colon implies that these acts are analogous. But while at first the speaker asserts that one character "stands for . . . the other," she immediately pulls back from this model of equivalence to a more provisional act of "imagin[ing]." (Rich also does not specify whether the poem's speaker is "the one" or "the other.") The use of the present participle intensifies the confusion: it is unclear who is "trying to keep faith" and when.

The poem's opening lines anticipate these slippages by implying a narrative, then complicating it:

> Little as I *knew* you I *know* you: little as you *knew* me you *know* me
> —that's the light we stand under when we meet. (59, italics added)

A past of "little" knowing yields to a present of knowing, but the two characters are also involved in a parallel and reciprocal process, even as the poem chronicles the particular moment when they "meet." In the next lines, the speaker depicts herself "look[ing] . . . " at and "watching" what surrounds her, a visual act later juxtaposed with the addressee's symmetrical act of "listening for voices within and against." But the poem also undermines this symmetry along with the poem's conventional vantage point by claiming that the "you" has been "drawn through the pupil of your eye," entering an organ that ordinarily perceives the outside world. The poem's final imagery of mirrors and reflection furthers the asymmetry: we do not know what is being reflected or to what extent the poet is able to reflect back what the addressee has witnessed.[10]

Even as "Comrade" considers the equivalence between "I" and "you," Rich emphasizes her own authorial power. The poet asymmetrically bears witness to the addressee's testimony, an act that is itself witnessed by the poem's reader. We learn of the addressee's testimony only through Rich's account of it, which frames and contains the testimony. Rich does not portray the comrade as autonomous or identifiable. Instead, the poem offers a belated (if also passionate) reflection on an already belated act of testimony, and it suggests that testimony requires this distance.[11]

Many other poems in the volume also challenge assumptions central to the poetry of witness and so by implication interrogate the efficacy of scenes of belated witness and testimony in trauma theory. They often do so in ways that recall another aspect of trauma theory—its concern with the ways poetic figures, especially address, represent literally traumatic events. In fact, influential trauma theorists Dori Laub and Shoshana Felman have much to say about the ways address conveys and also disrupts witness, especially

Holocaust witness, which is from the outset disrupted. Rich's poems often evoke the sense of obstruction and blockage central to such formulations.

Trauma theory several times associates the literal condition of belated survivorship with the figure of address. In fact, this association offers one of the clearest examples of the ways trauma theory links literal manifestation of trauma to particular figurative forms. According to Dori Laub, the Holocaust caused a "collapse of witnessing," which Laub identifies as the constitutive feature of the "Holocaust experience" (80). More specifically, the Holocaust "extinguished philosophically the very possibility of address, the possibility of appealing, or of turning to another" as well as "*bear*[ing] *witness to oneself*" (82). Yet this act of extinction enables the possibility that "survivors" can present "retrospective testimonies about the Holocaust" (84) before an "interviewer-listener" (85), permitting "something like a repossession of the act of witnessing" (85), which "*belatedly* [allows] the event . . . to be historically grasped and seen" (84).

Laub's insistence that an eradicated mode of witness (or address) can be belatedly reconstituted imposes a narrative of therapeutic healing onto an event that seems antithetical to such a narrative. It does so by implying a distinction between what I have been calling the first and second phases of witness. The Holocaust destroys the survivor's capacity to experience atrocities at the moment they are occurring, but it seems to leave intact his capacity belatedly to create a narrative that can be subsequently received by a sympathetic listener. This transformation of roles is evident in Laub's description of the antichronological capacity of the belated listener to take on "the responsibility for bearing witness that previously the narrator felt he bore alone" (85): the listener "becomes the Holocaust witness *before* the narrator does" (85). The act of receiving testimony thus undermines the ordinary chronology of listening. Although Laub at one point distinguishes "three separate, distinct levels of witnessing in relation to the Holocaust experience"—bearing witness "to oneself, . . . to the testimonies of others, . . . [and] to the process of witnessing itself" (73)—his definition of testimony also relies on the slippage between these "levels."

A related slippage between the roles of speaker and listener is central to the way poetry has sometimes been defined. In fact, Susan Stewart uses similar terms to describe what "evoke[s]" "the situation of poetry" (*Poetry* 111). An inconsistent address, Stewart claims, is central to poetry, since in poems, "actors become the recipients of actions, . . . speakers speak from the position of listeners, . . . thought is unattributable and intention wayward" (111). Poetry is thus defined by the passive listener's capacity to become a speaker and the reverse, an assertion that recalls Laub's notion that testimony converts the listener into the witness. The speaker in "Comrade" similarly "speak[s] from the position of" a listener in ways that make it unclear whose story is being told since "thought is unattributable and intention wayward."

Holocaust survivors offer testimony, Laub asserts, because they desire an *"addressable other"* (68), a phrase that evokes poetry's related concern with what Paul Celan has called "a 'thou' that can be *addressed*" (qtd. in Felman 38). Poetic address, though, is different from oral testimony: in poems, the interlocutor is not present but must be imagined. This difference is central to Shoshana Felman's discussion of Paul Celan's post-Holocaust poem "Death Fugue," published in the same volume as Laub's discussion of oral testimony, a discussion that extends Laub's claims while considering the distinctive features of poetic address.

Felman focuses on the tension between the destruction of address and its subsequent (re)creation in "Death Fugue." The poem, she claims, looks back at this destruction but also forward to the future (if dubious) scene of its receipt by readers. (The uncertainty of this receipt is also evident in Celan's well-known analogy between the writing of poems and the casting of a "message in a bottle" into the sea.[12]) Poetry, Felman claims, is "an event directed toward the creation of a '*thou*,'" and in this context, "Death Fugue" "is contingent upon various forms of apostrophe and of address" (32). But Celan's poem does not merely seek to "creat[e] an addressee" *within* the poem; it enacts address's inability to extend beyond the poem's limits or what Felman calls "the incapacity of '*we*' to *address*, precisely, in this poem of apostrophe and of address, the '*he*'" (33). These two modes—"apostrophe" and "address"—combine in the poem, making it "precisely, the event of creating an address for the specificity of a historical experience which annihilated any possibility of address" (38).

Essential to Felman's argument about "Death Fugue" is the general assumption that the figure of address articulates the literal condition of aftermath. Thus Celan's address figuratively renders the actual violence of the Holocaust: in "the radical disruption of address between the 'we' . . . and the 'he' . . . Celan locates the very essence of the violence, and the very essence of the Holocaust" (33). Because the *actual* violence of the Holocaust is inexpressible, the "radical disruption" of the figure of address expresses it. Address thus makes an uncontainable literal event figurative while bringing a past event into the present.

Several of Felman's claims strongly evoke Rich's poems, although Rich's poems were written in radically different circumstances.[13] Many of Rich's poems explore something like what Felman calls "creating an address" or what one of Rich's readers has called a general attempt throughout Rich's career to "mak[e] 'you' to find 'we'" (Hedley 145).[14] In the poems of *Dark Fields*, scenes of what Felman calls "incapacity" and "disruption" recur. Like Celan, Rich reveals her addressees' repeated failure to appear. And like Celan, Rich interrogates the function of address and exposes its artificiality in ways that articulate the asymmetry and inconsistency of witness.

Laub and Felman's arguments help illuminate Rich's method in *Dark Fields*, as well as my own in this chapter, but they do not fully explain it. Felman is interested in the overlap of apostrophe and address in Celan's poems, but Rich tends to shift between apostrophe to an absent character within the poem and address directed toward a reader outside the poem's boundaries. This shifting draws attention to the poem's constructedness, especially the fictional nature of its rhetoric of immediacy. But such shifts also reveal something quite different: by thematizing the containment inherent in poetic speech, Rich implies that the poem is itself, in ways that echo her career-long interest in the topic, a frame set around a particular and limited amalgam of experiences and words.[15]

Acts of framing have political as well as aesthetic functions, as Judith Butler makes clear in her consideration of the term in relation to representations of war. In *Frames of War*, Butler argues that acts of linguistic and visual framing (for example, by journalists and those who give them access to certain war scenes but not others) often attempt to contain war in ways that are politically expedient. The frame is, she claims, "the controlling fantasy of the state" but also "mark[s] its limits" (xvii) since this frame can be easily transgressed, revealing, at the "limit of the frame," "the precarious position of targeted lives" (xvi), which state discourse often disregards or attempts to suppress. For example, the photographs of torture at Abu Ghraib, which Butler discusses, distance the horrific scenes they convey from their viewers but also (partly through their casualness) bring them close; depicting a single moment, they allude to a larger narrative. For Butler "the point" of such photos is the contingency of their act of framing: they allow us "not . . . to locate what is 'in' or 'outside' the frame, but what vacillates between those two locations, and what, foreclosed, becomes encrypted in the frame itself" (75). Stewart's claim about address, to which I referred above, similarly implies that when actions and speakers shift roles, they undermine poetry's capacity to contain or frame its own speech acts. The frames of poems are especially susceptible to disruption, as Stewart and others have claimed, because they are permeable: they easily allow the reader to become not merely a spectator but a participant.[16] By exposing and interrogating acts of framing and containment, Rich expresses a related ambivalence about who and what can be represented in a poem and for whom.

In the remainder of this chapter, I will examine one of Rich's essays and several poems in *Dark Fields* that directly reveal patterns that recur throughout the volume. In the process, I will explore a range of ways Rich depicts the discrepancy between wishing to bear witness and acknowledging that it is impossible to do so. The recurrence of these concerns reveals not only Rich's intense engagement with them but the impossibility of simply or fully resolving them; the volume's poems keep returning to and reworking the same problem. This problem, these poems make clear in ways that become more explicit throughout my chapter, has to do with Rich's concern with boundaries. Often, the speaker occupies a position of frustrated watching: she observes a scene she cannot participate in or fully understand. This situation is intensified in poems that impel their readers into the poem while also forbidding entry, at times by invoking an addressee distinct from the reader. In what follows, I will consider these issues by examining three pairs of poems. The first two poems focus on the relation between poems and their readers, depicting negative or cautionary scenes of miscommunication, euphemism, and distance. The second pair more directly considers the poem's frame by depicting asymmetrical scenes of watching, in which the gap between watching and conveying what is seen is often poignantly evoked. In the final pair, scenes of historical remembering and reconstruction make explicit the tension between what Rich calls "then" and now" and between belatedness and anticipation. I end the chapter by considering a passage from Rich's subsequent volume that directly considers witness and its dangers, as well as the ethics of its own utterance and our response to it.

||||||||||||||||

As I have already implied, Rich's prose writings and her poems are deeply interconnected. The essay "Dearest Arturo," which Rich composed at the same time as many of the poems in *Dark Fields*, crystallizes a number of the topics central to the volume. The essay explores the disjunction between addressee and audience in ways that expose Rich's interest in both formal and political acts of framing.[17] As its title indicates, the essay adopts a letter format to address Rich's friend Arturo. But Rich immediately reveals that this format is a device that enables her to speak to her actual unknown readers: the essay's first sentence asserts, "I'm writing you tonight because I feel mired in the frustration of addressing that 'someone' to whom I must explain why poetry and politics aren't mutually exclusive. Maybe I can begin if I think of myself as talking to you" (*What Is Found* 22). Rich here makes it clear that Arturo, a character within the essay's frame, is in fact a substitute for the unknown "someone" who exceeds it. Something like apostrophe ("writing you") thus stands in for reader address ("addressing that 'someone'").

The essay's format seems even more artificial when Rich reveals, late in the essay, that Arturo is in fact dead; he died while she was writing the essay, although her "conversation" with him, she asserts, nevertheless "goes on" (26).[18] Rich enacts this conversation within the essay by citing Arturo's earlier words, to which she belatedly responds. Significantly, Arturo's words concern acts of projection and invention and thus echo Rich's own act of summoning Arturo up:

You've said, *The great justification for the act of reading and writing fiction is that through it we can be disciplined and seduced into imagining other people's lives with understanding and compassion, even if we do not "identify" with them.* Yes. (26)

Arturo's claim is that fiction gives us access to *"other people's lives"* by letting us *"imagin[e]"* their experiences, an assertion that echoes Rich's claim in "Comrade" that one character *"imagines . . . the other"* (italics added). More specifically, Arturo seems to be distinguishing imagining others from *"'identify[ing]'"* with them; his use of quotation marks distances the latter idea from his own beliefs.[19]

Arturo does not use the term *witness* here, but he reveals a gap between speaker and listener that recalls the one I associated above with Holocaust testimony. As Holocaust testimony re-creates the survivor's destroyed past experiences by conveying them to sympathetic listeners, fiction turns toward its characters in ways that allow its readers to *"imagin[e]"* situations of which they have no direct experience. The fiction writer, like someone giving testimony, sees what is not otherwise available to the reader (*"other people's lives"*) and attempts to convey this information to an undefined collective (*"us"*). Rich's essay engages in a similar process; she speaks to us now by seeming to continue a past conversation with Arturo. She thus seeks asymmetrically to convince us of her beliefs about politics and poetry (she bears witness before us) by recounting or bearing witness to Arturo's own earlier words (which are already about bearing witness).

In the process, Rich reveals the essay's various acts of framing, denial, and performance in ways that recall Bidart's "Curse," which I discussed in the introduction. Like "Curse," the essay exemplifies what J. L. Austin has called performative speech: it attempts to make Arturo present by acting as if he already is.[20] It thus relies on its own fiction, which, according to Arturo, involves both *"seduc[tion]"*—as Rich here invites her readers to collude in the fiction of intimacy—and discipline, which implies withholding and judgment. Just as fiction for Arturo speaks to its readers indirectly, through invented characters based on actual people, Rich's essay addresses us by pretending to avoid us: we, of course, are the impersonal, undefined, and unfamiliar "'someone'" that the essay attempts to convince.

||||||||||||||||||

A related strategy of indirection is evident in the first two poems in *Dark Fields*, both of which consider, in cautious and cautionary terms, the possibility of collective speech even as they retain distance from their actual readers. The first poem, "What Kind of Times Are These," chronicles the poet's inability or refusal to speak forthrightly to her readers, while the second, "In Those Years," depicts and condemns a collective "we" for their self-absorption. Both poems refuse simple, intimate, or forthright witness; they shift between observation and commentary and so evoke what I have been calling witness's asymmetry, eroding the bond between "you" and "I" and between "I" and "we" in ways that recall the similar patterns located by Felman in "Death Fugue." Yet Rich often began readings with these poems (Langdell 201). In the process, she mitigated the failure of connection and identification presented within the poems by inviting her actual audience members to distinguish themselves from those addressed in the poem. By exceeding the frame of the poem in this way, Rich implied an alternative to the poems' rhetoric of failure.

As the deictic "these" indicates, the title of "What Kind of Times Are These" (3) identifies a present and immediate moment, although the poem focuses not on these times but on how they have affected the narrator's mode of speech. Rich begins with a straightforward scene of witness: the poet is standing "between two stands of trees" in a place associated with the earlier "disappear[ance]" of "the persecuted." The speaker locates this place through other spatial and interpersonal deictics: it "is not somewhere else but *here*" (italics added), in "*our* country" (italics added).

But the poem turns, in the last two of its four quatrains, from bearing witness to the scene of trees and the disappeared to bearing witness for her readers. The speaker has, she makes clear, seen and understood the scene, but she refuses (or perhaps is unable) to convey its location to her readers, implying that if she does, you will destroy or coopt it. Then Rich interrogates her use of address in the poem: "why do I tell you / anything?" The answer pulls back slightly from her earlier hostility: "Because you still listen," if only to accounts of "trees."

The poetic impulse to describe abstract issues metonymically or metaphorically—to convey suffering, for example, by describing trees—is generally seen as a wholly aesthetic strategy. The speaker of Archibald MacLeish's "Ars Poetica," for example, suggests that the substitution "For all the history of grief / An empty doorway and a maple leaf" paradoxically makes poems more direct, letting them "not mean / But be." "What Kind of Times," in contrast, reveals the political implications of such figurativeness, implying that indirection makes otherwise intolerable realities palatable to resistant readers. Yet the poem's condemnation of its addressees is also figurative; it is meant to help Rich's actual readers recognize her euphemisms as such and thus begin to understand fully the implications of the events she hints at. That the poem's title alludes to another text, as Rich's note indicates, further distances the poem from immediate or spontaneous speech.[21]

While "What Kind of Times Are These" uses address to characterize the present moment, the volume's next poem, "In Those Years" (4) forgoes address, euphemism, and, for the most part, imagery. Instead, it recounts, using a retrospective past tense, the "los[s]" of "the meaning of *we*, of *you*" and the replacement of collective identification and empathy with a "reduced" and self-referential "*I*." In the process, the poem elaborates an asymmetry similar to that of "What Kind of Times" but suggests that by becoming conscious of our self-absorption, we may be able to remedy it.

The poem's denunciation of a current situation of narcissistic self-involvement is from the outset complicated. As the "Those" of its title indicates, the poem adopts a more complex temporal position than "What Kind of Times Are These." In fact, as the first line makes clear, its position of retrospection has been artificially induced:

In *those* years, people *will* say, we *lost* track [italics added in this line]
of the meaning of *we*, of *you*
we found ourselves
reduced to *I*. (4)

Here prolepsis (a projection into a future when "people *will* say") is the necessary precursor to an act of remembering ("we *lost* track") that allows the present moment—*these* years—to be retrospectively understood as "*those years.*" (This sense of displacement is intensified by the fact that the early insight about losing track, and indeed the whole poem, is attributed to an unidentified group of "people.") While trauma theory argues that traumatic events cannot be understood or witnessed at the time they occur, Rich goes further, inventing a future scene of belated retrospection that does not yet exist.

Rich links the provisionality of this scene to questions about the relation between the literal and the figurative later in the poem by describing one of its only specific events: "the great dark birds of history screamed and plunged / into our personal weather." Though Rich depicts these actions in detail, the birds are clearly figurative; disrupting "our personal weather"—the phrase conflates a physical with a psychological phenomenon—they impose "history," the speaker makes clear, onto the present moment. The birds thus convert a physical disruption into an allegorical one.

The physical reality of Rich's "dark birds of history" is further compromised by their similarity to Walter Benjamin's "angel of history," which also binds physical with figurative attributes. (The allusion also links an unspecified contemporary landscape to Europe in the 1940s.) The angel, like Rich's birds, is associated with meteorological disruption; but whereas Rich's birds move through and disrupt "personal weather," the angel is powerless: condemned to witness "one single catastrophe" with "eyes staring," he cannot "make whole what is smashed" because a "storm is blowing" (259). As a result, Benjamin's angel, like the speaker of "In Those Years," cannot occupy the present but is "propel[led]" by the storm's "violence" "into the future to which his back is turned" (260).

The outrage of "In Those Years" is paradoxically expressed, as in "What Kind of Times," through the indirection and figuration that Rich's speaker explicitly condemns. I discussed above the way the near-parallel structure of "Comrade" expresses both the temptation and danger of drawing equivalences. Rich's pronoun shifts here have a similar effect. Rich does not (as she did in "What Kind of Times") use the "*you*" that the poem's first lines

imply offers a way of escaping the limitations of "*I*." She also refuses the
"I" whose proliferation she condemns, employing instead a "we" that re
mains distinct from collective identity. In fact, Rich aligns this "we" with
the "personal":

> we were trying to live a personal life
> and, yes, that was the only life
> we could bear witness to[.]

Here, "personal" or private acts of "witness" have eclipsed the possibility
of bearing witness to or for others. The poem does not imagine an alternative to such private acts; the speaker engages only in flat reportage. It is
thus unsurprising that Rich depicts two asymmetrical acts of "say[ing]" and
witnessing: the "people" who early in the poem "say, we lost track" seem
unaware of the scene where "we stood, saying *I*." Speech here persists, but
no one listens to it; it is reduced to a rhetorical self-referentiality in which
the poet herself participates.

Because the poem makes clear, as I have indicated, that "*those* years"
are in fact the same as "*these*" "times," "In Those Years" can be read as a
reconsideration of Rich's stance in "What Kind of Times Are These." The
second poem, that is, looks back on events Rich has already described, belatedly reassessing her earlier decision to withhold information from her
readers. In "In Those Years," though, the poet reveals that she is to blame
as well as her readers; both they and she participate in the same pattern of
self-involvement and narrowed vision. In this context, the final assertion
in "What Kind of Times" that "you still listen" seems naive: the capacity to
listen is exactly what the later poem depicts as lost.

Yet the belated gaze of "In Those Years" also offers a way out, as is implied by Rich's readings of the poem before actual audiences. The simultaneously intimate and communal situation of a public reading may let Rich's
listeners first recognize themselves in the negatively portrayed "we" of the
poem and then separate from it. By listening to the poem, they affirm that
they are in fact capable of "still listen[ing]" and thus bind themselves to the
past (they are "still" doing what was done earlier). But Rich also implies that
they can learn to listen in a new and less "personal" way. This simultaneous

act of self-recognition and distancing invites Rich's listeners to locate the poem's frame, inhabit the interior of the poem, and then step outside it.

IIIIIIIIIIIIIIII

In both these poems, the act of witnessing is linked to address: both poems speak, or resist speaking, to their readers. In both, the idea of the frame remains implicit. But other poems more directly link acts of asymmetrical witness to exposing and manipulating the poem's frame in relation to often obstructed or mediated acts of seeing. "Sending Love" (33–39), for example, describes multiple scenes of transmission and receipt through imagery of reflection and transparency. Each of its four sections presents love's transmission differently. The second, longest section catalogs a series of situations in which named characters send love across distances, usually but not always in written form (including, for example, "a postcard" and in "braille"). What matters, as in "Dearest Arturo," is not receipt but the act of "sending it, sending it," which the section's parallel construction imbues with hope, even exuberance. Other sections depict speech and transmission in less positive ways. The poem's first, brief, verbless section describes an unwitnessed and inanimate "voice" emerging from a forest, while the third section offers a critique of the reasons for sending love.

It is in the final section, though, that Rich elaborates alternatives to these models of one-way transmission by considering scenes of spectatorship. Significantly, these acts of watching are indirect and partial:

Terrence years ago
closed the window, wordless

Grace who always laughed is leaning
her cheek against bullet-proof glass

her tears enlarged
like scars on a planet

Vivian hangs her raincoat
on a hook, turns to the classroom

. . . .

Victor fixes his lens
on disappearing faces

—caught now or who will ever
see them again? (39)

As the window, bullet-proof glass, tears, and camera lens distance and reveal their subjects, the descriptions of Terrence, Grace, and Victor both
establish and refuse boundaries. Frames are both artificial and powerful.
Terrence has, it seems, separated himself from what is outside the window,
and both the "bullet-proof glass" against which Grace leans and Victor's
camera lens separate these characters from what they see, while Vivian remains apart from (able to "turn . . . to") the classroom she also participates
in. For Grace, the window's glass distances, magnifies, and repeats her also-
transparent tears. The barrier of Victor's lens similarly permits both distance and access: separating him from what he sees, it enables him to "fix"
what is evanescent. This notion of evanescence introduces into the present
tense of the poem a sense of time's passage. The unspecified "disappearing
faces" Victor captures recall but mitigate the more violent and deliberate
acts of "making people disappear" in "What Kind of Times."

The poem does not specify what faces Victor is photographing; they
may be those of strangers or of Terrence, Grace, and Vivian. Victor's act of
watching is already asymmetrical; he first watches, then "fixes" what he
sees. Rich watches again what Victor has already seen, similarly capturing
these characters in snapshot-like vignettes. She does not seem to know, nor
do we need to know, why Terrence has closed the window, Grace is crying,
Vivian is filled with "love" entering her classroom, or Victor is taking his
photos. Instead, the poet's voice and gaze, superimposed over the already
distancing glass and camera, enable us to see these characters. Similarly it is
the poet who, by introducing the simile comparing Grace's tears to "scars on
a planet," interprets and understands the tears, in this case by interposing
another lens, that of the telescope, over the already mediated scene.

As the poem reveals a series of visual boundaries, it also temporally frames its protagonists. It is unclear in the fourth section whether it is Victor or the poet who realizes that his photos are attempts to undermine the "disappear[ance]" essential to time's passing. The ambiguity reveals the poet's commitment, like the photographer's, to representing and also "fix[ing]" what is fleeting. A clearer connection between her project and Victor's is evident in the final question (" —caught now or who will ever / see them again?"). Here Rich affirms not only the inevitability of disappearance but the urgency "now" of trying to mitigate it. The poem engages in a similar process; like Victor, the speaker transforms what she sees into something permanent, partly by offering insight into (and thus, in yet another sense, reflecting on) time's passage. While the poem here reveals the poet's capacity both to watch and interpret, this role is asymmetrical, in the end, because the poem is for us: by receiving its letter-like words, we grant it legitimacy and allow its "voice" to be heard. Rich implies that this act of reception also enables "love."

While "Sending Love" elaborates the connections enabled by brief transmissions (letters, snapshots, vignettes), "Revolution in Permanence (1953, 1993)" (23–24) uses similar imagery of seeing (especially descriptions of nonintersecting gazes) to reveal the asymmetrical but intimate transhistorical bond between the present-day speaker and the now dead Ethel Rosenberg. As in "Sending Love," scenes of watching and framing recur, and here too the poem's concern is with the connection between containment and escape: the poet watches Rosenberg "through a barn window" but cannot hold her. Other explicitly asymmetrical scenes of witness recur. The poet early claims that Rosenberg "stares down past a shattered apple-orchard / into speechless firs," but she also asserts that "What she is seeing I cannot see, / what I see has her shape." The near-symmetry of these lines, like those in "Comrade," draws attention to the similarity of the characters. But because the speaker cannot see what Rosenberg sees, she is impelled figuratively to transform her, locating Rosenberg's "shape" in unrelated objects, including the landscape "Last night," an act that recalls the metaphoric transformation of human disappearances into trees disparaged by the speaker of "What Kind of Times."

At the poem's end, a pair of nonintersecting gazes more directly exposes the problem of figuration. The speaker claims of Rosenberg,

I've thought she was coughing, like me,
but her profile stayed still watching
what held her in that position. (24)

By conflating immobility (the "profile stayed still") with persistence (it "still watch[ed]"), the speaker emphasizes Rosenberg's evasiveness. Rosenberg here looks outside the poem's frame, exceeding both the poet's gaze and ours. Rich refuses to convert this act of one-way seeing (through a window) into reciprocation or reflection by identifying her resemblance to Rosenberg. Yet the scene also blurs the two characters' gazes by implying that Rosenberg has, in escaping the poet's gaze, impelled Rich to subsume and thus belatedly reinvent her. Thus, the phrase "what held her in that position" refers both to a material, physical constraint of which Rosenberg may have been aware and also to a figurative constraint belatedly understood by the poet; Rosenberg may be "held," for example, by her own biases, class, or religion. The title contains a related pun on "revolution," which implies both physical movement and an uprising of people.[22]

Rich's note on the poem distinguishes Rosenberg's identity as a "real woman" from her presence in the poem as "a secular vision" (77). In fact, Rosenberg is both "real" and figurative in the poem. She evades the poet's belated attempt to contain or frame her even as she is framed (and reanimated) by Rich. The "firs" near the barn through whose window the poet watches Rosenberg are "speechless," and the poem explores the related difficulty of finding a way to speak about someone else's forty-year-old experiences. Like the modes of contact in "Sending Love," Rich's connection with Rosenberg is one-sided and belated. In fact, both poems explore the unknowability of others in ways that imply the naivety of the claim, implicit in much "poetry of witness," that others can be known. The result, as these poems reveal, is often loneliness and a sense of separation. But Rich also affirms the poet's task as a chronicler not only of the facts of what occurred but of the obstacles to knowing these facts.

||||||||||||||||

In the two pairs of poems I have so far considered, acts of anticipation and memory are bound to asymmetrical scenes of witness. The five-poem sequence "Then or Now" (25–31), which directly follows "Revolution in Permanence," more explicitly juxtaposes, as its title indicates, two different time frames—the time of the Holocaust and the present. Yet, unlike "Revolution in Permanence" and Rich's earlier poems on the Holocaust, "Then or Now" refuses to connect these two moments.[23] Instead, the two time frames remain distinct; the speaker appears only in the present moment, and past events are described in their own poems.[24] This separation enables Rich to reflect more directly than in the poems I discussed above on what her poems can and should do, especially in relation to others' experiences. Like "Revolution in Permanence," the sequence reveals the speaker's chronological distance from past events. But Rich here implies that belatedness is also a figurative mode that disguises the truth of these events. It is a stance, perhaps even a mode of subterfuge.

"Sunset, December, 1993" (29), the sequence's third poem, begins by considering the risks and benefits of "draw[ing] / parallels," perhaps between past and present:

Dangerous of course to draw
parallels   Yet more dangerous to write

as if there were a steady course, we and our poems
protected: the individual life, protected

poems, ideas, gliding
in mid-air, innocent.

Here, as in other poems in the volume, the nearly but not entirely parallel syntax enacts the danger Rich describes: the alternative to drawing parallels is not refusing to draw them but rather adopting the illusion of writing from a "steady" and "protected" position. Drawing parallels thus paradoxically undermines the symmetry of parallelism by impelling the watcher to become involved in what has been observed.

Although the poem mostly refuses analogies or metaphors, it ends with a discussion of a particular past event:

> Dangerous not to think
>
> how the earth still was   in places
> while the chimneys shuddered with the first dischargements.

The speaker does not directly locate these chimneys in concentration camps. Nor does she spell out the disturbing equivalence or "parallel" implied by this description, although the chimney smoke's contamination of the air evokes the ways poems "glid[e] / in mid-air," and the earth's endurance recalls the poet's similar effort to find a "steady course." The implication is that poems create an illusion of "innocen[ce]" visually echoed but ultimately belied by the chimneys, although "Sunset" does not explicitly "draw parallels" between poem writing and the chimneys' "dischargements." In fact, Rich's point seems to be that such parallels are impossible: the Nazis' actions (for which the chimneys are a synecdoche) coexist but cannot be reconciled with picturesque sunsets.

"Sunset" draws attention to the poet's task by reflecting on what poems can and cannot do, implying that the poet must look both at the events she describes and at her poems' future effect on readers. The sequence's final poem, "And Now," more directly distinguishes these two modes of witness. As the poem progresses, it enacts the discrepancies between these modes in ways that reveal the difficulty of reconciling the present act of bequeathing the poem to its readers with the past-tense recording of others' actions.

The poem's structure reveals this asymmetry. The first lines affirm an immediacy and intimacy evident as a passionate confusion of reader with lover and of public with private modes of love:

> And now as you read these poems
> —you whose eyes and hands I love
> —you whose mouth and eyes I love
> —you whose words and minds I love—

The poem's addressee is at once singular (possessing a "mouth") and multiple (possessing "minds"). The literal and figurative also join: the beloved eyes, hands, and mouths are visible parts of the body but also synecdoches for the addressee's capacity to see, touch, and speak. But then Rich turns, in the second part of the poem, to a description of what the speaker needed to do before writing the words that her readers are now reading:

> don't think I was trying to state a case
> or construct a scenery:
> I tried to listen to
> the public voice of our time
> tried to survey our public space
> as best I could
> —tried to remember and stay
> faithful to details, note
> precisely how the air moved
> and where the clock's hands stood
> and who was in charge of definitions
> and who stood by receiving them
> when the name of compassion
> was changed to the name of guilt
> when to feel with a human stranger
> was declared obsolete.

As the poem enumerates the speaker's acts of "listen[ing]," "survey[ing]," "remember[ing]," and "not[ing]," the addressee vanishes (it is evident here only in the initial and strongly negative imperative "don't think"), as does the tone of celebration: this part of the poem reads as a defense of Rich's poetic process. The "I" also vanishes; it appears only in the first half of this final passage, and the poem's late use of the passive voice further undermines agency. Instead, even as she defends her poetics, the speaker allows her authority to be coopted by the disembodied others whose unspecified actions she attempts to record, both those "in charge" and those "who stood by receiving them." In the process, the effortless mutuality of the early lines yields to a more formalized and obstructed mode of communication. As "definitions" are bequeathed and received, the possibility of "feel[ing] with a human stranger"—something like the connection elaborated by the poem's first lines—is "declared obsolete."

The poem thus enacts an explicitly temporal asymmetry; by looking back at what happened, the speaker loses sight both of her readers and of her own earlier capacity for "compassion." The present-tense reader, like the poet as "I," does not return at the poem's end, and the speaker's repeated attempt ("I tried . . . tried . . . tried") to "stay / faithful to [these] details" fails insofar as the details themselves obliterate her as a speaker. The point seems to be that remembering is inextricable from loss.

But the poem can be also read in another, nearly contradictory way. Rich often ends the poems of *Dark Fields* by asserting what others say or believe, often in ways that emphasize the irony of these statements. Here, for example, the declaration that empathy with strangers has become "obsolete" may be inaccurate insofar as the poem has spoken from the outset to a plural group of readers. Or rather—and the difference is important—the poet is speaking not to the readers of this poem but of "these poems." We are here meant to recognize that Rich is engaged in a larger project that has to do with intimacy and connection. But the reader's recognition of this fact requires distance from the poem's particular argument and thus, as in several other poems I have discussed, a separation from the poem's protagonist. The poem begins by addressing its readers, and its ending may indirectly invite them to respond with outrage or distress to the lost possibility of empathy.

This way of reading the poem, though, is inconsistent with a reading that focuses on its explicit lament about what has been lost. In fact, "And Now" affirms both the loss of compassion and the possibility of a different future. It also affirms both the impossibility and necessity of compassion with strangers. Rich's previous volume contains a poem ("Dedications") whose celebratory and omniscient speaker depicts a scene in "a waiting-room / of eyes met and unmeeting, of identity with strangers" (*Atlas* 25). Rich here pulls back from the baldness of this claim (as well as from the certainty of the poem's anaphora, "I know you are reading this poem") to the more curtailed possibility of "feel[ing] with" a singular "human stranger." Her point is that this kind of feeling can be achieved only by breaking the poem's frame and trusting the reader to derive from the poem what it does not actually say.

Here, then, the asymmetry between what others say and what the poet says, as between the poet as silent observer and as passionate lover, engenders a mode of connection that requires that the poem's frame be transgressed by readers who can both insert themselves into the poem and distinguish themselves from its addressees. The resulting bond thus requires imagination rather than, as in "Dedications" or Arturo's statement about fiction, "*identi[t]y.*" And the poet must in turn imagine her reader actually receiving not only "these poems"—those she has already completed—but also this poem, the one she is now writing, whose receipt she can only anticipate.

The poetry of witness, as I indicated above, runs several risks, including overconfidence and polemic. Perhaps the greatest danger involves a too easy or too complete appropriation of others' experiences, an appropriation that undermines the very premises of connection and sympathy essential to witness. At times, Rich's poems pull back abruptly from the compassion and intimacy they seem to advocate; at others, they dwell perhaps excessively on who is looking and through what lens. The curtailed scenes of witness in this and other poems in *Dark Fields* express Rich's doubts that her poems will be heard and received. But they also preserve her poems from the dangers that come from assuming that bearing witness is easy.

||||||||||||||||

In a section midway through the poem "Camino Real" (*Midnight* 30–33), published in the volume after *Dark Fields*, Rich cites one of American poetry's most famous claims about witness, Walt Whitman's "I am the man, I suffer'd, I was there" (225). This phrase, from part 33 of *Song of Myself*, exemplifies the ideal of sympathetic identification: the speaker asserts that he "understand[s]" the experiences of others ranging from "the large hearts of heroes" (224) to "the hounded slave" (225). But Whitman's assertion is dangerous, according to Mutlu Blasing, because it confuses the individual with the collective and thus collapses the difference between witnessing poet and other:

To say, *I am the man, I suffer'd, I was there* . . . does not merely subjugate one's experience to others', painful as that democratization is; it also subjugates and colonizes others' experiences to one's "omnivorous" self. . . . Since synecdoche works two ways to say, "I am him *and* he is me," it preys on the self and the other alike; it resists victimization and repeats it. (61)

Whitman's claim thus implies a mutual cannibalization that recalls the scenes of eating and being eaten in Bidart's "Curse": coopting others, the poet is obliterated by them in ways that, in Blasing's terms, repeat and thus trivialize the very notion of victimization. Charles Altieri associates a related problem with testimonial poetry. By adopting the position of the "representative X" or member of one group, Altieri claims, "poets often ignore those aspects of their experience which they might share with other groups."

As my preceding discussion has shown, Rich is clearly aware of such dangers. By offering an explicit corrective to Whitman's uncritical identification with others, "Camino Real" presents an alternative to a glib or unconsidered poetry of witness. While Whitman famously claimed, "what I assume you shall assume, / For every atom belonging to me as good belongs to you" (188), in "Camino Real," Rich offers a different and wholly depersonalized catalog of actions: "O to list collate commensurate to quantify: / *I was the one, I suffered, I was there.*" Rich retains the infinitive (also present in "Comrades") throughout the poem's next stanzas:

> never
> to trust to memory only
>
> to go back   notebook in hand
> dressed as no one there was dressed
>
> over and over to quantify
> on a gridded notebook page
>
> the difficulty of proving
> such things were done for no reason

that every night
"in those years"
people invented reasons for torture[.] (*Midnight* 31)

Although no protagonist is identified, it seems that the poet is depicting herself as a journalist, anthropologist, or even a statistician. This role recalls her attempt to "listen" and "survey" in "And Now." Here, though, rather than attempting, as she did there, "to *remember* and stay / faithful to details," she determines "never / to trust to *memory* only" (italics added). Her need to "quantify" and "prov[e]" further distinguishes Rich's speaker from Whitman's. Whitman assumes a readership sympathetic to his methods and words, but Rich's speaker affirms her difference both from those she observes and from her audience, as is evident in her acknowledgment that she is "dressed as no one there was dressed."

I have through this chapter identified a number of techniques that distance Rich's poems from actual lived experience. Here, the ambiguities of the infinitive make it unclear whether "Camino Real" is describing a past action or giving advice and whether its protagonist is the poet or someone else. Nor does the speaker (as in "And Now") specify the "things" that were done or to whom. As in earlier poems, Rich does not chronicle or bear witness to particular incidents; even the final reference to "torture" is nonspecific. Instead, her focus is on a method of bearing witness that can convince skeptical readers.

Whitman's version of witness is essentially instantaneous: there is no gap between witnessing the other suffering and suffering oneself. But Rich describes a process that involves going "back" in time as well as belatedly reevaluating what occurred "'in those years.'" The quotation marks around this phrase reveal its familiarity; Rich implies that speaking this way helps those who come after rationalize their actions, perpetuating torture by enabling the belated "invent[ion of] reasons" to explain what was in fact "done for no reason." But the quotation marks also recall Rich's earlier use of this phrase in the poem of that title in *Dark Fields*, implying that Rich understands that she too has ignored the evidence of torture. I located a similar mode of self-criticism in "In Those Years," which revises the accusatory tone of "What Kind of Times." But here Rich focuses on the tendency—likely her own—to conceal actual events by setting them into the past; the position of belatedness, she implies, makes it easy to avoid what is difficult. The blurring and instabilities of belatedness are dangerous, she more generally implies, because they can be deployed by those in power to conceal past atrocities. Forché associates the poetry of witness with "claims against the political order . . . made in the name of justice" (Introduction 31). Rich's claim here is "political" and subversive; it arguably evokes an underlying sense of "justice," although it also chronicles justice's failure. Yet the poem is also deeply cynical, partly because it insists on the damage done not only at the time of torture but during subsequent retrospection about it.

Yet belatedness is also necessary to the effort "to go back" to the past and reassess what occurred then. This section associates the potentially creative act of "invent[ion]" (something perhaps similar to Arturo's "imagin[ing]") with the ways those in power belatedly rationalize acts of "torture." But the poem also engages in a different and opposing act of invention: by exposing the duplicity of the unidentified "people" it describes, it creates an alternative to their self-justifications. Rich implies that it is simplistic to recover the past or retell history. Yet the poem also offers a set of instructions for a circumscribed but resistant mode of witness. In the end, its act of "invent[ion]" may not eradicate the torturers' but can at least be set alongside it.

||||||||||||||||||

In her study of acts of framing, Judith Butler draws—as does Carolyn Forché in her 2011 statement about witness—on Emmanuel Levinas's definition of ethics as a mode of what Butler calls "communication between" one person and another (*Frames* 77). This mode, Butler claims, "follows" at least partly "from being addressed and addressable" (181). Rich's poems are insistently figurative; their concern with their own capacity to speak to and for others is inextricable from their preoccupation with their status as poems. Address is always figurative in poems; it reveals the distance between the poem and ordinary or spontaneous speech. But Rich's address also resists this figurativity by expressing a genuine and ethical desire to speak to her readers.

In shifting between modes of address in ways that expose and often violate the poem's frame, *Dark Fields* considers the human need to bear witness even when doing so seems artificial or useless. Testimony is always solitary in poems, but it also affirms the speaker's faith in an unidentified, unknown, and possibly unsympathetic listener. Faith in this possibility is essential to Rich's 2010 idea of what poets believe:

> Someone writing a poem believes in a reader, in readers, of that poem. . . . But most often someone writing a poem believes . . . that an "I" can become a "we" without extinguishing others, that a partly common language exists to which strangers can bring their own heartbeat, memories, images. ("Someone")

Strongly recalling the terms in which Felman described Celan's "Death Fugue," as well as the manipulations of the pronouns *I, you,* and *we* in "In Those Years," Rich here expresses the poet's yearning not only for the reader's presence but for mutuality. The constant shifting in *Dark Fields* between a rhetoric of faith and doubt is partly an aesthetic strategy: it preserves these poems from the extremes of polemicism and hermeticism of which they have nevertheless sometimes been accused.[25] But Rich's statement suggests something different: her poems' inconsistencies enact the ethical but also deeply political actual challenges of a poetry that risks "believ[ing]" not only in its readers but in us.

Chapter Three

"I am the ghost who haunts us"

Prosopopoeia and the Poetics of Infection in AIDS Poetry

Frank Bidart's poem "The Second Hour of the Night" (27–59) published in his 1999 collection *Desire*, mostly juxtaposes two narratives concerning different characters, one focusing on frustrated mourning and the other on sexual violence, central themes of the volume and of Bidart's poetry more generally.[1] But toward the end of this thirty-page poem, with no warning, an "I" enters and begins to speak. Rich's inconsistent use of address, as I argued in chapter 2, enables her to consider the poet's capacity to witness the experiences of others and to convey those experiences to her readers. But Bidart uses address differently: his speaker addresses someone explicitly identified as dead. And while the addressees in *Dark Fields* tend to remain at a distance, Bidart's speaker seeks, and seems to achieve, actual physical contact with his addressee. This section of the poem does not, as many elegies do, implore the dead other to approach or bid him goodbye. Instead, the speaker describes a present-tense and immediate encounter with an unidentified addressee, one who seems to resemble that of several other poems in the volume who has died of AIDS:[2]

> courteously
> [you] ask (because you are dead) if you can briefly
>
> borrow, inhabit my body.

When I look I can see my body
away from me, sleeping.

I say *Yes.* Then you enter it

like a shudder as if eager again to know
what it is to move within arms and legs.

I thought, *I know that he will return it.* (58)

The passage sets forth a model of transaction: the addressee, having
died, desires a loan, one that the speaker grants both because his body is
already "away from me, sleeping" and because he "know[s]" it will be later
"*return[ed]*." There seem to be other bonuses for the speaker; the act of
entry, itself "like a shudder," makes the speaker himself shudder, and he
may also feel something like the addressee's "eager[ness]." Such experiences
imply that the speaker is willing not only to lend his body but vicariously
to experience its sensations, which both are and are not his own. This confusion offers one rationale for the loan. Another, more powerful one is that
it allows the speaker to reanimate the dead addressee, if only temporarily.

The scene of ghostly visitation in "The Second Hour" echoes similar
scenes in the American poems about AIDS on which I will focus in this chapter. The recurrence of ghosts in postwar poems, I argued in the introduction,
not only juxtaposes but merges the literal with the figurative. Bidart here
describes a literally impossible narrative as if it is real, using matter-of-fact
language. But this casualness also reveals the scene's fictiveness, although
the speaker here seems to have forgotten that the dead cannot actually return, much less borrow the bodies of the living. Bidart acknowledges this
impossibility by implying that the scene was dreamed; the speaker's body
is "away from me, sleeping," a notion that extends Bidart's earlier and more
ambiguous assertion that ". . . grace is the dream, half- / dream, half- // light,
when you appear."[3] The paired similes that describe the addressee's "ent[ry]"
into the speaker's body—"like a shudder as if eager"—also impose doubt,
as does the last line's shift to the past tense ("I thought"), which disrupts
the passage's apparent immediacy. In these ways, Bidart frames—encloses
and sets apart, in ways that recall the similar tendency in Rich's poems—a

scene that is also vivid and physical. This act of framing both mitigates and reveals the scene's strangeness.

By denying that the addressee is in fact dead, this passage refuses to acknowledge the belatedness of its situation, although it mixes different time frames, as is especially evident in the past, present, and future tenses in the line "I thought, *I know that he will return it.*" Instead, Bidart depicts a paradox about agency that recurs not only in Bidart's poems but in the other poems about AIDS I will consider below. The poem chronicles a simultaneous act of yielding and mastery, a "*seeking to be allowed to S U B M I T.*" To use terms employed by other poems discussed in this chapter, the speaker here consents to being physically (if not mentally) possessed by the addressee in a way that suggests that he has invented and thus possesses him. This paradox is made evident through tensions about animation: the speaker willingly deanimates himself so the dead addressee can come back to life.

"The Second Hour" mostly normalizes the situation it describes by presenting it in simple and declarative terms. But Bidart's poem "Like" (*Metaphysical* 11–12), which I discussed in the introduction and which reads as something of a gloss on "The Second Hour," explicitly considers the contradictions involved in ghostly animation. In this more recent poem, Bidart considers in compressed and abstract terms the extent to which the creation of ghosts or "spectre[s]" can compensate for the literal experience of bereavement. The poem describes a situation in which the dead, as in "The Second Hour," retain sentience after death. But they do so, it seems, to resist the survivors' reliance on figuration or "symbolic // substitution," which Bidart locates both in the survivors' creation of a ghostly "spectre" to replace the dead and, more generally still, in the "*like*" of simile. The poem asserts that specters both push the plural "dead" away and also, paradoxically, confirm the continuing presence of these dead, an act of persistence that is here less positively depicted than in "The Second Hour." Part of the problem seems to involve the success with which the specter approximates the actual dead other; because this revived version is "so like what [the survivor] watched die," the summoned-up specter, or the *act* of summoning it up, impels "the unique / soul you loved [to endure] a second death." Thus, using "*like*" or figuration does not, in the end, undermine the fact of death or the pain of bereavement, as the poem opens by claiming: "Woe is blunted not erased / by *like*." Nor can the dead be vanquished by the survivors' use of "*like*." Instead, this act of substitution makes the dead angry (they "hate" being replaced) and thus even more present.

By superimposing several time frames—the time after death, the time in which the dead are reanimated as "spectres," and the time of "second death"—"Like" makes explicit a belatedness that is more often implicit in American poems about AIDS and the AIDS dead. The poems written between the late 1980s and the late 1990s by Mark Doty, Paul Monette, D. A. Powell, Thom Gunn, and James Merrill that I will discuss in this chapter also often excise the physical reality of death by describing scenes in which the dead return in ghostly form, a tendency that also recurs in poems about AIDS by other poets.[4] These poems, which I have chosen for discussion because they make such scenes explicit, mostly excise the fear and uncanniness generally associated with ghosts, especially literary ones. Instead, the poems' speakers welcome familiar ghosts into domestic and intimate spaces, often, as in "The Second Hour," the bedroom. In the process, the speakers of these poems also evoke other transgressive impulses—among them, to yield to the dead and to consent to be obliterated. But these poems also contain these impulses by revealing their ghosts to be imaginary; they have been summoned up so the living survivor can obscure his actual, solitary condition of bereavement.

The poems by Plath and Rich I examined above situate their speakers at a temporal remove from the often historically remote events they describe in ways that expose their position of belatedness. AIDS poems, as I have already implied, are often structured to deny their speakers' bereavement. Nor are acts of remembering or particular memories central. Instead, these poems merge past with present in ways that deny absence. Yet they clearly originate in the condition of "aftermath" (xxi) that Ross Chambers has argued characterizes all AIDS writing. More exactly, AIDS poems support Chambers's assertion that this condition of aftermath is manifest in AIDS writing through recurrent scenes of "perpetually surviv[ing] a trauma that is never over" (43) or what Melissa Zeiger calls a pattern in AIDS poems of "summon[ing] ghosts while insisting upon the finality of death" (131).

This strenuous denial of an undeniable and ongoing situation of after-math evokes a related tension in much modern elegy. As Jahan Ramazani and R. Clifton Spargo have argued, modern and contemporary elegies often refuse to separate from the dead and thus, in Ramazani's terms, "tend . . . not to achieve but to resist consolation, not to override but to sustain anger, not to heal but to reopen the wounds of loss" (*Poetry* xi). As a result, modern elegies remain caught in something like Chambers's liminal and re-petitive position of aftermath, "neither abandon[ing] the dead nor heal[ing] the living" (Ramazani, *Poetry* 4). Spargo describes elegy in terms that more directly recall the terms in which I have been describing AIDS elegy: eleg-ists, he claims, repeatedly and melancholically "imagin[e] . . . an impossible recovery of the dead, sometimes quite literally a retrieval of the dead body" (*Ethics* 12). But AIDS poems go further still, refusing not only separation but grief in ways that create something approximating what both Mark Doty and D. A. Powell, as well as Spargo in another context, have called anti-elegy.[5]

The recurrent ghosts in AIDS poems recall the posthumous characters in Plath's late poems, as well as Rich's observation of the dead Ethel Rosenberg in "Revolution in Permanence." AIDS poems rely, as do Plath and Rich, on metaphor and apostrophe, which evoke and interrogate analogy and con-nection. But even more frequent in AIDS poems is the figure of prosopo-poeia, which in Susan Gubar's general terms enables "the dead [to] speak" (177).[6] Paul de Man has called prosopopoeia the "master trope of poetic discourse" (qtd. in Fuss 22), partly because speaking for the dead is deeply counterlogical and thus draws attention to the artifice of poetic utterance; prosopopoeia must constantly deny the fact that the apparent speech of the dead is actually the speaker's own voice. As such, prosopopoeia over-lays denial and acknowledgment in ways consistent with the invocation of ghosts. As do ghosts, prosopopoeia asserts animation while implying its failure, often, as at least one critic has argued, through a rhetoric not only of animation but deanimation.[7]

Diana Fuss implies a similar analogy between literal and figurative man-ifestations of posthumousness in a discussion of what she calls "corpse poems," which she defines as "first-person poetic utterance[s], written in the present or past tense, . . . spoken in the voice of the deceased" (1) and often employing prosopopoeia (22). But corpse poems, especially modern ones, also resist the premise that the dead can speak: "the fiction of the speaking corpse allows survivors of traumatic events to express their own feelings of premature death" (21). Corpse poems, Fuss here implies, thus displace the belated (and also anticipatory) laments of a solitary speaker. This solitude is sometimes evident through not only prosopopoeia but apostrophe, speech *to* (rather than *by*) the dead. In AIDS poems, too, both animation and prosopopoeia are always temporary.

AIDS poems therefore more radically blur literal with figurative belatedness than do the poems I discussed in earlier chapters. By exposing both the figurativity of the actual ghosts they invoke and the artificiality (or ghostliness) of the figures on which they rely, these poems insist on their own artifice in ways that recall other scenes of posthumous performance, including Lady Lazarus's "great strip tease" and the staged address in Rich's "Dearest Arturo." Concerns with performance are often explicit in AIDS poems, as "The Second Hour" makes clear. Rich's poems, I argued above, privilege what Arturo calls "*imagining*" over "*identif[ication]*" and so complicate straightforward acts of witnessing. This complication recalls several recent characterizations of queer poetry, which insist on related, but more elaborate, acts of imagination and fantasy.[8] As such, AIDS poems intensify the tendencies of other poems, including those written earlier.[9]

But the blurring of the real and the wished for, the literal and the figurative in AIDS poems is not only aesthetic. It also vividly evokes the bodily and political reality of AIDS, in which, as in the 9/11 attacks discussed in the introduction, the literal and the figurative are already entangled. Because AIDS is spread by intimate contact, it tends to confuse the positions of lamenter and lamented. All elegies consider, at least implicitly, the poet's own mortality: they not only chronicle the past but function as anticipatory self-elegies. But in AIDS elegy, the bereaved survivor, often identified as the former lover of the dead, is more obviously a potential casualty. Sex and the blurrings of identity it enables are thus associated with death, as is implied by Bidart's speaker, whose act of allowing the addressee to "inhabit" his body, an act accompanied by a "shudder," evokes a sexual act as well as self-annihilation. (Bidart's more recent poem "For the AIDS Dead" discusses more directly his own strategy of indirection in reference to AIDS.[10]) More-over, the virus's long incubation period creates other confusions between (abstract and intellectual) knowledge and (bodily) experience; AIDS may be diagnosed in asymptomatic individuals as the result of a test, a situation in which knowledge precedes physical manifestation. But it may also be man-ifest physically first, through discrete symptoms that must be subsequently linked and confirmed by testing. Nor can the test explain where or when infection occurred. And recent advances in AIDS treatment have further blurred the distinction between the HIV-positive and the AIDS-infected.

Moreover, AIDS has been from its first identification inextricable from the language in which it has been described, as many have argued. The syndrome's earliest name, GRID, or gay-related immunity deficiency (Alt-man, "New"), associated a physical syndrome with a particular population and by implication its lifestyle. The conflation of the literal and metaphoric in subsequent rhetoric surrounding AIDS has been often noted, as when the cultural phenomenon of AIDS is described in literalizing and medical-ized terms; for example, AIDS is said to "infect the *morals* of the greater population" (Sturken 150), or when AIDS advocates have attempted to re-appropriate this rhetoric, adding what one critic calls a "counterdiscourse of criticism and defiance" to an existing "discourse of hysteria and blame" (Sturken 147).[11] It is often claimed that AIDS cannot be separated from its figurative "meaning"; it is in one critic's terms "*simultaneously an epidemic of transmissible lethal disease and an epidemic of meanings and signification*" (Weeks 135). Other critics feel that AIDS exists solely in and through lan-guage; it is, according to one well-known formulation, exclusively "an epi-demic of signification" (Treichler 42).[12] As such, according to Lee Edelman, AIDS rhetoric radically undermines the distinction between "the biological, associated with the literal or the 'real,'" and "the literary, associated with the figural or the fictive" (302).

Since questions about poetic transmission long predated AIDS, such con-flicts are perhaps especially liable to being explored by poems. As I indi-cated above, Susan Stewart has argued that poems are deeply preoccupied with the provenance of their inspiration, partly evident in the persistent Western trope that poetry results from the muse's possession of or entry into the poet (*Poetry* 113). Stewart associates these terms of physical transgression with anxiety about literary creation. Partly for this reason, there exists a "tension . . . between mastery and surrender" related to "the idea of poetic will," especially "the question of . . . agency" and who "is speaking" (111). This tension is often evident as a fear of a "contaminat[ion]" between the distinct positions of "poet" and "reader" ("Lyric" 34) and a sense that "one's helplessness is contagious" ("Lyric" 36).[13] The trope of possession is especially evident in the work of queer poets beginning with Walt Whitman, who used this figure to depict (and disguise) otherwise inexpressible erotic counters, as Mark Maslan and Michael Moon have argued.[14]

In the remainder of this chapter, I will examine the ways a range of poems explore these issues. The figurative strategies through which these poems depict (and disguise) the literal manifestations of AIDS are, as I have implied, deeply political; they influence how the disease is understood by both the afflicted and the larger culture. Yet AIDS poems complicate the simple equation of explicit subject matter with politically progressive views and of difficulty with political obfuscation. They do so by considering, among other topics, the political implications of a poetics that foregrounds figuration and indirection. I will focus on the implications of what I call a poetics of immunity and infection, terms I have adopted because they evoke both the physiology of infection and its figurative potential. Mark Doty, who has made his HIV-negative status known (*Heaven's* 2), tends to refuse literal descriptions of infection or illness, relying instead on metaphoric constructions. In these poems, AIDS is already figurative, a stand-in for more general conditions of grief, illness, and survivorship. But while such poems enact a defensive rhetoric of immunity, they also emphasize blurring and merging in ways that complicate their own defensiveness. Other poems, including those by Paul Monette and D. A. Powell, more fully embrace what I call a poetics of infection. Often narrated by speakers who reveal their HIV-positive status and name AIDS directly, these poems allow the AIDS dead not only to speak but to permeate the living. Yet such scenes of permeation are generally, as in "The Second Hour," temporary and associated with dream and wish. All these poems thus blur infection with immunity, revealing the dynamics of infection that underlie defensive assertions of immunity and the reverse. In the process, they raise questions about the aesthetic and political role of poetry, questions also central to Rich's *Dark Fields*. Rich's poems are often indirect and nonspecific. But AIDS poems consider the topic of indirection, asking whether and how a deeply figurative and personal poetry can engage with a literal issue that has both political and personal ramifications.

I have structured this chapter to move from the more distanced, defended, and figurative poems of Doty through Monette's more open poetics of contagion and fantasy to Powell's explicit embrace of infection and also artifice. I end with readings of poems by Thom Gunn and James Merrill that elaborate and even celebrate the sense of permeability and mutuality that other poems resist.

||||||||||||||||||

I claimed above that tensions about the condition of belated survivorship are often enacted in AIDS poems through dynamics of possession and yielding. Such dynamics are central to Doty's AIDS poems from the 1990s and also evident, albeit indirectly, in his subsequent work.[15] AIDS is never directly named in these poems; instead, Doty emphasizes acts of displacement and depersonalization, which help defend the poems' speaker from contagion, as well as from the need to remember the past. In fact, it is difficult to know whether many of these poems are actual or anticipatory elegies or something else entirely because they so emphatically disavow personal details, as well as narrative and closure. Several poems in *My Alexandria* (1993) allude to fears about an unspecified illness (74–76) and to dying young men (65–67). Doty's subsequent volume, *Atlantis* (1995), was written, as he has said elsewhere, when "[the AIDS] epidemic was the central fact of the community in which [he] lived" ("Souls" 72) and more exactly during his partner Wally's terminal illness, but they do not mention these "fact[s]." Doty prefers to describe the landscape, including the movements of fog and tide, which enact and also depersonalize his experiences through imagery of erasure and continuation. (In contrast, Doty's prose memoir, *Heaven's Coast*, contains detailed and chronological descriptions of his partner's illness and death.)

Many of Doty's AIDS poems identify their speaker not as a writer but a reader or detached witness attempting to interpret and understand nearly illegible experiences. In the process, Doty merges agency with passivity and possessing with being possessed. In *Atlantis*'s "Grosse Fuge" (20–28), for example, the speaker calls the MRI of his sick friend Bobby "an image I can't read," an illegibility that contrasts with his attempt in the same poem to read a "nameless season." Only late in the poem does he convert these scenes of passive reading into an active one of writing. What he has experienced, he makes clear, informs his own attempt at creation: in a world characterized by repetition, "What can I do but echo / myself, vary and repeat?" To speak, Doty here claims, is to "echo," an act that involves no agency, but also to "vary" in ways that evoke Beethoven's fugue of the title, which Doty here imitates and extends.

Elsewhere, Doty more directly disavows his agency as a poet through acts of prosopopoeia and near-prosopopoeia, recalling the ambivalent imagery of possession in "The Second Hour." It is not we who chronicle death, Doty states in his prose memoir, but death that "transliterates us" (*Heaven's* 64). Doty here does not grant death the capacity to translate experiences into comprehensible form. Instead, he depicts the more technical conversion of one alphabet to another. We, he suggests, are the inanimate text over which a personified death labors, though our transformation may not, in the end, be momentous. Doty here grants death the capacity to speak, but the animation is also compromised; the poet's personification of death enables death more easily to do its ordinary work of deanimating our already textualized (and thus deanimated) selves.

Bidart's "The Second Hour" describes a transactional model: the speaker lends his body with the understanding that the loan is temporary. Related models recur in other AIDS poems, at times punning on possession; often, material possessions enable the protagonist to possess other, less tangible entities. Doty's long poem "The Wings" (*My Alexandria* 39–51), for example, is mostly concerned with "buying things" (at an auction, a yard sale, and the like), as well as with recurrent imagery of wings and angels. But in the unnumbered fourth section, Doty describes the AIDS quilt in ways that link material possessions to questions about whether the dead can be possessed or reanimated. Doty begins by describing a viewing of the quilt at a public "Exhibition Hall," but this scene of spectatorship quickly yields to a meditation on the ways the objects sewn into the quilt embody, and partly personify, the dead.

> It's the clothing I can't get past,
> the way a favorite pair of jeans,
> a striped shirt's sewn onto the cloth;
>
> the fading, the pulls in the fabric
> demonstrate how these relics formed around
> one essential, missing body.
>
> An empty pair of pants
> is mortality's severest evidence.
> Embroidered mottoes blend
>
> into something elegaic [sic] but removed;
> a shirt can't be remote.
> One can't look past
>
> the sleeves where two arms
> were, where a shoulder pushed
> against a seam, and someone knew exactly
>
> how the stitches pressed against skin
> that can't be generalized but was,
> irretrievably, you, or yours.

The speaker refuses to take possession of the observed scene. Instead, the visible clothing sewn into the quilt ("a favorite pair of jeans, / a striped shirt") evokes an imagined "one essential, missing body" notable because it "*can't be held*." The quilt in this way joins literal, present, tactile objects to figurative absence. Yet the passage turns at its end to something quite different: as the present tense yields to the past tense, the speaker separates from the now-absent dead. The act of viewing the quilt and the quilt's existence itself thus reveal a belated condition of survivorship at odds with the poem's repeated refusal to "get past" the quilt's visible emblems. Moreover, the last line's shift from the detached and generalizing pronoun "one" to the more intimate "you" reveals the speaker's capacity to be possessed (or even metaphorically infected) by what he sees. By implying that "you," the animated dead other, and "yours," the persistence of his possessions, are equivalent, the last line suggests that animation is possible only temporarily, in relation to what Ross Chambers has called in the context of the AIDS quilt "objects left behind" (xxix). The "empty pair of pants / is mortality's severest evidence"; it affirms the fact of death. Yet the emptied, billowing clothing also recalls the living body, "the sleeves where two arms / were, where a shoulder pushed / against a seam." The poem refuses wholly to animate or even name the dead, but it also explores the quilt's prosopopoeiac capacity, as one critic has claimed of it, to speak "*for* the dead in an act of substitution" (Kermode 227). The clothes remain clothes, although the poet's attempt to understand or read them—in ways consistent with the quilt's more general capacity to be "textual—or at least discursive" (Kermode 227)—also permits a moment of closeness, as the intimacy of address reveals.

In another poem in the same volume, "Fog" (33–36), a more sustained act of personification reveals a similar tension between literal and figurative possession. Here, though, the dead speak directly, in a clearer approximation of prosopopoeia, although this speech occurs only via the mediation of the Ouija board, which also provides a context and explanation for it.[16] The board, as James Merrill's extended exploration of it in his epic *The Changing Light at Sandover* reveals, raises questions of animation and voice that are also central to poetry; while the dead speak to the living through the board, these voices often seem to be projections of the poet's own. Merrill describes bringing out the board to forestall marital ennui (5–6), but the protagonists of "Fog," Mark and Wally, use it "Three weeks after the test," before they have learned its results. They succeed in summoning "A cloud of [dead] spirits," although the identities of these spirits are less important than the "incongruous / and exactly spelled" words, "*energy, immunity, kiss. //* Then: M. *has immunity. W. has.*" Rather than actually animating the dead, these words emphasize the act of transmission and their own textuality. On a literal level, the protagonists get the information they want from the board. But on a poetic one, these words prevent the speaker from having to disclose his partner's status; he twice expresses his wish "not to say the word."

Both receiving and sending messages, the speaker in "Fog" plays a double role. The poem depicts a literal scene of transliteration, in which the board does not speak but spells out its messages letter by letter. But Doty also transliterates these messages by putting them into his poem. Doty's memoir's use of the term "transliterates" involves, as I just suggested, an ambivalent prosopopoeia that personifies death while deanimating "us." The prosopopoeia of "Fog" is similarly bound to deanimation. Wally and Mark are "the public health care worker's / nine o'clock appointment," and this worker writing down the "*P*" of "positive" is a "phantom hand." (Merrill uses the term *hand* to identify the transcriber of the Ouija board's messages.) These deanimating terms function partly as social commentary: they reveal the ways medical interactions eradicate the humanness of both patients and health care workers. But they also evoke another, unstated and proleptic deanimation: the diagnosis implies that Wally will die soon.

The poem's prosopopoeia thus defends against the diagnosis and what it implies. But as Doty's speaker reveals he has "*immunity,*" this apparent defense against contagion is belied by the poem's imagery of invasion and merging. Blood, Doty claims, "can't be seen except" when it is

no longer itself.

Though it submits to test, two,
to be exact, each done three times,

though not for me, since at their first entry
into my disembodied blood

there was nothing at home there.
For you they entered the blood garden over

and over, like knocking at a door
because you know someone's home.

Here the blood is both alive (it "submits") and not (it is "disembodied"). It is a "garden" entered by the unspecified "they" who administer the test "for" an unspecified "you," although these characters also stand just outside a "home" inhabited by a personification of AIDS itself. The blood must "submit to test" and be "entered . . . over // and over"; it is thus doubly permeable, both removed from the body and invaded by the virus. Elsewhere in the poem, the speaker attempts to substantiate the board's assertion "*God in garden*" by viewing the flowers in his actual garden as imbued with an animating force. He is, he claims, "almost convinced" that a "god" is there, almost, but not quite, because he recognizes that such acts of animation represent attempts to push away the threats—and reality—of permeation, infection, and death.

"Fog" directly announces Doty's physiological "immunity," but Doty's subsequent volume, *Atlantis*, read as a whole, abstracts this condition and renders it figurative. The volume thus expresses something like what Sarah Brophy identifies as a more general recurrent "*fantasy* of immunity" in AIDS writing (4). The poems in *Atlantis* hardly mention illness. Instead, they describe a coastal, tidal landscape that continuously unmakes and remakes itself in ways that undermine closure, partly by allowing what is lost or submerged to reemerge. Such scenes recall Lee Edelman's claim that AIDS rhetoric demonstrates a recurrent pattern of "tropological substitution" (312), including metaphorical language. According to Edelman, this pattern refuses the "literality" of "death," in an attempt to "claim . . . immunity against contamination" (312).[17] Certainly in *Atlantis*, metaphor allows the poet both to transform dangerous material and to contain what threatens to leak out or contaminate him. (Doty has elsewhere acknowledged and also defended his reliance on metaphor.[18]) Yet because this imagery itself insists on contamination and blurring, it is only partly effective as a defense, as Doty repeatedly acknowledges.

While "The Wings" asserts that the quilt's sewn-on clothes offer "evidence" of "mortality," the poems of *Atlantis* tend to marshal "theor[ies]" (98), "evidence" (73, 87), and "argument[s]" (83) to deny death's finality. Often they do so by posing generalizing questions about what it is to be human, some of them answered prosopopoeiacally by inanimate objects in the poems, often contradicting or deflecting the poet's arguments.[19] Moreover, the poet's questions tend themselves to be ambiguous; often conditional and negative, they partly reject the alternatives that they propose or express doubt about their own logic. In the process, these poems reveal both Doty's defensiveness and his openness to what "Nocturne in Black and Gold" (94–98) calls what is "volatile . . . / permeable, leaking out."

"Homo Will Not Inherit" (*Atlantis* 76–79) explores several related paradoxes. The poem is occasioned by a "xeroxed" notice including an image of Jesus along with the phrase "Homo Will Not Inherit." The poem's speaker coopts, then extends this claim, refusing the earthly inheritance Jesus promised the meek for an embrace of "the margins / which have always been mine." This is arguably a defensive act, as is evident in the speaker's defiant tone, though it also enables Doty to explore the literal and figurative possibilities of permeation and boundarylessness. Doty here transforms the homophobic into something lyrically beautiful, partly by excising any mention of AIDS as well as the literal meaning of the placard, which likely implied AIDS to be a divine punishment for homosexuality. Nor, other than in the title and citation from the posted document, does Doty refer to the sociopolitics of queer culture, although the poem's systematic transformation of homophobic imagery is arguably political in that it recalls Chambers's claim that AIDS rhetoric often articulates the political via the "rhetorical intervention" of tropes and figures (xxvi).

The speaker's act of taking possession of the margins is, Doty makes clear, belated and thus redundant; perhaps because these margins were imposed on him by a perennially defensive culture, he has "always" possessed them. Yet affirming possession also involves ceding control. After physically locating the "edges no one wants, no one's watching" (they are "downtown anywhere," in a nighttime "secret city" alongside the "public" one), the speaker engages in an act of quasi-prosopopoeiac self-animation. He has, he says, been

> possessed of the god myself,

> I have been the temporary apparition

salving another, I have been his visitation, I say it
without arrogance, I have been an angel

for minutes at a time . . .

Significantly, Doty here depicts himself not as ghostly but angelic, recalling
James Berger's general claim that angels "reassure," whereas ghosts "engulf
[the survivor] in . . . unhealed wounds" (*After* 53).[20] The speaker begins by
depicting himself as the recipient of godliness, although the preposition "of"
in the phrase "possessed of" (rather than the more conventional "by") suggests that he does not yield completely. He then transforms being possessed
into possessing (or being infected by) the god's attributes. The speaker becomes first "the . . . apparition," then "his visitation," and then "an angel."
Self-erasure is thus the precondition for resurrection. The speaker's willingness to allow himself to be animated by the god recalls the ways the dead
addressee is animated by the speaker in "The Second Hour." Here too being
possessed is reassuring. But Doty also qualifies this account by acknowledging that his transformation is "temporary," lasting only "minutes."

"Homo Will Not Inherit" thus both enacts and suppresses bodily transformation: as it belatedly converts hate speech into affirmation, it transforms the literal facts of infection (the poem takes place in the vicinity
of "bathhouse[s]," associated with the transmission of HIV) into something
figurative and beautiful, evident in "the column of feathering steam /
unknotting itself," "shimmered azaleas of gasoline," and the like. By adopting a provisional, partial ghostliness, the speaker defensively diffuses the
actual threat of AIDS. Doing so refuses the elegiac, as does Doty's prose
characterization of another poem in *Atlantis* "written some six months after
my partner of a dozen years had died of AIDS" as "a sort of anti-elegy" that
affirms not death but what "goes on" ("Souls" 72–73).

||||||||||||||||

Unlike Doty's anti-elegies, the poems in Paul Monette's 1988 sequence *Love
Alone*—one of just three poetry volumes he published before his death in
1995 and the volume for which he remains best known—are, the book's
subtitle indicates, *Elegies for Rog*. The preposition is ambiguous: these are

poems about Monette's partner, who died of AIDS in 1986, but they are also meant for his receipt, at least according to the rhetoric of animation that informs them. The volume thus presents a fundamental ambiguity from the outset; it is both a response to Rog's death and a denial of it, achieved through a rhetoric of reanimation and prosopopoeia far more insistent than in Doty's poems. While Doty mostly considers infection indirectly, as in the description of the animated garden in "Fog," Monette's AIDS poems focus at length on infection's literal implications. Like Doty, though, Monette also transforms the literal facts of illness and death into a figurative mode that enables proximity. Taking place between Rog's remembered death and Paul's anticipated one—Monette is explicit about his HIV-positive status—the poems of *Love Alone* are often temporally unstable. They confuse remembering with anticipation, partly by rendering Rog as still alive and capable of speech, at least in contained and artificial settings. Doty's essentially metaphoric poems distinguish tenor (the ordinary world) from vehicle (how it is interpreted by the poet), but in Monette's unpunctuated, loosely blank verse lines, the dead and living Rog are easily confused. This confusion is especially evident in the poems I will discuss below. (Like Doty's, Monette's prose memoir, *Borrowed Time*, recounts Rog's illness and death in detailed and chronological terms.)

As I argued above in relation to Bidart and Doty, the motif of possessing and being possessed in AIDS poems is often linked to animation and prosopopoeia. Monette's "The House on King's Road" (43–47) links the poet's consideration of an actual possession—the house shared by Paul and Rog—to his belated attempt to animate Rog. Doty's "Homo Will Not Inherit" focused on the metamorphosis of solitary speaker into an angel, but here the poet's capacity to reanimate Rog affirms that Paul as survivor is also a ghost.

The poem associates the facts regarding the ownership of the titular house, the deed to which is stored in "the hall / of records," with an assertion of mutual and shared purpose: "two men ceased to be single / here in a house free of liens." This assertion impels the poet to ask a question about the future: "how can / Death untwine them or the room in the room / where they have one name[?]" The next, more intimate question seems to acknowledge

Rog's absence and inability to speak: "oh my love tell me / where you are." But then the speaker antichronologically answers this question by describing an actual, ordinary location in the house; Rog is again alive, "in the study writing Follain / laughing on the phone." Yet we know—and the speaker also knows—that this belated act of animation expresses the speaker's wish rather than what is literally and currently true.

This moment reveals a recurrent tension in AIDS elegy; the poetic act of reviving the dead exposes its own figurativity and thus the irrevocable absence of the dead. Elsewhere in "The House on King's Row," a similar tension is more directly explained:

> my gentle housemate
> lost at the front door still I bawl *I'm home Rog*
> not that I really expect to meet you . . .
> . . . .
> *fixed roof* your diary scrawls *skimmed pool pasta*
> *for supper* stuff you wouldn't suppose worth
> the ink yet somehow it breaches the wall
> within the wall more than memory more than
> the pivot of event calls us home shoring
> time with casual embraces . . . [.] (44)

The situation of address is both belated (the poet "still . . . bawl[s]" to Rog, suggesting grief) and displaced (Paul depicts himself rather than Rog as "lost"). The poem also denies the reality of Rog's absence by using the present tense and by granting Rog something like proposopoeiac speech; Rog's "scrawl . . ." seems to respond to (and echo) Paul's "bawl." Rog's diary "breaches the wall," or rather the figurative "wall / within the wall" separating him from Paul, enabling Rog posthumously to speak, or at least write.

Yet like Doty's animation of the clothes sewn onto the quilt, this act is also deeply provisional: Rog's diary may still exist, but Rog does not. The strain is evident in the devolution of Monette's syntax at the end of the passage cited above. Among other ambivalent lines, the referent of "calls us home" is unclear. It may refer to Rog's voice (insofar as the diary undermines "memory" by insisting on the present moment) or to the poem itself, which has "pivot[ed]" from the fiction of presence to an acknowledgment of the persistence of "memory."[21]

Elsewhere in the poem, Monette extends this sense of slippage to Paul's future death. Describing Rog's sense "a month before you went" that *our happy life* was lost, the speaker offers a belated rejoinder: "it's here it's here I know because I am / the ghost who haunts us I am the last window." Here Monette confuses Rog's actual ghostliness—insofar as it is he who is dead—with Paul's figuratively similar, future state. Rog's apparently posthumous voice, "bawl[ing]" and "crie[s]" have in fact been created (or at least transmitted) by Paul. This situation has proleptic implications, as when Monette explicitly associates ghostliness with belatedness:

> let the material go
> what you cannot buy or have in your name
> is the ghost of a touch the glancing stroke
> as a man passes through a room where his love
> sits reading later much later the nodding head
> of the one on the other's shoulder no title
> usurps that place this is its home forever[.] (46–47)

Here the syntax is ambiguous: it is unclear whether the imperative "let . . . go" signals advice to Rog, some other addressee, or the poet himself. Nor is it clear who is touching whom and whether this touch is real or imagined, although it must be relinquished along with the rest of "the material." In this way, the poem unmoors ghostliness from Rog, intimating that Paul too must "let the material go" in anticipation of a future that is not only "later much later" but "forever." Such tactics imply a wholly figurative alternative to the literal, "material" possession of the house. Here the dead possess the living and the reverse. But Monette also refuses wholly to embrace this dissolution of the literal. By indicating that this transformation occurs on a "stage" or "set," he frames and contains haunting; ghostly presences can persist within his poems because these presences are not in fact real.

Several other poems in the volume also both depict and contain the possibility that Rog can be revived and enabled to speak. In "No Goodbyes," as the title indicates, the speaker attempts to undermine separation and thus the fact of his own belated survival. The poem shifts from memories of Rog alive ("he ate he slept") to an urgent address that implies that Rog is listening even as it affirms he cannot be "rouse[d]": "oh why / don't all these kisses rouse you." Then the speaker explores what seems like a fantasy of presence:

> I won't I won't
> say it all I will say is goodnight patting
> a few last strands in place you're covered now
> my darling . . . [.] (5)

An ordinary recalled bedtime here blurs into the final "goodnight" of death, and bed "cover[ings]" evoke burial. But a few lines later, Monette explains this apparent blurring: the speaker is, he says, "still here . . . / singing your secret names till the night's gone." The scene just described is, we understand, a flashback; the shift above into the future tense ("all I will say is") in fact abandons what is revealed to be only a fantasy that Rog is still present.

This moment foregrounds Paul's continuing capacity to "say" and "sing," even following Rog's death. "Three Rings" contains a similar temporal shift, but here Rog prosopopoeiacally speaks. Paul, at his dead partner's grave, hears Rog posthumously addressing him. He

> froze mid-moan
> saw it all in a blaze YOU WERE CALLING ME
> my sailor brother oh I didn't know Death
> had reached your lips muscles gone words dispersed
> still you moaned my name so ancient wild and
> lonely it took ten weeks to reach me . . . [.] (32)

Here Rog's "moan[ing]" resembles Paul's: Paul "froze mid-moan" while "still you moaned my name." So too the poem's implied situation of address to Rog (or apostrophe) becomes a corresponding address by Rog to Paul (or prosopopoeia). Despite Paul's "ten weeks" alone following Rog's death, Rog's voice is "still" present: "*now* / I hear each melancholy wail a roar like / fallen lions" (italics added).

But, as the graveside scene in "No Goodbyes" disrupts the bedside one, Monette here undermines this sense of mutuality. Rog's moans only seem to be occurring here and now. In fact, they are

like a signal sent by a dying star bursting
here in my dead heart a bloom of black light
calling WE ARE A MILLION MILES AWAY
SAY WE ARE NOT ALONE[.] (32)

As starlight is experienced long after it has been emitted, so too Rog's words, the analogy reveals, were spoken while he was alive but only now, belatedly and posthumously, deciphered. The passage thus confirms Paul's belatedness—he only now understands Rog's earlier cries—and also contains the poem's act of prosopopoeia. Paul has, we understand, merely pretended that Rog was speaking because he wanted to hear his voice; the words were actually spoken only "here in my dead heart."

Monette has described his poems as explicitly political, citing his wish to "have this volume filed under AIDS [rather] than under Poetry, because if these words speak to anyone they are for those who are mad with loss, to let them know they are not alone" (xi). Yet central to his project of conveying the reality of AIDS is a bodily confusion more extreme than that in "Homo Will Not Inherit" and other poems by Doty. Even as he remains committed to an activist agenda especially urgent at the time of the poems' composition, Monette acknowledges and also perpetuates the blurring of literal with figurative that Edelman and others associate with AIDS rhetoric. To speak publicly to a broad audience about AIDS, that is, requires both breaking down boundaries, including that between the literal and the figurative, and also revealing the political utility of such acts.

D. A Powell's 1998 *Tea* relies on a similar rhetoric of infection but does not contain it. In a sense, this strategy pertains directly to Powell's decision to include in his poems the kinds of explicit descriptions of promiscuity, sex acts, and sexual desire that both Doty and Monette avoid. (This tactic is consistent with Powell's other poems about AIDS and his poems more generally.[22]) Powell also refuses to pull back from the sense of transgression and excess that Monette more provisionally associates with ghostliness, repeatedly presenting speakers who are, in Stephen Burt's terms, simultaneously "resurrected" and "survivor[s]" (85). But even as Powell undermines distinctions between self and other, now and the future, and the living and the dead, he reveals that the desire to animate the dead prosopopoeiacally can be expressed only figuratively.

The excesses and challenges of Powell's project are evident in his nonce form: he was able to write these poems, his introduction to *Tea* states, only by turning his notebook sideways (xi), permitting unusually long lines. Like Monette's, Powell's lines are unpunctuated, but while this practice fosters connections and double meanings in *Love Alone* (a single word or phrase often connects both to what precedes and follows it), in *Tea* Powell refuses connection by splitting each line into clauses separated by white space. Powell also fragments his poems' voice by combining different registers into a single poem. As such, these poems are more emotionally oblique and syntactically difficult than Monette's and much more so than Doty's. Such a strategy is both distancing—these poems cannot be easily digested or summarized—and politically significant; Powell speaks from within a culture whose private vocabulary and references he often adapts but does not explain within the poems.[23]

The political implications of Powell's form are evident in "[Dead boys make the sweetest lovers.relationships unfold like stroke mags:tales less complex]" (8). (In this poem, like most in the volume, the title is the first line, with punctuation added.) Here Powell identifies several modes of representation. This topic recalls Doty's concern with representation and writing, although Powell's poems, as he explains in the volume's introduction, refuse the kind of metaphoric connection central to Doty's poems.[24] The poem ends with a contrast between "games [that] evolve into storylines," "the novel you write," and "autobiography." But Powell does not choose between these genres. Instead, he enumerates them in relation to the more urgent question of whether "dead boys" can be brought back to life. Powell uses terms familiar from other AIDS poems; he considers ghostliness (an unidentified "he is only ghost and polaroid") as well as the possibility of a "brief resurrection." But the poem's literal situation remains deeply ambiguous. It is not clear whether the poem is animating a dead lover or whether this lover has been effectively replaced by a photograph or substitute "relationships." Nor is it clear whether the poem's ghost is meant to be understood as the posthumous incarnation of an actual dead lover or, in ways that may contradict Powell's disavowal of this figure, as an implied metaphor for something unmentioned in the poem.

The poem considers possession, but Powell does not contrast possessing with being possessed (as do Bidart and Doty), nor does he contrast material with other forms of possession (as does Monette). Instead, the speaker insists on the pleasure that comes from owning things. "Relationships," the poem asserts, are "like stroke mags" in that "several might be possessed and managed at once: properties / to be landed upon turn after turn." As in the game Monopoly, the act of "possess[ing] . . . properties" multiplies them until "nudes prop themselves against the bed."

Relationships with dead boys here grant pleasure to the speaker without threatening him. However, the poem's epigraph from D. A. Miller suggests something different: Miller's assertion that the death of a gay man never "stopped the elaboration of someone else's fantasy about him" reveals that, despite his mercantile attitude and his initial assertion that "dead boys" can be converted into "the sweetest lovers," the speaker cannot animate the dead but only create inanimate copies of them. The stroke mags substitute for actual presence, the Polaroid is just a photo, and the nudes on the bed are dummies. Thus, unlike Doty, who tends to valorize making, speaking, and reading, or Monette, who repeatedly enacts a prosopopoeia he then explains away, Powell *describes* an act of prosopopoeia he does not participate in. Just as new "relationships" offer "tales" that are "less complex" than earlier ones, Powell's poem "lack[s] a certain tension"; its depicted act of possession involves repetition rather than excitement, as the properties in Monopoly are "to be landed upon turn after turn." In the process, Powell reveals, as do Doty and Monette, the limits of both ghostliness and prosopopoeia. But he considers more directly than they do the process by which actual or literal occurrences are converted into what his epigraph calls "fantasy." As such, the poem partly dismantles the very tropes on which it relies.

A similar ambiguity is more directly enacted in "[and eventually I would take him back.into the reliquary of my mattress.winter terms]" (20). Here, Powell blurs a scene beside a sickbed with an erotic encounter so that it is unclear whether the poem is really about sex or illness. The poem seems to chronicle the speaker's recollection of nursing (and also having sex with) someone beloved and now dead, a recollection that contaminates the world he belatedly inhabits. But this is not the only possible reading of the poem; as several lines imply, it is unclear whether the poem's "he" is dead or alive and whether the speaker wishes to hold him closer or cast him off.[25]

The poem in these ways demonstrates Powell's interest, as he asserts in the title of the section in which this poem appears, in "equat[ing] sex and death" (11). But the poem also disrupts this equivalence. The rhetoric of illness is especially evident in the vehicles of its similes, including "he stung like the briefest injection" and "the world white as aspirin." Elsewhere objects associated with illness and hospitalization (including "purple splotches," "hospital waste," and "capillaries") are more radically displaced, as in the final phrase "capillaries burst their deciduous branches," which may refer to actual capillaries or use them as ways of describing tree branches. Such images emphasize a fundamental ambiguity, as is also evident in the first line's phrase "the reliquary of my mattress," in which it is unclear whether the tenor is the mattress or the reliquary. Nor is the time frame clear. Powell several times uses "would," a term that may refer to a habitual past event (implied by the poem's first clause, "and eventually I would take him back") or a hypothetical future one (perhaps alluded to in the later phrase "I would use my teeth"). The poem also uses several verbs (including "spread" and "burst") that take the same form in the past and present tense. As a result, it is unclear whether the events described are memories or fantasies. The recurrent images of injection and penetration intensify the confusion: we do not know who or what is entering whom.

Similar images appear in "[sleek mechanical dart:the syringe noses into the blue vein marking the target of me]" (63), but here the speaker intensifies the sense of permeability by applying images of injection and penetration to himself. Looking ahead to the future possibility of his own AIDS infection instead of back at the past illness of others, the speaker reverses the earlier poems' imagery of insertion. Instead, the "syringe" takes "what's inside me. inside me or coming out," an experience that leads to a recollection of "a thousand happy tourists in-&-out[ing] me" and then a sensation of "feel[ing] taken in." This imagery literally describes the AIDS test, which removes the speaker's blood, then imposes his diagnosis on him. But it also figuratively erases the boundary between interior and exterior, an erasure Powell extends by refusing, unlike Doty, to reveal the test's outcome.[26]

More emphatically than the other poems I have considered, "[sleek mechanical dart]" undermines the distinction between the dead and the living by confusing animation with deanimation. In the first line, the syringe is personified (it "noses in . . ."), but it also deanimates the speaker, converting him into a "target" and later, a text of body parts and "an alphabetsoup" that must be read by others. "Aliveness jars" the speaker, having apparently entered him from outside. His blood is similarly alive with the ghostly traces of others.

The test thus reveals the speaker to be simultaneously alive and dead. Certainly he anticipates his death: during the "fortnight" waiting for the test results, he "draw[s] up a will," "develop[s] false symptoms," and anticipates "the waist of a coat [he]'ll bury in" as well as the "parties" he'll "throw . . . where death blindfolded is spun." The poem has already depicted the speaker as a text, and here the rhetoric of deanimation and posthumousness is increased. Perhaps this imagery of posthumousness explains Powell's more general refusal, like Doty's, to label his poems elegies.[27]

Powell's poems, I have been arguing, not only allude to scenes of infection but fully adopt infection as a poetics, emphasizing contact with the infected, dying, or dead and relying on syntax and imagery that facilitate linguistic as well as thematic ambiguity. In contrast to Doty and Monette, who tend to confine scenes of ghostly animation to artificial or theatrical spaces, Powell's poems resist the possibility of a truth or reality outside the poem. Yet Powell's poems also pull back from the prosopopoeia evident in the other poems I have considered. Powell nearly allows the dead to speak proposopoeiacally but does not, perhaps because this gesture is itself so artificial and theatrical. As such, Powell's poetics of indirection and infection is arguably both more and less effective as a rhetorical strategy than Doty's more decorous deployment of similar images. In fact, the juxtaposition of the poems I have considered seems to reflect a tension between poetry and the physical, political, and social reality of AIDS. Certainly, all these poems work—and expose how hard they are working—to turn this predicament into a linguistic construct distinct from both the literal dynamics of the disease and earlier rhetoric about it.

⸿⸿⸿⸿⸿⸿⸿⸿⸿⸿⸿⸿

I have been arguing that ghosts join the literal with the figurative as they make presence simultaneous with absence. Another recurrent image in AIDS poems—the ash of cremation—enacts a similar paradox. Such ash both literally embodies the dead—it is what the dead body has become—and symbolizes the process of relinquishing them. It evokes the once-living person even as it reveals that this person is now inanimate. But unlike ghosts, which are imagined, ash literally exists; it can be seen and touched. Ash is also bound more directly to narrative: the scattering of ashes is often a part of memorial rituals, separating the mourner from the dead and the speaking voice of the poet from the mute one elegized.

Similar features may be present in all poems about ash, as well as those about other funeral rituals. But they are especially acute for poets writing about AIDS, as is revealed by both Thom Gunn's "Words for Some Ash" and James Merrill's "Farewell Performance." As both poems chronicle the ash's dispersal, both describe the illusion that the ash is alive. And both poems address the dead, implying a sentient listener contradicted by the fact of the ash's existence, although both poems contain this animation within situations defined as theatrical.

To speak to the dead involves both connection and distance, as both poems make clear. The title of Gunn's poem, "Words for Some Ash," and the dedication of Merrill's ("For DK") rely on the same ambiguous preposition as Monette's subtitle, *Eighteen Elegies for Rog*; the preposition *for* implies a gift bestowed on someone capable of receiving it, yet the fact of death makes such a gift impossible. Gunn's "words" are merely for "*some* ash," a collective, undefined, and inanimate entity that cannot receive them. They are also for their recipient in another sense: the poem accompanies, or even replaces, the ash with its own textual materiality. This situation recalls the tension between possession and relinquishment I have been tracing throughout this chapter. Here, though, the emphasis is not on possessing, taking, or buying. Instead, like Bidart's "The Second Hour," these poems chronicle acts of bestowing and dispersal.

"Words for Some Ash," one of a number of poems in Gunn's 1992 sequence *The Man with Night Sweats* in which Gunn explores dynamics of absence and presence in the context of AIDS, is a ballad in six trimeter quatrains, a form Gunn adopts often in the sequence. The poem chronicles a narrative of relinquishing. It begins by describing the speaker's memories of the addressee, an ill, "poor parched man." The poem turns midway through to this man's current condition—"Now you are a bag of ash / Scattered on a coastal ridge"—and then describes the speaker's hope that the ash's encounters first with "rain," then "unseen streams," and finally the ocean "shore" will restore what the friend lacked in life by reanimating him in another form. The account thus makes belated restitution for the addressee's suffering using the subjunctive of prayer.

Puns, however, complicate this narrative by affirming the simultaneity of animation and deanimation. In the penultimate stanza, for example, the speaker describes the ash's movement into streams, in which the particles "bound / Briskly in the water's play." The line describes animation: the ash is able to "bound," moving freely and with apparent intent. Yet the word "bound" also implies that, lacking volition, the ash is obligated or "bound" to follow currents it cannot control. The following lines, which end the poem, explicitly affirm this failure of animation by using the language of animation:

> May you lastly reach the shore,
> Joining tide without intent,
> Only worried any more
> By the currents' argument.

At its final, wished-for resting place, the ash (and so the remembered suffering friend) will be released from human suffering. Yet this release is expressed through the evocation of the human qualities of "worr[y]" and "argument" and so recalls the addressee's experiences when alive. Moreover, the use of "you," implying an intact and sentient addressee, at the moment of the ash's imagined dispersal reveals the speaker's unwillingness to accept this dispersal. In fact, it is the poet who is not only describing but imagining this journey, which has no existence outside the poem. In this way, Gunn reveals his poem to be an artificial and contained space in which the performance of relinquishment can also be contained.

James Merrill's "Farewell Performance," one of two elegies he wrote for his friend David Kalstone, who died of AIDS in 1986, reveals a similar thematics of performance more directly, as the title indicates.[28] The poem interweaves two narratives emphasizing different kinds of performance. The first involves a dance troupe's final performance, after which its members are repeatedly called on stage by an audience unwilling to acknowledge that "it's over." The second remembers Kalstone (who "would have loved" the dance performance) and describes scattering his ashes. These two narratives interweave, and the poem's vocabulary of illness (the first line is "Art. It cures affliction") reveals Merrill's interest not only in the parallels but the interactions between these narratives, often in chronologically impossible ways that emphasize the speaker's belatedness. For example, Kalstone is described as having "caught like a cold" the dancers' "lust for essence," although the dance performance postdates his death. (The poem does not disclose either that Kalstone died of AIDS or that Merrill was HIV-positive, as he knew when he wrote the poem [White 223].)

The poem insists both on Kalstone's continuing presence and his absence, a doubleness embodied, as in Gunn's poem, by the ash. The addressee has been "in the furnace parched to / ten or twelve light handfuls," yet this apparently inanimate "gravel / sifted through fingers" is also "mortal." The previously living friend and his current deanimation are conflated in the subsequent description of the ash as a "coarse yet grayly glimmering sublimate" that simultaneously evokes the chemical (a sublimate involves a change in state, something like the human body's dissolution into ash), the philosophical (the friend has become sublime or transcendent), and the psychological (his continued presence allows the speaker to disguise or sublimate his sense of loss).

Merrill's description of scattering the ashes, the only moment in the poem in which he uses "I," also emphasizes the simultaneity of animation and dissolution. While "Peter . . . grasped the buoy," the speaker "held the box underwater, freeing / all it contained." Gunn evokes a similar sense of freedom, but Merrill goes further, imbuing the drifting ash with bodily wholeness:

> Past
>
> sunny, fluent soundings that gruel of selfhood
> taking manlike shape for one last jeté on
> ghostly—wait, ah!—point into darkness vanished.

The "gruel of selfhood" is from the outset both temporary (as "gruel," it exists to be consumed) and permanent; it is a kind of clay from which "selfhood" can be shaped or modeled. Then the speaker animates it. "Taking manlike shape," the ash's diffuse particles reassemble into an intact man or, more exactly, the illusion of one, an illusion that affirms its own artifice: the shape is final (the "last jeté") but stylized, a dancelike "jeté on / ghostly . . . point." Anticipating the dancers' similar departure from the stage, Merrill emphasizes finality, although the dancers also attempt to delay their departure, or rather the audience's applause does.

The poem's conflation of the addressee's "farewell performance" with the dancers' reveals a third mode of performance; Merrill's poem is also a "farewell performance" and thus is also both artificial and staged. This overlaying of performances complicates the poem's initial assertion. Art can cure affliction only by catching the affliction, then infecting someone else: it cures through contagion. Or perhaps the poem reveals that art does not in fact cure affliction or, by implication, mortality, since the dancers look back to Kalstone's death while the audience members proleptically look ahead to the moment when they will "join the troupe" of the dead. Just as ash makes past wholeness simultaneous with future obliteration, art also requires the fact of death though it seems to deny or "cure" it. Like the dancers, whose performance is temporary, the poet is also a performer, imposing grace and beauty temporarily over "darkness," affirming his belatedness even as he delays the endpoint. Merrill's title asks us to read this poem, like Doty's poems valorizing artistic making and artifice, as an *ars poetica*. All the other poems I have considered in this chapter in the same sense insist on their capacity to perform (and defer) the incontrovertible fact of mortality.

In its last stanzas, "Farewell Performance" shifts to an anticipatory mode. The audience members "jostle forward / eager to hail [the dancers], // more, to join the troupe." But the illusion created by the dancers falters: "up close their magic / self-destructs," not only because their sweating bodies and faces are visible but because "they've / seen where it led you." The overlaid gazes of audience and dancers thus reveal the difficulty of chronicling the future fact of death.

In "An Upward Look" (*Scattering* 96), the final poem in Merrill's last volume and thus one imbued from the outset with proleptic poignancy, Merrill more directly considers the implications of looking forward to, but also back from, death. Like several other poems in Merrill's final volume, "An Upward Look" can be read as an anticipatory self-elegy: Merrill was dying of AIDS when he wrote the poem, although he does not directly acknowledge this fact. The poem is concerned with balancing opposites; its lines are split in two, creating uneven halves. The question of how these halves relate is central to the poem, as Merrill indicates:

> How did it happen
>
> in bright alternation   minutely mirrored
> within the thinking   of each and every
>
> mortal creature   halves of a clue
> approach the earthlights . . .[.]

Though "each and every // mortal creature" can be described, these creatures remain separate, the singular "clue" split into "halves." Contradictory elements—evident as "alternation" and "mirror[ing]"—coexist, not reconciled but simultaneous.

As the fractured syntax and juxtapositions of Powell's poems allow "I" and "you" as well as death and ghostly continuation to blur, "An Upward Look" unmakes or, to echo the poem, "dissolv[es]" not only particular associations but also the distinction between the literal and the figurative in ways perhaps more extreme than the poems I have so far considered. From the first phrase, "O heart green acre," it is unclear whether the poem is addressing the speaker's heart, an actual green acre, or a beloved. This heart, like a biblical field, has been "sown with salt," apparently unmaking its greenness, but elsewhere Merrill describes the regenerative "Salt of the earth" and salt thrown over the shoulder for luck.

Other imagery in the poem explores a similar instability:

First the grave   dissolving into dawn

then the crucial   recrystallizing
from inmost depths   of clear dark blue

The term "grave" may function as an adjective instead of or as well as a noun. When read as a noun, it remains ambiguous; the salt-like recrystallization that follows the grave's dissolution may affirm the finality of death. Or it may affirm salt's association with transformation. The poem's logic of "alternation" allows these contradictory elements to persist.

Another image midway through the poem punningly describes "this vast facility   the living come / dearest to die in." The term "facility" is both a euphemism for a medical institution and a term signifying ease, comfort, and an ability to speak. Merrill here links these meanings. The fact of dying also joins them; it makes confinement and liberation simultaneous, along with infection and its eradication. So does language, as Merrill here reminds us; insofar as Merrill's dense, punning, unlocated poem offers a reprieve, it is one derived from the "bright alternation" of lyric itself. Here, more explicitly than in the other poems I have considered, transformation and prosopopoeia are simultaneously evoked and contained. And here too, the rhetoric of posthumousness and ghostliness enables an apparently literal possibility of transcendence, of passing over and through, that is perhaps obtainable only in extremis, not (only) in the throes of mourning but on the verge or threshold—these common terms signal borders and then traverse them—of death.

Chapter Four

"Deep into the lateness now"

Likeness and Lateness in Jorie Graham's
Region of Unlikeness

Not only has belatedness recurred in the postwar poems I have been discussing, it has been generative of them. This generativity evokes trauma
theory's assumption that traumatic events remain present long after they
have been experienced and that those who have witnessed them can revive
these events by giving belated testimony to them. Such claims in turn recall
the tensions about witness I described in chapter 2, as well as those inherent in the prosopopoeia I discussed in chapter 3: by arguing that trauma remains able to speak, trauma theory makes it speak again through the voices
of belated witnesses. The thematics of belatedness in the poems discussed
in previous chapters—although evident differently in the work of different
poets—suggests something similar. All these poems in different ways reanimate the past even as they acknowledge its remoteness.

Jorie Graham's 1991 volume *Region of Unlikeness* engages with these issues, which are also evident in both earlier and subsequent volumes by Graham. But belatedness is often implicit in these other poems, which depict
the past as disrupted and obscured.[1] In *Region*, though, this topic is explicit;
the terms *late* and *lateness* recur (along with *delay* and *after*), and virtually
all of its twenty-four poems consider aftermath or the distinct but linked

idea of waiting.[2] This rhetoric recalls the recurrent occasions of prolepsis and anticipation I have noted in earlier chapters. Here, as there, waiting destabilizes both the present moment and the act of remembering. But Graham's general emphasis in *Region* is not on keeping the past alive. Rather, her poems insist that it is too late to do so.

Graham emphasizes the irrecoverability of the past by linking the situation of being "late" to what she repeatedly calls being "like." Graham here recalls the concern with tropes of likeness I have identified in the chapters above. I argued in chapter 1 that Plath replaces metaphor with more provisional simile, metonymy, disrupted synecdoche, and pun in ways that tentatively offer an alternative to the logic of analogy. The inconsistent address and scenes of asymmetrical witness in Rich's *Dark Fields* interrogate a different kind of likeness by considering the extent to which "I," "you," and "we" share similar concerns and desires. And AIDS poems imply that, insofar as the dead persist and prosopopoeiacally speak after death, they resemble the living despite the evident discrepancies between them and those who survive. Such figures, I have been arguing throughout this book, both articulate the literal condition of belatedness and demonstrate its utility as a poetics to be deployed by postwar poets.

As Graham's volume makes this connection explicit, it both analyzes the imbrication of belatedness with figuration and enacts the problems that arise from it. Metaphors and especially similes recur throughout *Region*, but rather than signaling absolute equivalence, they reveal its limitations. Graham explores these limitations in a range of ways. At times, her speakers yoke unlike elements in similes that seem forced or implausible; at others, they directly acknowledge the inadequacy of their own similes. Graham also comments on the nature of likeness, as the title *Region of Unlikeness* makes clear; likeness is inadequate—its opposite is affirmed—but the act of negation reveals that it is also central to the volume.

In ways quite different from the other volumes I have considered, *Region* also proposes an alternative to analogical thinking or "likeness" by emphasizing particular and often artificial spaces that physically locate abstract ideas. This impulse is also evident in the volume's title, which associates unlikeness (already a nominalized adjective) with a physical "region." The claim in the poem "History" (35–36) that an unspecified woman is "deep into the lateness now" is typical of the volume; it not only implies the simultaneity of "lateness" with the present "now" but also depicts lateness as "deep" and thus by implication a place that can, and perhaps must, be physically entered. Such acts of spatialization gesture toward an alternative to metaphor, one that replaces the depth often associated with metaphoric modes of representation with a flatter and more metonymic mode that emphasizes contiguity rather than resemblance.[3] At times, Graham offers alternatives to metaphor or likeness by insisting on spatial, metonymic connections. But these connections are often abstract or conceptual, and the places to which Graham refers are often, as in the depth associated with lateness in "History," not actual or physical. Instead, they concretize abstract ideas. The poems thus rely on something like what Mary Kinzie has called "metaphorical abstraction . . . ," which she defines as "thoughts represented as abstractions." Such abstractions, she claims, "behave more like beings in a material embodied realm than like ideas, owing to metaphorical implication." Although, as apparent "beings," they evoke animation and prosopopoeia, metaphorical abstractions are in fact "the reverse of personification" (436).

Several readers have noticed the imagery of lateness and waiting in *Region*, while others have remarked on its preoccupation with metaphorical and spatial ways of understanding.[4] But these features have not for the most part been linked. One exception is implicit in Helen Vendler's gloss of the epigraph from Augustine from which Graham's volume draws its title, one of several that comprise a foreword to the volume. This epigraph—"I trembled with love and awe, and found myself to be far from you, in a region of unlikeness" (qtd. in *Region* xi)—Vendler claims, implies that Augustine's description of temporality is articulated through and by the problem of analogy. The epigraph cogently expresses several tensions I have already associated with Graham's volume: it links a psychological condition of "trembl[ing] with love and awe" with a physical one (Augustine is "far from" God), then engages in an act of spatialization, as I have already described.

Vendler claims that the epigraph's reference to unlikeness recalls a lost but remembered region of likeness that paradoxically renders the linguistic act of analogy unnecessary. Instead, this region of likeness

> would be a place where no metaphors would be needed, where thing, thought, memory, imagination, and language would all coalesce in the oneness of eternity. But in temporality, as we yearn forward and the object of desire or the object of memory perpetually recedes, we are shaped by the absence of the object of our longing. ("Mapping" 233)

According to this logic, Graham's reliance on what Vendler calls "metaphor" —and by implication simile—marks not the essential or literal likeness of things, as might be supposed, but the failure to bind entities that are in fact fundamentally unlike. Vendler implies that this linguistic failure is the result of belatedness: to inhabit a region of unlikeness is to occupy a postlapsarian state by definition too late, which reveals the inaccessibility of "the oneness of eternity." Condemned both to recollect (recognizing what Vendler calls the "object of memory" even as it "recedes") and to "yearn forward," "we" remain caught, as the speakers of Graham's poems often are, between an unavailable past and an unknown future.

Vendler's reading of Augustine conveys the relation between a temporal condition defined by loss and the failure of language to reconnect the parts of a disjointed world. It is unsurprising that Graham's volume focuses on a similar relation. Certainly *Region* demonstrates that to come after is to be caught in language. The volume also demonstrates the verbal and tropological entanglements that derive from the attempt to speak from and about belatedness; although this volume has been called Graham's most autobiographical, the actual events that it depicts are often unclear or confusingly overlaid.[5] Scenes of disrupted spectatorship recur, but they function differently from similar scenes in AIDS poems. The scattering of the dead friend's ashes in the poems I discussed above by Gunn and Merrill forms part of a ritual designed to help the survivor both take leave of and demonstrate his continued attachment to the dead. But Graham's poems repudiate such notions. Instead "history"—this term also recurs—becomes a way to justify a series of wholly self-referential performances.

The volume thus implies a chronological development through postwar poetry that evokes but extends the increasing emphasis on imagination and performance that I noted in chapter 3; in ways that will be even more explicit in my next chapter, Graham reveals that performance responds to and derives from the failure of analogy and depth. As I noted above, Graham replaces metaphoric ways of understanding with metonymic ones. D. A. Powell, whose poems I explored in chapter 3, similarly repudiates metaphor in an apparent attempt to regain intimacy with the dead. (He also relies, in the poem "[and eventually I would take him back]," on simile.) But Graham's disavowal of likeness has a different purpose: her poems expose not only the irrevocability of lateness but the inadequacy of analogy, especially as a way of depicting belatedness.

Graham explores the issues I have been describing in "Holy Shroud" (71–74), which focuses, as do a number of the volume's poems, on the difficulty of verifying apparently literal events and objects. The poem's second half considers the Shroud of Turin, believed for centuries to be that of Jesus. As Graham describes in the poem, in 1894, the amateur photographer Secondo Pia took photos of the shroud, which revealed what the poem calls a "negative image," a "face" on the shroud, apparently of someone crucified. The photos thus seemed belatedly to provide evidence of the shroud's true provenance by making visible an image of a history that could not until then be objectively corroborated. Yet this apparent evidence—what might be called the literalization of an idea—was not visible on the shroud itself. Instead, the face's image could be seen only on Pia's photographic negatives and so relied on this intermediate medium. Pia's photos thus bore a complex relation to narrative: they seemed belatedly to confirm the shroud's authenticity by referring back to the time of Christ's crucifixion, an event that is itself significant only proleptically, when understood in terms of his subsequent resurrection. (In contrast, carbon dating of the shroud has revealed it to be no more than eight hundred years old.)

The poem's ending emphasizes the uncertainty associated with this mediated and deeply belated position. Here a crowd gathers, expecting to see Jesus's face on the shroud. But the face is not visible.

> —When they held [the shroud] up to us
> we saw nothing, we saw the delay, we saw
>
> the minutes on it, spots here and there,
> we tried to see something, little by little we could almost see,
> almost nothing was visible,
> already something other than nothing
> was visible in the *almost*.

While "nothing" is at first visible, Graham converts this absence, along with time, into something "visible" on and via the shroud. At first, the absence is spatialized (and thus undermined) by being converted to "the delay." Then the delay itself is broken into its component parts: it contains visible "spots here and there" as well as "the minutes" that apparently constitute the delay, which are also superficially evident "on" the surface of the shroud. But then something else is revealed, or nearly, an unspecified "something" that is first "almost see[n]," then further spatialized "in the *almost*." Graham thus creates a narrative of spatialization that emphasizes both surface and depth. The effect is that the reader, like the crowd in the poem, must shift between what is literally visible ("nothing," some "spots") and the poet's apparent interpretation of this scene, which transforms it into something figurative. The result is, typically of the volume, vertiginous: we don't know what the viewers in the poem, and by implication we, are actually looking at.

This complex scene of seeing both "nothing" and "delay" offers an alternative to the logic of likeness earlier in the poem. The poem begins with another scene of observation: the speaker "watch[es]" birds flying through "the discarded / photobooth" at "the back of // the mall." (Even this description is complicated, though, in that the birds located *near* the photo booth take on attributes *of* photos by "slipping from still to blur.") The poem then shifts to a description of the shroud via a simile, which functions, as similes often do, as a kind of hinge linking the poem's otherwise unrelated parts; the birds' flight is compared to "when the face which is His . . . emerged."

The simile, a figure of likeness, thus links an apparently observed scene to one that reveals the unreliability of watching. This discrepancy is typical of *Region*, which frequently emphasizes juxtaposed or overlapping acts of looking in ways that recall the asymmetrical witness of Rich's *Dark Fields*. But while Rich and the other poets I have considered depict incongruities in seeing to affirm an underlying reality, Graham is more interested in the construction of the poem itself. Her speakers' compulsion to look redundantly at what she calls "the look *on* things" (*Region* 66, italics added) excises the seen object altogether, emphasizing instead an often solipsistic act of looking *at* looking.

In "Holy Shroud," "delay" is indistinguishable from the modes of interpretation and language that make delay itself visible. Belatedness thus, to recall my book's general claim, here engenders a poetics. But this poetics is self-defeating in that Graham's speaker transforms a literal, actual situation of delay—the wait for the shroud's invisible face to be made visible—into something that exposes the impossibility of accurately depicting this condition. Calling to mind the ineradicable figurativeness of ghosts in AIDS poems, this gesture reveals the inescapability of figurative modes of understanding. Despite the speaker's apparent wish to be done with likeness, her reliance on figuration affirms that the poem is an act of interpretation, which is also, it seems, a self-referential and even solipsistic performance.

I will consider these issues at more length in the remainder of this chapter through close readings of a number of exemplary poems from the volume, in conjunction with prose statements and writings by Graham that articulate her poetic goals and practice. I will first examine two poems in which Graham directly connects lateness to likeness, then explore two that foreground watching, and end with two poems describing theatrical performances.

||||||||||||||||

Vendler's association of "metaphor" with distance from God and thus fallenness implies a sense of loss that Graham's volume mostly turns away from. Instead of lamenting belatedness, Graham manipulates this condition by disrupting what she repeatedly calls "narrative," "story," or "history" in ways that separate belatedness from the grief or powerlessness often associated with it. Her protagonists at various times cannot get access to the past, are caught in intermediate states of waiting, or are compelled to repeat the same actions, sometimes in increasingly disjointed ways. Such disruptions are frequently articulated through a turn away from likeness to more fragmentary figurative structures. In particular, the breakdown of narrative is often expressed through the breakdown of simile, which is replaced by violent images of incorporation that evoke the similar imagery of Bidart's "Curse" and Powell's AIDS poems and confuse, as in "Holy Shroud," the exterior (or literal) with the interior (or figurative).

Yet Graham also at times acknowledges the nostalgia associated with the condition of belatedness. In a discussion of narrative in the introduction to *The Best American Poetry, 1990*, which she edited while writing the poems of *Region*, Graham asserts that contemporary poetry enacts "the incredible tension between the desire to return to 'slower' uses of language and the historical values they still transmit, and an equally strong desire to rebel against the very nature of language—its slowness, its referentiality" (Introduction xx). Poetry, Graham implies, wishes both to go back in time ("to return") and to repudiate this past ("to rebel"). Calvin Bedient has similarly linked Graham's concern with what he calls "*story (plot, outline)*" to both "cover-up" and "consolation" (289–90).

The contradictions of this double wish are extended by Graham's ambivalent description of contemporary culture elsewhere in the same introduction. This culture is filled, she asserts, with "sound bites, shortcuts, clips, trailers, minimalist fragmented 'dialogue,'" which appeal (and perhaps also contribute) to "the speeded-up, almost decimated attention span of the bored, overstimulated viewer" who is constantly "clicking past, 'grazing' the channels" (Introduction xix). This situation, Graham makes clear, involves loss; the "attention span of the . . . viewer" was formerly more robust. Indeed, Graham seems to condemn such tendencies by implying that poetry offers an antidote to them. Thus, poems can "coax the reader into a new—shall we say *awakened?*—state" and "force the reader out of a passive role and back into the poem as an active participant" (xxvi). The imagery of coercion, though, reveals the difficulty and even the violence inherent in such interventions, as Graham has elsewhere implied.[6]

Moreover, elsewhere in the introduction, Graham conflates rather than contrasts contemporary poetry with the culture in which it participates. Poetry, she claims, affirms a "realm" similar to that of contemporary culture —here too Graham employs a spatializing term—"outside the linear and ending-dependent motions of history, narrative, progress, manifest destiny, upward mobility" (Introduction xxv). Here, then, the "decimat[ion]" of contemporary culture offers a useful model for poetry, in which it participates. Graham uses similar language in a poem in *Region*, "Who Watches from the Dark Porch" (97–108), in which a first-person speaker suggests, "Let's graze the channels? Let's find the/storyline composed wholly of changing/tracks, click" (102–03). But here the editorializations are excised, and it remains unclear whether the poet condones or condemns this statement.

Often, the poems of *Region* fracture what Graham's introduction calls "history, narrative, [and] progress" without advocating either coherence or fragmentation. Many poems, including "Holy Shroud," begin by describing a specific, ordinary event or recounting an ordinary vignette. But then Graham disrupts chronology, frequently, as in "Holy Shroud," by superimposing alternative and contradictory time schemes. Different media (often photographs or film) tend to intervene, obscuring the truth of what "really" happened. The speaker also repeatedly explores the ways that these disruptions undermine the capacity of traditional modes of representation and analogy to depict past events.

"The Hiding Place" (19–21) makes something like this point directly. The poem first chronicles a series of past events, then reveals the unreliability of the speaker's memory of them, and finally redescribes the scene in alternate, nonnarrative terms. The figurative thus overtakes the literal as the poem progresses, converting an act of recollection into an exploration of the figurative techniques available to a speaker whose certainty about the past has been compromised. It is perhaps unsurprising that Graham turns to spatial figures, given the poem's topic: it describes a "hiding place" that is both particular and concealed.

The poem begins with a straightforward narrative account of the "*distur-bances*" in 1968 Paris, in which the speaker participated: "I spent 11 nights sleeping in the halls"; "Once I watched the searchbeams play on some flames"; "In the [jail] cell we were . . . crowded." Midway through, though, she begins to interrogate the validity of these supposed memories:

> I remember the cell vividly
> but is it from a photograph? I think the shadows as I
> see them still—the slatted brilliant bits
> against the wall—I think they're true—but are they from a
> photograph?
> Do I see it from inside now—his hands, her face—or
>
> is it from the news account?

As the speaker associates her apparent memories with the media that represented them, she abandons the declarative syntax of the earlier part of the poem. While affirming what she "remember[s]" and "see[s]," she repeatedly disrupts these assertions with "but" and with a question about whether her memories come "from a photograph." The speaker's assertion that she "see[s]" the shadows "still" punningly extends this chronological disruption by conflating the continuous ("I / see them still") with the immobile (what she sees is the still or "photograph"). As the third question ("Do I see it from inside now . . . ?") turns from still photos to a narrativizing "news account," Graham spatializes seeing; her question about whether she can "see . . . from inside" implies that seeing, like lateness in "History," has an interior.

That this spatialized mode is an effect of lateness is apparent when Graham returns to the remembered scene but excises its narrative, partly by describing it in sentence fragments:

> The strangest part of getting out again was *streets.*
> The light running down them.
> Everything spilling whenever the wall breaks.
> . . . .

The open squeezed for space until the hollows spill out,
    story upon story of them
        starting to light up as I walked out.

What is interesting to the poet is not her act of "walk[ing] out"—a vestige
of the poem's "story"—but the visual effects made evident "as" this occurs.
But the scene is not static. The light is mobile: it "run[s] down" the streets,
and other entities "spill," "break," and "squeeze," confusing agency and sequence. It is unclear whether the streets already contain violence (implied
by association of the "spilling" with the already broken wall) or whether
the poet creates it (insofar as the "hollows spill[ing] out" are the result of
"squeez[ing]" "the open . . . for space"). The speaker also severs the term
"story" from narrative in that the visible "story upon story" refers at least
partly to the apparently stacked stories of the building. (The ambiguous "of
them," though, leaves open the possibility that they refer, at least vestigially,
to Graham's account.) The poem thus adopts some of the flattening and
spatializing attributes of the photographs it describes. But spatialization
also offers the poet a (metaphoric) way to articulate her uncertainty about
what is "true." Graham's introduction's ambivalence about belatedness is
here extended; the sense of loss often associated with the failure of memory
is here so excessive and fragmentary that it is hard to recognize as memory.

Although "The Hiding Place" describes a simple scene of remembering,
it gestures toward what Graham has elsewhere called "two versions of time,
cyclical and linear" (Gardner, Interview 236); the speaker, having seen the
ineffectiveness of the "linear" or chronological, adopts a more repetitive
and punning "cyclical" mode. Graham defines these two "versions" of time
in terms of another opposition: the Old Testament, she claims, is "propelled
by the will of the beginning" and "exfoliates off the power of *beginning*, of
creation," while the New Testament exemplifies a temporal mode "tugged
indefatigably by the end" or "predictions, prefigurations of 'something' at
the end" (236). The more complex poem "Detail from the Creation of Man"
(84–88) explores this relation between beginning and end. More exactly, it
considers both what the poem calls "delay" (which looks back toward the
past) and "waiting" (which looks ahead to future events). Graham explains

in her interview that the two different "versions of time" she has defined are "married to each other" (Gardner, Interview 236), but "Detail from the Creation of Man" goes further, depicting them as inextricable.

Graham begins, as in "Holy Shroud," with a description of an ordinary experience, the speaker's extended observation of a nest whose eggs gradually hatch. Graham refers to "the start" of her account, as well as "the end," what is "near the end," and "the very end." This act of narrativization complicates but also confirms what she identifies as the experience's repetitiveness ("I go down there every day" for "three weeks"). Moreover, the starting point is imbued with foreknowledge, paradoxically of the failure of knowledge itself: "Even at the start, even before [the eggs] hatched, / whatever there was to *know* / was gone." For this reason, "the ending cannot be undone."

The poem also contains a separate, more extended discussion of a "picture . . . from the façade at Orvieto," containing two panels, a prelapsarian scene of Adam "being made" and a postlapsarian one, in which "God has just called" Adam and Eve, who are hiding from him after having eaten the forbidden fruit.[7] Graham several times links this second account to the earlier description of the nest, often awkwardly, as when a "road, dusty like the one behind our house" but also associated with Eve, "leads to the knot which is this nest," or later, when Adam and Eve, whom the speaker identifies as "a knot of flesh, . . . want to *be* / the nest again" (italics added). (Here, as elsewhere, we do not know exactly what nest is being described and whether it is literal or metaphorical.) Recurrent references to fire link the poem's different scenes in similarly awkward ways. The nest functions as a literal object or metaphoric tenor when it is described as a weaving of "flame with bits of dirt in it." But it is also a vehicle, as when an actual "fire I once saw" is associated with "gold mosaic tile" that is also part of the façade, which "made a nest, too."[8] A reference to an undefined "It [that] burned at every stage, / all gold enameled tile and fire" a few lines earlier is even more unstable; here it is unclear whether Graham's tenor is the road, the nest, or the mosaic. Like the hinge-like simile linking bird flight to the face of Jesus in "Holy Shroud," such analogies ultimately expose the strain and slippage implicit in analogy itself, as is revealed clearly when Adam's "foot is fire // becoming mud, then . . . flesh." In these passages, Graham reveals the contingency of the likenesses she constructs, features made more acute when the poem is read as a reconsideration of a poem earlier in the volume entitled "Detail from the Creation" (29–31).[9]

The poem links such failures of analogy to problems of sequence by conflating or overlaying multiple time frames. A description later in the poem of the concealed Adam and Eve emphasizes the inextricability of foreknowledge, waiting, and belatedness in ways that complicate Graham's interview's claim that Old Testament stories allude primarily to *"beginning"* and "creation." Here, Graham gestures forward, not only to the inevitable moment of the couple's discovery by God but also to the story's foreknown (but not depicted) "end," in which they are exiled from Eden. This temporal overlaying is articulated partly through a shifting series of metaphors.

> A knot of flesh, [Adam and Eve] want to be
> the nest again, but they can't, they're the thing
> *in* the nest now, the growing pushing thing, the
> image, too late.
> Their hair falls over them but it is nothing.
> Their arms fold down over their selves,
>
> tight—
> They hide. They are what waiting is. (87)

Adam and Eve "want to be / the nest." But their predicament—as already fallen and also as mythical characters depicted in a certain way by an artist —prohibits this metaphoric transformation, as well as the agency implicit in "want." Instead, they are metonymically located *"in"* the nest, a situation that also enacts their earlier wish to be deanimated: "they're [a] thing." This assertion recalls the similar displacement in the passage's muted earlier claim about lateness, which also refuses both agency and personification; not Adam and Eve but "the / image" of them is "too late." In fact, their lateness seems here to be manifest as waiting; because representation ("the image") comes after the fact, Adam and Eve are transfixed, objectified, eternally caught in the moment in which the artist—both the creator of these representations at Orvieto and Graham herself—has conveyed them.

Descriptions like this one tend to be obscurantist; they impel the reader to shift between the literal thing described and the act of describing it. That such obscuring is part of Graham's intention is evident in a simile about time early in the poem. An image that conflates "road," "knot," and "nest" is

> something like Time
> writ down in scrawl not meant to
> clear,
> communicate. (85)

Here, the simile ("like Time") describes an illegibility that evokes the syntactically confusing lines that precede this one: we feel that not only Time's but Graham's textual "scrawl" is not "clear" and does not "communicate." Time, Graham here insists, creates this sense of obscurity, and the poem's stance toward Adam and Eve involves a distance that Graham retains throughout the poem. This distance is partly evident in Graham's tendency to make these characters exemplify specifically temporal attributes ("They are what waiting is"). Such descriptions thus involve a sense of coercion and violence similar to that which I noted in Graham's introduction; here Adam and Eve wish to "hide," vanishing not only from God's gaze but the poet's by "fold[ing] up into their bodies, tight." But they cannot, partly because the poem's categorical assertions about what these characters "are" eradicate the possibility of their escape or concealment.

The poem's depiction of contained violence may be an effect of Graham's belated appropriation of preexisting source materials, or more specifically her awareness of this appropriation. Graham implies something like this midway through the poem, acknowledging that by leaning close to the nest, the speaker has left a "scent" that may be "sufficient cause" for the birds' mother to "let" the hatchlings "die." She asserts, "I knew I should leave" the vicinity of the nest, but she does not. The implication is that the poet is engaging in a dangerous, even immoral act; she keeps visiting the nest and its birds, it seems, because they provide her with poetic material, and she dwells on the images of Adam and Eve for the same reason. Before or after visiting the nest, she claims, she sometimes hears reports on "the news" about "tortur[e]," rape, and other devastation. Such events are depicted in sketchy terms partly because the reader already "know[s]" what she is describing. But there also seems to be no way for Graham to reconcile these events with the rest of the poem. This failure is both aesthetic and ethical. The speaker's position of belated foreknowledge—of already knowing how it will end—seems to allow her to rationalize disregarding the real-life effects of her actions. Perhaps this disregard is implicit in her belated project: she is in this poem retelling a story (via a description of previously created visual representations of it) that has already been told countless times.

"Detail from the Creation of Man" thus reveals a speaker projecting her own belatedness onto her poem's protagonists, an act that reinscribes belatedness's redundancy. In fact, this redundancy and the failures it engenders are logical effects of the always mediated, channel-grazing culture Graham elsewhere embraces. Asserting metaphoric equivalence, Graham implies, offers a similar escape from actual events. Thus, just after describing the fragments she has heard on the news, the speaker attempts to begin again, commanding, "Let x equal perhaps. Let y be the // dizziness." Such an attempt, though, gets caught in language. "This story," Graham asserts, is both "verbal" or constructed of language and "fleshy" or reliant on something like analogy. So are all stories: they expose but are alienated from reality, partly because they offer too-late renditions of what has already been rendered. And the poet, Graham here implies, not only participates in but exploits this alienation.

||||||||||||||||||

As "Detail from the Creation of Man" considers directly the imbrication of belatedness with language and in particular with the attempt to find connections between distinct events via analogy, it also emphasizes watching. The speaker is "looking around at all those / woods," while God is "looking for" Adam and Eve after their transgression, an act distinct from the fact that, as an omniscient God, he "sees them of course." Such overlaid situations of watching evoke Rich's sustained interrogation of witness, and several of Graham's poems depict what in chapter 2 I called asymmetrical witness: the speaker watches others watching in ways that draw attention to the reader's similarly voyeuristic but more detached position. More emphatically than Rich, though, Graham exposes the limitations of such acts of seeing, often by depicting scenes of watching not actual events but renditions of them in photos, films, theater, and paintings. In this way, Graham insists that literal, historical events are not in fact available either to the poet or her readers.

Rich uses such scenes of watching and listening to consider her actual readers, and a related sense of asymmetry may help explain Graham's ambivalence about her readers, whom she at times celebrates, as I implied above, and at others associates with an explicitly belated exhaustion, as when she claims in an interview that

> for me the reader is one who has heard it all before, who is no longer really capable of extended reading. . . . A reader who can practically no longer tell the difference between something true and something false because of the surfeit, the information glut, the sensoral glut. (Gardner, Interview 232)

Graham insists that, rather than keeping the past alive, belatedness—specifically a familiarity with what has already occurred—interferes with communication. Having already "heard it all before," the reader resists hearing it again. This situation leads to a failure of ethical discrimination; the reader can "no longer" make previously possible distinctions between the "true" and the "false."

Although the volume's first poem, "Fission" (3–8), does not directly reveal antipathy toward its readers, it undermines the possibility of seeing in ways that echo Graham's interview's cynical description of her reader. Like "The Hiding Place," the poem depicts a spectacle—the adolescent speaker's 1963 attendance at a screening of the film *Lolita*, which is interrupted by a cinema employee's announcement that "the President's been shot"—whose multiple "layers" ultimately undermine the distinction between the audience members and what they see. The poem tells a story with what Graham within the poem calls a "plot" and an emphasis on what her interview calls "true" historical and autobiographical events. But Graham spatially and temporally disrupts these narrative elements. This disruption recalls the material attributes of film, which, as the poem notes, creates the illusion of motion from a series of still images projected at "twenty-four frames / per second." While film achieves the illusion of movement and narrative, the poem does the reverse by breaking its story into a series of snapshot-like tableaux.

The poem overlays scenes of watching and being watched to reveal the impossibility of singular or definitive witness. The film's camera watches Lolita watching, focusing on her "lowered lids" as "the man" in the film "looks down" at her, and the speaker watches all this, as the repeated phrase "I watch" makes clear. But she is also part of the spectacle; the "house-lights" make her visible to others, as when, once she has risen, the film's "image[s] licked my small body from the front, the story playing / all over my face my / forwardness," while "the squad car now faintly visible on the screen / start[s] the chase up, / all over my countenance." Watching is thus abstracted, dissociated from both particular watchers and a speaker unable to assimilate her acts of watching into coherence. In the process, in ways similar to the volume's other poems, watching itself is given agency: the "possibility of never-having-been-seen" is what allows "the glance [to be] let loose into the auditorium."

Spatialized connections intensify the poem's confusion of watching and being watched; the poem mostly foregoes simile and metaphor, and thus the possibility of likeness, in favor of accidental overlay. Two kinds of figures recur, emphasizing both superficiality (one image replaces an earlier one) and depth (new images contain old ones) or, to recall "Holy Shroud," relations involving both *in* and *on*. The poem begins by describing "the real electric lights . . . upon the full-sized / screen," as well as the "corridor of light filled with dust" that "flows down from the booth to the screen." When the "houselights come on—midscene," the prepositions emphasize both depth ("the picture . . . keeps flowing *beneath*") and surface (the lights "lap *against* the other light" of the projected film without obliterating it). Later, "the theater's skylight is opened and noon slides *in*" and "*overpowers* the electric lights" (italics added). But while the "story up there grays, pales" before being whited out, the film keeps playing, its images "laying themselves across [the announcer's] face" as well as the body of the speaker. These spatializations give depth to what is flat: the two-dimensional film is manifest through a three-dimensional column of light; the different lights cover without obliterating each other; and through it all, the film "keeps flowing."

Graham here seems, more clearly than in poems like "Detail from the Creation of Man," to be espousing a metonymic model—that privileges accidental, superficial adjacency—rather than a metaphoric one based on underlying similarity and depth. But the poem does not wholly repudiate likeness, as several uses of the term in the poem make clear. Instead, Graham implies that likeness persists as a trace. Early on, the speaker describes the different light sources "touch[ing]" her but "unable to // merge into each other / over my likeness." The failure of the visible to integrate into singularity—an integration that might be achieved through analogy— reveals the speaker's physical "likeness" or how she appears to others, an appearance that seems to obstruct the possibility of "merg[ing]." Later in the poem, likeness is more completely abstracted from referentiality. The speaker describes the "infinite virtuality of light . . . / some *likeness* . . . but not particulate, / a grave of possible shapes called *likeness*." Though likeness is not dead, it is evident in or as "a grave." This proximity to death and perhaps obsolescence seems to be what enables the grave to be named *likeness*. Graham here transforms likeness from a mode of equivalence into a pure signifier. It exposes neither what Graham's interview calls the "true" nor the "false" (232) but reveals rather the actual process of deriving figures. Here, then, Graham destabilizes the distinction between the literal and figurative, partly through an implied rhetoric of ghostliness.

At its end, "Fission" furthers this blurring by listing the "ever-tighter wrappings // of the layers of the / real," which include "what is" and also "what the words say that is." The integrity and depth of "the real" are here displaced; what matters is the "layers" in which it is wrapped. The final admonition "Don't move, don't // wreck the shroud, don't move" advocates an immobilism that forestalls the flux and instability that have threatened to overwhelm the poem. Such stasis is accomplished by a focus on the superficial "shroud"; the term foreshadows "Holy Shroud," which appears later in the volume. Here the shroud literally conceals the reality of death, as it does figuratively in "Holy Shroud."

In "Fission," the "real" persists, albeit so wrapped in "layers" that it is hard to locate or identify, and the possibility of likeness, however partial, evokes the speaker's actual face. But "From the New World" (12–16), another of the volume's early poems, implies that the literal does not exist at all. By more radically undermining seeing and witness, as well as narrative and chronology, Graham impels what her interview calls "surfeit, . . . information glut, . . . [and] sensoral glut" (Gardner, Interview 232) to replace the distinction between "true" and "false." What remains is an interplay of surfaces, which include (and partly dismantle) likeness itself.

While "Fission" focuses on actual historical events—the film *Lolita* exists, as does the fact of Kennedy's assassination—"From the New World" focuses on a historical situation more deeply imbued with doubt. The poem describes the 1987 trial in Israel of John Demjanjuk, a Cleveland auto worker alleged to have been the notorious Nazi criminal Ivan the Terrible. Although he was convicted based largely on the testimony of relatives of those killed and other concentration camp inmates, this conviction was overturned in 1993 (after Graham's volume was published); he was then subsequently found guilty.[10] The poem focuses on this sense of doubt, which is also central to "Holy Shroud." Graham explores the implications of the trial but also describes other, apparently autobiographical events, including the teenaged speaker's realization that the Holocaust has occurred, her aged grandparents' illness, and their move to a nursing home.

Although the poem's speaker, unlike that of "Fission," maintains a detached and omniscient position, she depicts multiple scenes of watching. In ways far more radical than in Rich's poems, this multiplication dismantles the validity of witness as a strategy for understanding. These scenes also extend the "layer[ing]" evident in "Fission," as is especially apparent in one description of the trial:

>   Then the man standing up, the witness, screaming it's him
>   It's him
> I'm sure your Honor I'm sure. Then Ivan coming up to him
>   and Ivan (you saw this) offering his hand, click, whoever
> he is, and the old man getting a dial-tone, friend,
>   and old whoever clicking and unclicking the clasp the
> silver knobs,
>   shall we end on them? a tracking shot? a
>
> close-up on the clasp a two-headed beast it turns out
>   made of silvery
> leaves? . . . (15)

After an account of what the male "witness" says and Ivan's response, the passage turns to a scene in which the speaker attempts to corroborate her own capacity to witness by addressing a "you" who also "saw this." The scene of watching is then further disrupted: the speaker reveals herself to be not an immediate witness but part of a collective "we" manipulating a camera, implying that the "you" who "saw this" may in fact have seen the trial only on television. Partly to mark this fact, the passage abandons the narrative marker "Then" for a paratactic "and."

The passage also dismantles the witness's early assertion of certainty ("it's him it's him / I'm sure") by shifting from Demjanjuk, the man on trial, to Ivan to an undefined "old man" to a still more ambiguous, ungendered "old whoever" elsewhere identified as the speaker's grandmother. The media through which the speaker perceives and attempts to capture the scene are also unstable, since the camera seems both photographic (its shutter "click[s]") and cinematic (the speaker must determine whether to use a "tracking shot"). Then this "click"—the term here recalls Graham's several other uses of the term—is transformed, first into the repeated clicking of the phone's disconnect button and then the "clicking and unclicking" of a handbag clasp. Rather than illuminating the courtroom scene, these transformations reveal the instability not only of objects but language. The signifier *click* here overcomes what it signifies in ways that reveal the observers' sensory overload and distraction. As is often the case in *Region*, the documentation of an already existing situation also perpetuates it; we are impelled redundantly to watch again a scene that the speaker acknowledges we already "saw," the itself belated attempt to identify the perpetrator of atrocities committed decades ago.

"From the New World" mostly avoids similes and metaphors, but it considers, as "Fission" also briefly does, likeness as a topic. The poem has often been read as an exemplification of what James Longenbach has called "analogical thinking" ("Jorie Graham" 88); Longenbach claims that the poem's apparent "superimpos[ition]" of disparate "narratives" ends up "equating" them (89).[11] But Graham in fact uses "superimpos[ition]," a spatial strategy, as an alternative to "equating," a metaphoric one. Graham explicitly repudiates likeness midway through the poem:

> I went into the bathroom, locked the door.
> Stood in front of the mirrored wall—
>
> not so much to see in, not looking up at all in fact,
>   but to be held in it as by a gas,
> the thing which was me there in its chamber. Reader,
>   they were all in there, I didn't look up,
> they were all in there, the coiling and uncoiling
>   billions,
>
> the about-to-be-seized,
>   the about to be held down,
>
> the about to be held down, bit [sic] clean, shaped,
>   and the others, too, the ones gone back out, the ending
> wrapped round them. (13)

The passage, like others I have discussed, interrupts an early narrative account ("I went into the bathroom, locked the door. / Stood in front of the mirrored wall—") in ways that reveal the speaker's belatedness. The "billions" of victims are physically present in the confined space of the bathroom, disrupting temporal boundaries; their ghostly apparition makes them present now. But, in ways consistent with the concern with both delay and waiting throughout the volume, Graham also insists that the victims occupy a temporal limbo between what has not yet happened and what has already occurred; some are nominalized as "the about-to-be-seized, / the about to be held down" while others have "the ending / wrapped round them." By physicalizing these temporal states, Graham challenges the possibility of equivalence and interpretation. In fact, the moment in the passage that comes closest to asserting equivalence—the speaker's assertion that "the thing which was me [was] there in its chamber"—is ambiguous. "The thing" may refer to the ghostly "billions" the speaker is the process of summoning up, but it may simply refer to her own body. Certainly the passage emphasizes physical containment; the word *in* recurs, linking identification (finding oneself in others) with external, physical acts of "coiling and uncoiling," "go[ing] back out," and "wrapp[ing]."

That this refusal of what Longenbach calls "equating" is in fact one of the poem's subjects is also evident when, late in the poem, Graham's speaker attempts to defy her own belated position and instead imagine "something completely / new, but what—[?]" (16). This "completely / new" thing can be represented only spatially and referentially: it is, the speaker notes, "underneath" what already exists. Then follows a list that seems to represent the speaker's attempt to find the right simile:

> *Like* what, I wonder, to make the bodies come on to make
> room,
>
> *like what*, I whisper
>
> *like* which is the last new world, *like, like*, which is the thin
>
> young body (before it's made to go back in) whispering *please*.

The term *like* is first used as a conjunction; it gestures toward a missing vehicle ("*what*"), signaling the speaker's wish to find an analogy that can make the undefined (and dead) "bodies" return. But then, in the passage's third line, Graham turns "*like*" into a noun: here likeness is personified as a singular "body."

The passage thus presents a double animation: Graham animates *like*, which then animates the dead bodies. This act is quite different from Graham's tendency elsewhere to deanimate living characters, including Adam and Eve in "Detail from the Creation of Man." But the animation is here partial (only the physical "thin / young body" is fully evoked, along with its whisper) and temporary (the body soon will be "made to go back in"). The poem thus evokes but ultimately refuses the prosopopoeia that I argued above is essential to AIDS poetry and that I began this chapter by associating with trauma theory. In fact, the personified "like"—a wholly tropological construct—ends up replacing the literal, historical events the poem purportedly describes. "*Like*," the speaker acknowledges, "is the last new world"; it makes newness simultaneous with lastness in ways that recall Graham's conflation of "lateness" and "now" in "History." The speaker's foreknowledge, too, is an effect of her belatedness; having already seen what comes after this world, she, like the exhausted, belated readers she describes in her introduction, already knows what will happen next.

Graham's prolepsis is partly defensive: it demonstrates her capacity to assert her mastery of the Holocaust, an event that would seem to preclude mastery. As Graham spatializes and embodies likeness, detaching it from "*what*" or referentiality, the literal events of the Holocaust and the Holocaust as a historical event slip away. Like Demjanjuk's true identity, the truth cannot be confirmed. What is left is the poet's impulse to link a series of scenes with no inherent resemblance to one another. No trope can fully capture the literal, but Graham reveals that, without a sense of what she calls in her interview "true," the poet, like this poem, is left with mere "surfeit," an unassimilable excess.

ıııııııııııııııı

In these poems, film and television often obscure what really occurred in ways that emphasize layering, artifice, and disguise. Something similar is evident in a description Graham has given of her creative process. When she writes a poem, she remarks, she begins with an actual "man and a woman in a room, no longer speaking to each other." But Graham claims,

I'm not interested in re-telling a story filled with the narrative of blame and occasion. Rather I'd go at that scene with the desire to inhabit the occasion. . . . To be willing to inhabit that scene, in willing uncertainty, to be able to describe it, to linger, to use everything that we consider *technique* in poetry to inhabit it until the scene cracks open and you know what it is about the *human condition* that the scene is revealing. ("Conversation" 6–7)

Graham here dismisses narrative quickly. The backstory to such a scene, she claims, is an old and tired story of "blame, who did what to whom and why, what was done to them as children" (6). Instead, Graham spatializes the scene, converting it into something like a stage set. Like a director or stage designer, she decides whether to "build the walls up" and "turn electric lights on or not" (7). The transformation of an actual room into an artificial space is, it seems, the precondition for a more radical act of remaking in which "the scene cracks open." This act is an apparently necessary precursor to the revelation of its deeper truth or reality, here identified as something larger about the "*human condition.*" To write a poem thus involves transforming a situation into a stage set, manipulating that space, and then finally destroying it. Having in the process converted "story" to fixed "occasion" and thus excising chronology from the scene, she can "linger," staying there for as long as she wants.

Graham here affirms her faith that the poet can derive something true about "the *human condition*" from an observed scene. Graham's poems about theater go further; they suggest that performance offers not a version but a replacement of the literal. "Act III, Sc. 2," a poem I discussed briefly in the introduction, is situated midway through a theatrical performance, likely of a five-act Shakespeare play, in which the temporally indefinite conditions of waiting and lateness have overwhelmed the possibility of genuine action or characterization. Moreover, this scene is itself watched by a spectator who is also waiting, if only for the performance to be over. Perhaps more than elsewhere in the volume, temporality overwhelms the poem; its recurrent spatializations are clearly attempts to locate and define the condition of belatedness. Here is the first part of this fourteen-line poem, the volume's shortest:

Look she said this is not the distance
we wanted to stay at—We wanted to get
close, very close. But what
is the way in again? And is it

too late? She could hear the actions
rushing past—but they are on
another track. And in the silence,
or whatever it is that follows,

there was still the buzzing: motes, spores,
aftereffects and whatnot recalled the morning after.
Then the thickness you can't get past called *waiting.* (66)

The poem is from the outset deeply ambiguous. We are not sure which of the poem's words are spoken by the "she" or who she is. Nor do we know her relation to the play referenced in the title. This confusion is essential to the poem, which juxtaposes seriality (as the use of "then" indicates) and paralysis; the poem's "she" is stuck, perhaps as a member of a larger audience, awaiting an ending that has not yet arrived.

This character's attempt to understand this temporal predicament is articulated at first through physical and spatial terms ("the distance" and the wish to "get / close"). Then she shifts to temporal language: "is it // too late?" When the narrative shifts from the apparent speech of this protagonist to an omniscient account of her experiences ("She could hear"), time is again depicted spatially, as a "track" on which "actions / [are] rushing past." The conflation of these modes is also evident in the description of "whatever . . . follows" in terms both of visible "motes, spores" and of temporal "aftereffects and whatnot recalled the morning after." The excerpt's final line directly conflates physical "thickness" with temporal "*waiting*" by renaming the former (it is "called") in terms of the latter. Throughout,

Graham implies that lateness can be understood only figuratively, via the likenesses implied by its spatializing language.

The centrality of likeness to the poem is made clearer in the final stanza, in which Graham refers for the first time to a situation that appears to be a performance, while adding a new character, "you":

> Then the you, whoever you are, peering down to see if it's done yet.
> Then just the look on things of being looked-at.
> Then just the look on things of being seen.

The phrase "peering down" physically locates the unspecified "you" at a height; this addressee is apparently observing the play referred to in the title. Or perhaps the "you" is a character in the play, whom "she" is watching, eager for it to end. Certainly the "you," like the "she," has a role to play, as is evident in the overlaying of "looks," which recalls the similar situation in the cinema in "Fission." More exactly, in ways that recall Rich's tendency to expose then transgress her poems' frames, the poem's final two lines align the positions of actress and "you." But the confusion is more drastic: conventionally stable "things," which exist to be "looked-at," seem at least partly imbued with agency. Their awareness of "being looked-at" is evident in their "look," a term that punningly conflates deanimation (they are looked at by others) with animation (they can look at others).[12] As such, these lines nominalize and literalize the colloquial, imperative "Look she said" of the opening line in ways that further liken "she" to "you." That is, the bored spectator eager to know "if it's done yet" resembles the actress onstage, who is also "waiting."

Graham here radically destabilizes the scene of performance. We do not know whether the scene described in the poem is actually occurring or whether it is an implied metaphor, a way of expressing the more general condition of being caught midway through an undefined narrative. Either way, this condition is aligned with a performance that seems to require the participation of all who come into contact with it. The poet too, Graham implies, is an actress engaged in a similar performance for us, her "you" or addressees. But if our position resembles that of the play's spectator, we need not, and indeed seem not to be expected to, applaud the poem's performance. Instead, the poem implies that our experience of reading resembles that of "the bored, overstimulated viewer" apparently condemned in Graham's introduction. We want this poem to end, but we also know that its ending is likely to be as inconclusive as those of other poems in the volume. This mixture of anticipation and foreknowledge—waiting and lateness—aligns us with the similarly belated poet in other poems: aware that it is too late, we keep reading to confirm what we already know. In "Detail from the Creation of Man," Graham distinguishes God's act of "looking" for Adam and Eve from the fact that he already "sees" them. Here, though, Graham seems to equate "the look on things" with "being seen," undermining the difference between the superficial and the deep.

Or perhaps these concepts remain distinct and the poem indirectly affirms the necessity of seeing. If this is the case, "Act III" seems to emphasize not only the importance of watching but of witness, even if it is reluctant or impotent. This possibility gestures toward a potential escape from the limbo of a situation that is both too late and unconcluded. Certainly in *Region*'s final poem, "Soul Says" (125), performance seems to gesture more clearly toward liberation. I have been arguing that throughout *Region*, the act of creating likenesses ultimately affirms unlikeness. But in "Soul Says," the separation of vehicle from tenor frees simile from the need to represent literal objects or events. In the process, "Soul Says" converts the situation of belatedness into an opportunity for verbal play.

"Soul Says" explores aftermath, as its subtitle, "(Afterword)," makes clear. Midway through, the speaker, whom Graham's note confirms to be Prospero (130), "[lays down his robe]"; the phrase is a stage direction from Shakespeare's *The Tempest*, in which Prospero abjures not only what Shakespeare calls his "magic garment" but his "art" (1.2.26–28). Before this point, Prospero has emphasized art's capacity to create "brittleness, shapeliness," and "meaning," as well as "idiom" and "the alphabet of ripeness"; art evokes both "what is" and "what could have been." But after the robe is laid down, the poem changes. It becomes mostly parenthetical, apparently unvoiced, and seemingly without artfulness; it occupies something akin to the region of unlikeness identified by Vendler. Song, however, recurs, both a specific one that "she sang" and an undefined sound that "soothe[s]." Here are the final lines of the poem, and the volume:

Now then, I said, I go to meet that which I liken to
(even though the wave break and drown me in laughter)
the wave breaking, the wave drowning me in laughter—

The act of "liken[ing]" here occurs because of (and also despite, as implied by the phrase "even though") what has literally occurred; the act of the wave breaking and drowning him is set verbatim into Prospero's speech. But the simile's tenor is undefined; it is only identified as "that which" the speaker "go[es] to meet." What matters instead is the vehicle (the wave), which is repeated and located—at least mostly—in the actual world.

Yet this emphasis on the present moment is illusory: Prospero's shipwreck has in fact already occurred, and Prospero has already survived it. The passage indicates this sense of belatedness and redundancy in the phrase "I said," which implies that the poem itself is restating what has already been expressed. These lines also imply a future moment of meeting ("I go to meet"). In this way, Prospero's explicit affirmation of the present relies on an awkward conflation of past and present. Prospero asserts earlier that "(. . . the hurry is stopped)." But then he goes on: "(and held) (but not extinguished) (no)." The poem's ending reveals something similar; "the hurry," or time's forward motion, cannot, even here, be fully eradicated.

Nonetheless, "Soul Says" implies an alternative to the figurative impactedness of many of the volume's earlier poems through a release into "laughter" and an act of likening that seems to disregard verisimilitude in favor of wholly verbal repetition. If this act of redundancy offers, in this final poem of the volume, a partial solution to the problems of lateness and waiting Graham has been tracing (and also perpetuating), it is highly provisional. Perhaps most crucially, it is expressed not by Graham as speaker but within an invented dramatic monolog spoken by a wholly literary character. The poem's title implies Graham's wish for a simple and direct mode of speech, in which the "soul" can say. But the soul itself is a figurative concept, and its speech is therefore always indirect. Despite its assertion that it has relinquished art, this belated "Afterword" confirms that art cannot be cast away, even after its apparent relinquishment. Nor can the compulsion to "liken" ideas to things be abandoned. Instead, likeness persists, perhaps because we must keep reiterating, as in Vendler's reading of the volume's title, our fallenness. But the persistence of art also enables the creation of more and different, if impacted and conflicted, poems.

||||||||||||||||

The impulse to spatialize has been sometimes linked to the explicitly political project of enabling those previously silenced to speak. The evocation of specific locations, it has been argued, offers a vivid and intimate way to appeal to diverse audiences. But Graham's spatializations function differently; in the poems of *Region*, they are figurative rather than literalizing. More specifically, the belated collapse of the literal repeatedly impels Graham's speakers to turn to the figurative, a turn that signals the impossibility not only of narrative but of action. I referred above to the disturbing news reports heard in passing by the speaker of "Detail from the Creation of Man." Her inability to dwell on these reports or their implications is meant to reveal that the narrator's personal concerns overwhelm and thus trivialize "real" events, a danger of which the poet is clearly aware. But the same risk is run by Graham's poems more generally: political and historical events, like ordinary, literal objects, are mostly triggers for explorations of language and figuration.

All poems, it could be argued, do something similar; because they exist only in language, they can never approximate reality. In fact, poems may reveal their estrangement from literal events most clearly when they attempt to convey these events. Certainly the poems I have examined in other chapters also refuse to advocate specific political action. Although Rich's poems offer a direct critique of contemporary culture, they are often disembodied and oblique. The AIDS poems I examined originate in and articulate a particular set of social and political concerns and at times critique contemporary public attitudes and policies, but they are primarily personal responses, emphasizing grief and loss rather than calling for specific action. Graham's disavowal of the literal, however, feels more extreme and, perhaps as a result, ethically problematic, as several readers have noted.[13]

I began this chapter by suggesting that *Region* offers a kind of endgame of belatedness. In these poems, it is too late for outrage and defiance, which Plath manipulates; for appeals to the reader, in which Rich retains faith; and for pathos, which is abundant in AIDS elegies. By exploring something like the aftermath of aftermath, Graham's poems instead depict speakers impelled to dismantle their own poetics even as they yearn to make actual experiences meaningful and whole. Perhaps as a result, the poems' wholly verbal performances often seem disconnected from the possibility (or hope) of sympathetic response.

Yet performances, even belated ones, require audiences. Even after he has laid down his robe, Prospero's soliloquy continues, in both Graham's version and Shakespeare's original. Poetic performances are similar: they proleptically retain faith in their readers, the actual ones who have not yet arrived. Graham's contradictory statements about the potential of poems to affect their readers reveal, as I have been arguing, her ambivalence about this issue.[14] So does her unwillingness—at least in this precursor to her subsequent volume, *Materialism*—fully to commit to a "region" from which likeness has been excised. But perhaps the poems themselves signal this next step. If they cannot, that is, offer true or literal chronicles of actual events or define a position from which to comment on them, they nonetheless persist, especially in the redundant, self-conscious, open form Graham here explores, as material objects.

Chapter Five

"Spectral scraps"

Displacement, Metonymy, and the Elegiac in
Susan Howe's *The Midnight*

Figuration in postwar poems, I have been arguing throughout this book, does not signal the equivalence between things and ideas, nor does it align the past with the present. Instead, it marks the difficulty of identifying a fixed underlying reality (the "true" nature of things or ideas). Postwar poems often interrogate equivalence, as is evident in Plath's partial, inconsistent similes of Jewishness; in Rich's slippage from identification with others to distance from them; in Doty's negative, interrogative metaphors; in Gunn's depiction of ash as both thing and symbol; and in Graham's direct interrogations of "likeness." Several, including Plath, Monette, Powell, and Graham, also explore metonymy as an alternative to metaphor and simile. For Plath, metonyms fracture metaphoric coherence; for Monette and Powell, they affirm, at least provisionally, adjacency to and contact with the dead; in Graham's *Region of Unlikeness*, recurrent scenes of juxtaposition and overlay more directly reveal the poet's wish for spatial alternatives to a metaphoric mode associated with nostalgia and exhaustion.

In her 2003 sequence *The Midnight*, Susan Howe offers a way out of the lingering and often conflicted allegiance to metaphor and simile that characterizes the work of the poets I have thus far considered. For the most part, *The Midnight* focuses on actual physical objects and their spatial position.

The volume thus presents a metonymic model based primarily on spatial connections, albeit in a fragmentary way consistent with the disjunctions of metonymy. Yet Howe's superficial, indirect poetics does not excise memory or history. Instead, in ways that recall Fredric Jameson's claim that postmodernism depicts time through spatial images, the volume offers oblique access to the past, challenging but also offering a resolution to the tensions between the literal and the figurative that I have argued postwar poets repeatedly explore in the context of belatedness.

Howe's writing is often associated with experimental and "Language" poetics.[1] Certainly, Howe's work reveals an interest in disjunctions of voice and persona; she has throughout her career explored other texts and integrated parts of them into her sequences. Both the prose and poetry sections of *The Midnight* mix original with appropriated language, generally with attribution in the prose sections and without it in the poems. The titles of the volume's two prose sections, "Scare Quotes I" and "II," make explicit their dependence on other texts by authors ranging from Shakespeare to Robert Louis Stevenson to the American philosopher Charles Sanders Peirce, and the first two poetry sections draw heavily, as Howe explains in the volume's first prose section, on a treatise on bed hangings.[2]

Juxtaposition is clearly crucial to the volume's structure. By separating the prose and verse sections, Howe raises questions about the rationale for and logic of their joining. In fact, the connection between these sections often feels superficial, even arbitrary, perhaps recalling the fact that several were originally published separately, at least one in quite different form.[3] That such issues of placement and connection are important to the sequence is evident throughout the volume in Howe's references to the topic of joining. These references extend Howe's longstanding concern with geography, space, and mapping, which several readers have noted and which is also evident in the titles of earlier sequences, including *Hinge Picture* (*Frame* 31–55), *Secret History of the Dividing Line* (*Frame* 87–122), and *Frame Structures*.[4]

Howe does not here employ the technique of overlaying words and lines of text that has characterized both previous and subsequent volumes. Instead, with the exception of a single page near the sequence's opening (2), she retains conventional spacing and word placement. The poems tend to be centered on the page, each of approximately the same length, with lines of approximately the same length. Within the prose sections, Howe includes photographs, many of superimposed objects and damaged and subsequently repaired old books. These photos complicate Howe's citations of language from some of the same books, revealing her interest not only in what is *in* these books but also in their material properties.

The two photographs that open the sequence concisely introduce these tensions between visual and verbal modes of representation, as well as between flatness and depth, by reproducing a textual, material object that both reveals and obscures. The first photo depicts the title page of Robert Louis Stevenson's *The Master of Ballantrae*, a book that Howe considers throughout *The Midnight*, blurrily visible through its interleaf; on the verso of this page is the reverse of this image. The two images resemble, but imperfectly, an actual interleaf, a textual element that, Howe explains in a double-sided discussion that follows and visually mimics the introductory photos, was "placed" by "bookbinders . . . between frontispiece and title page."[5] The interleaf, Howe explains, is a physical object that can be seen, touched (it is made of "tissue"), and heard (it is characterized by "rustling"). But it is also associated with time insofar as the interleaf, which recalls anachronistic printing practices, has become "obsolete." This situation is repeated by the process of reading; the interleaf disrupts "reading forward: no, the interleaf beckons you *back*" (73).

The interleaf thus makes the temporal condition of obsolescence physical and tactile. Providing what Howe calls a "transitional space," it joins not only two physical spaces (identified by Howe as "image and scripture" and "word and picture") but the physical and the temporal; as a "spectral scrap intact in a handed down book," the interleaf has "acquired an enchanted aura quite apart from its original utilitarian function." The "spectral" quality of the interleaf, like the recurrent imagery of ghostliness in many of the poems I discussed above, joins past to present and absence to persistence. In ways that evoke the temporal slippage associated with ghosts in AIDS poems, the interleaf also evokes the "double bind" of someone who wishes both to be "put . . . to sleep" and to be "waken[ed]" from the dead (144). But because interleaves, unlike ghosts, really exist, they literalize a ghostliness that many other poems acknowledge to be figurative, although Howe's volume does not include an actual interleaf but only the reproduction of one.

What Howe's early discussion of the interleaf calls "transitional space[s]" recur throughout *The Midnight*; the sequence discusses the provisional interiors created by bed hangings, represents overlaid book pages, and considers at length a man on the sidewalk unable to decide which way to go (115).[6] These objects and scenes join surface to interior, inside to outside, and living to dead. At times, they embrace the wholly superficial, but at others, they gesture toward depths that Howe often associates with the effort to remember the past.

Although Howe does not use the term *displacement* in *The Midnight*, the term concisely expresses this simultaneous concern with surface and depth by referring both to physical and psychological modes of understanding. The *OED* defines *displacement* as both the literal "removal of a thing from its place" and the figurative "substitution of one idea or impulse for another . . . the unconscious transfer of intense feelings or emotions to something of greater or lesser consequence." Howe implies the former meaning in the epigraph to her 1974 sequence *Hinge Picture*, which cites Marcel Duchamp's description of his interest in "the displacements 1st in the plane 2nd in space" (*Frame* 32). Duchamp here locates displacement or the disruption of spatial constancy both in a two-dimensional "plane" and in a three-dimensional "space." But Howe is also interested another, nonphysical kind of displacement, which the *OED* defines as "substitution," a notion that evokes Freud's use of the term to describe the unconscious processes by which "insignificant details" and objects come to stand for "important," repressed, and often painful material (qtd. in Laplanche and Pontalis 122).[7]

Metonymy is generally defined as a figure that involves the replacement of one idea or word with another that reveals a "material, causal, or conceptual relation" to the original (Martin, "Metonymy"). Metonymy involves both proximity and juxtaposition; by describing one thing in terms of something adjacent, it emphasizes relations that, to recall Howe's epigraph from Duchamp, occupy the same two-dimensional "plane." For these reasons, the displacement involved in metonymy is primarily "literal," as the early theorist Boris Eichenbaum argued. In fact, Eichenbam's 1923 definition included the term *displacement*: metonymy, he claimed, involves "a displacement, or lateral semantic shift, that lends words new meanings without leaving the literal plane" (qtd. in Martin). But this superficial and "literal" notion of metonymy often coexists, especially in discussions of poetry, with a psychological sense of displacement that implies depth; poets employing metonymy, according to one gloss of Roman Jakobson's use of the term, "project their being on an outer reality that their emotion and perception displace from the normal" (Martin).

Discussions of metonymy often connect the outer with the inner in inconsistent ways. In a discussion of Proust, Paul de Man associates metaphor with "substitutive totalization" and "metonymic association" with "mere contiguity" ("Semiology" 31). While Jakobson similarly claims that, in contrast to metaphor, metonymy is based on "contiguity," he emphasizes that, in the speech of aphasics, contiguous objects (for example, "knife" and "fork") are "project[ed] from the line of habitual context into the line of substitution and selection" (125).[8] Jakobson also associates metonymy and metaphor with both "substitution" and "combination" and connects metonymy with Freudian displacement (132).[9] Other readers have emphasized that the two concepts are often difficult to distinguish in practice and that metonymy often blurs into or wraps around metaphor.[10]

In the introduction, I associated the postwar period with a number of attributes more narrowly associated with postmodernism, including a resistance to the idea of a singular history and a refusal to mourn the past's current inaccessibility. The term *postmodern* generally refers to a period beginning in about 1960, and it is more often applied to fiction than to poetry. Few of the poets I have until now considered have been associated with postmodernism or make its features evident, with the possible exception of Graham.[11] But Howe's emphasis on spatialization and metonymy aligns her work with at least one strand of postmodern theory. Postmodernism has often been defined in terms of the substitution, or partial substitution, of spatial for temporal modes of understanding. Fredric Jameson, for example, claims that contemporary culture and experience are "dominated by categories of space rather than time" (16). But while Jameson here opposes the spatial to the temporal, he elsewhere claims that spatial representations do not repudiate temporality. Instead, they reveal "the will to use and to subject time to the service of space" (154). The distinctively postmodern "displacement of time" and "spatialization of the temporal" are, he goes on, "often" evident "by way of a sense of loss": rather than repudiating memory, postmodern representations indicate that "what is mourned is the memory of deep memory; what is enacted is a nostalgia for nostalgia" (156).

Jameson associates what he calls the postmodern "spatial turn" (154) with a shift from "vertical" to "horizontal" connections (168), asserting that "the supreme formal feature" of "all the postmodernisms" is "the emergence of a new kind of flatness or depthlessness, a new kind of superficiality in the most literal sense" (9). He relates this flatness with a more general re-pudiation of "depth models," including "the Freudian model of latent and manifest" (12). This depthlessness, Jameson goes on, is "not . . . merely met-aphorical" but "can be expressed physically and 'literally'" (12); it is often evident in "the material—or better still, the literal—signifier in isolation" (27). Such terms evoke the traditional distinction between metaphor, often associated with analogy and therefore depth, and metonymy, generally seen as flatter and more arbitrary, a tension vividly enacted, as I claimed in chap-ter 4, in Graham's poems.

Several theorists more have more directly associated the postmodern "spatial turn" with a shift in modes of figuration, associating the postmod-ern with the metonymic, or at least with a metonymization of metaphor. For example, Craig Owens identifies "the projection of metaphor as meton-ymy," or the tendency to depict fundamentally metaphoric relations in met-onymic terms, with what he calls postmodern allegory. This mode involves both spatial contiguity and a temporal "amalgamation of the present and the past" (211), as well as "an ambition that must be perpetually deferred" (235).[12] Owens here echoes Jameson's insistence that temporality is central to postmodernism.

Howe's sequences often explore related tensions between spatial and temporal modes of understanding, as is revealed by the spatializing terms in which they have often been described, which include "paratactic" (Megan Simpson 185), "palimpsest[ic]" (Vanderborg 62), and "palimtext[ual]" (Davidson 68).[13] All these terms involve visual modes that emphasize, to different extents, juxtaposition and overlay. They also reveal a recurrent concern in Howe's work with the possibility of recovering and making visible fragments of old texts, as well as other hitherto lost or forgotten items. Belatedness thus remains central to Howe's poetic project, these earlier readers indicate, even though it is mostly evident through the manipulation of space.

Howe uses similar terms early in *The Midnight*'s first prose section, in which she directly describes the link between acts of remembering and her own manipulations of time and space:

> I am assembling materials for a recurrent return somewhere. Familiar sound textures, deliverances, vagabond quotations, preservations, wilderness shrubs, little resuscitated patterns. Historical or miraculous. Thousands of correlations have to be sliced and spliced. (85)

Howe's focus is not on metaphoric relations, resemblance, or the relation between the literal and the figurative; instead, she emphasizes the often visible ways that surfaces join. But the passage also joins surface with depth and the spatial with the temporal. Howe's description of an apparently literal and diverse series of "materials" includes some that are visible ("wilderness shrubs") while others are intangible ("deliverances," "preservations"). Some involve hearing ("sound textures") and some seeing ("shrubs"). Some are textual ("vagabond quotations"), while others involve the physical world ("familiar sound textures"). Howe's description of "assembl[ing]," "correlations," "slic[ing]," and "splic[ing]" emphasizes the superficial and also random links between these objects; as the term "spliced" indicates, things that have been spliced can never be fully or organically integrated. The rhyme of "sliced" with "spliced" furthers the emphasis on surfaces: these ideas seem linked partly because they look (and sound) alike.

But these superficial and spatial ways of joining also involve—by displacing—temporal relations that have to do with depth. More exactly, they engage in the metonymic work of converting what several definitions of metonymy call "contiguity" into "substitution." The difficulty of this process is evident in Howe's phrase "recurrent return somewhere." The phrase implies that the poet engages in a redundant act that reverberates through time. But it is unclear what "return" Howe seeks, since the term *recurrent* is temporally unfixed, evoking both past and future: something new, it seems, may follow the "slic[ing] and splic[ing]" of yet-unidentified "correlations." Several items in the apparently random list of materials also reveal the past's continuation into the present. "Preservations" gesture toward a previous act of memorialization, and insofar as "patterns" have already been "resuscitated," they imply that the speaker's attempt to do so now repeats what has already occurred.

In the remainder of this chapter, I will consider in detail the ways Howe explores the processes of memory through a poetics of displacement and metonymy, whose tactile and spatial emphasis offers a cleaner, if less direct, mode of representation than do the figurative strategies I have considered above. I will begin by considering Howe's spatialization of belatedness in the context of the volume's ambivalent relation to elegy. I will then consider Howe's use of photographs, which both conceal and enact her position as survivor. I will next explore the way spatialization functions in the sections of the book that do not consider maternal absence, especially in the context of the volume's recurrent references to spectrality and textuality. And I will end by closely reading a series of poems that give voice to the dead mother's books in ways that join the motifs of bereavement and spectrality, arguing that these poems propose spatial and metonymic relations as an alternative to both loss and forgetting.

|||||||||||||||||||

In ways more extreme than the AIDS poems I examined in chapter 3, *The Midnight* recalls but does not wholly exemplify the attributes of elegy; the sequence can, in fact, be read as metonymically adjacent to this poetic subgenre, aware of its features while not participating in it fully. The volume was composed four years after the death of the poet's mother, the Irish-born actress Mary Manning, at the age of ninety-three, and it describes and assembles representations of many of her belongings, including books, papers, photos, and an address book. Throughout *The Midnight*, Howe also describes scenes of bereavement, absence, and maternal death, often displaced onto other characters and situations. Such materials and scenes might have provided another poet with the raw material of elegy, a series of sources to be analyzed and refracted through the poet's consciousness. But Howe's sequence does not engage in such synthetic acts. Howe appears throughout almost exclusively as an archiver and collector, and the documents and details included in the volume are generally described objectively or presented verbatim, rather than interpreted or responded to by the speaker. Howe refers to her mother almost exclusively by her unmarried stage name, and when she includes her own childhood memories of her mother, she does not describe herself in relation to Manning or disclose her feelings about her mother's death.

Howe thus refuses the emotions that often characterize elegy—including grief, anger, and regret—and instead engages in repeated and multiple acts of displacement. Yet elegies are at least partly characterized by just such acts. While they may originate in strong emotion, their existence offers evidence of their capacity to suppress or reimagine such emotion. This is Peter Sacks's somewhat controversial claim: "the objective of elegy," he asserts, is "to displace the urgent psychological currents of the work of mourning into the more apparently placid, aesthetically organized currents of language" (145–56).[14] Sacks locates the evidence for this "deflection of desire" in "the creation of . . . trope[s]" (7), especially metaphors that transform elegiac insufficiency into the possibility of asserting compensatory power (7–8). The rawer trope of metonymy in *The Midnight*, however, emphasizes neither "compensatory power" nor "elegiac insufficiency." Rather, it allows Howe to present the unassimilated residue of her mother's life, which resists being made to signify.

In fact, deflection and displacement recur throughout the sequence, often associated directly with maternal death. One sentence just before the start of the final section of poems associates something resembling displacement with both remembering and "commemorat[ing]": "Long ago Ogham stones were erected to commemorate the dead in rune-like ciphers then memory for voices then the rapid movement of ballads" (150). It is significant that none of these media refer directly to "the dead" whom they seem to "commemorate."

Nor does Howe directly mention her elegiac project or her mother here. But the next sentences address an ethereal and apparently dead other whose presence, like that of the ghostly Catherine in *Wuthering Heights*, can be sensed by the bereaved speaker: "I have no option to be faithful to you unlucky half human half unassuaged desiring dark shade you first Catherine. You are my altar vow" (150). The addressee is here ambiguous; the reference is to a "first Catherine" rather than Catherine herself, and the speaker does not indicate whether the "dark shade" she addresses is Catherine, her mother, a spouse (implied by the "altar vow"), part of the speaker, or someone else. It is also unclear from the negative construction of the opening phrase "I have no option but to remain faithful" whether the speaker succeeds in her attempt at faithfulness. Certainly the attempt seems only partly to affect the ghostly "dark shade," who remains "half unassuaged" and "desiring." Although this situation evokes the longing for presence directly expressed by AIDS elegy, Howe instead emphasizes the necessity of substitution and the difficulty of direct speech in relation to the dead.

When, earlier in the sequence, Howe directly considers the topic of substitution, she also distances it from both death and the mother. Howe is considering the idea of "di-alethia" or "two(-way) truth," which partly seems to explain the fact that "at the heart of language lies what language can't express" (70).[15] Then follows this statement:

> O light and dark vowels with your transconsistent hissing and hushing I know you curtain I sense delusion. Fortunately we can capture for our world some soft object, a fuzzy conditional, a cot cover, an ode, a couplet, a line, a lucky stone—to carry around when camping (70).

Instead of attempting to look *through* language, Howe here looks *at* it. Howe's emphasis is not on language's capacity to convey what "exists" in the world but on its materiality, evident in "hissing and hushing" sounds and synesthetically visible "light and dark vowels." Language is, she claims, "transconsistent," extending but also undermining consistency in a way that recalls the doubleness of the interleaf and metonymy's capacity to transform superficial spatial arrangements into modes of connection; language is both tactile (a "curtain") and conceptual (a "delusion"). The sense of concealment is echoed by Howe's use of the term "capture," which implies that language easily vanishes. In contrast, Howe's list of the objects that can substitute for language emphasizes tactility (what is "soft" and "fuzzy"), fortuitousness (what is "fortunate" and "lucky"), compactness (what can be easily "carr[ied] around"), and usefulness (what is helpful in activities like "camping"). These actual objects, Howe implies, replace language's failure to convey them.

Howe does not refer directly to her mother here, but the passage's implications about concealment, substitution, and evasion echo her direct descriptions of her mother. The tension between a superficial mode of substitution and a more psychological notion of loss is especially apparent in her account of her mother's recitation of a sonnet by Michael Drayton: "Now it's too late I remember the way she vocally italicized each 'glad'" (63). Recalling the mother's speech requires sensory displacement; Howe depicts the voice's sound ("vocally") in terms of printed words on a page ("italicized"). This act seems antichronologically to restore the sonnet to its original textual form, enacting Howe's assertion that the memory has arisen because it is "now . . . too late." Yet, as Howe's failure to italicize the word *glad* indicates, this belated restoration is inaccurate; in Drayton's sonnet "Since There's No Help," the word is not italicized. To remember, Howe thus implies, involves not only restoration but revision and even erasure. What Sacks calls elegy's "deflection of desire"—here the desire for the mother's continuing presence—is evident through Howe's depiction of the mother's recitation of preexisting words. But Howe's act of remembering also reiterates the loss, since in remembering, she presses the recited words back onto the page and thus into silence.

A few pages later, Howe engages in another act of textual displacement by associating bereavement with the ballads her mother recited; Manning was, Howe asserts, a "marvelous reciter of ballads" (65). The ballads Howe describes tend to depict both maternal death and the possibility that this death can be overcome or found to be impermanent. In "Lord Randal," maternal "good[ness]" fuses with threat (the "good mother" has "coeval ties to the murderer" [65]) to undermine the finality of death. The mother's position at "the locus between life and death" (65) is depicted differently in other ballads; in one, "the victim is a slaughtered child," but "Sometimes a dead mother hears her children weep so she comes back" from the dead (66). Ballads reveal the more general "way you splinter things when you're in a position of abject melancholia" (65). Such discussions evoke Howe's poetic response to her mother's death; certainly she here and elsewhere tends to "splinter things." Here too, then, Howe uses preexisting texts to voice a condition of bereavement she never identifies as her own. This act confirms her belatedness: the only thing that can be told is what has already been many times retold. As such, Howe's bereavement itself seems redundant.

A related sense of displacement is evident in Howe's extended prose description of the response of the nineteenth-century landscape designer Frederick Law Olmsted to his mother's death when he was six years old. This response was, Howe reveals, itself displaced; Howe describes not Olmsted's sadness at his mother's death but the "remedy for sadness" he devised involving "solitary walks" that taught him to enjoy "the edges of woods" (48). Howe also cites Olmsted's description of his participation, "soon after" his mother's death, in the funeral procession of a child he did not know personally (67): after the funeral, Olmsted "stole out alone to the burying ground and kneeling beside the new grave asked God to wake [the dead child] up so he could lead her home to mother" (67–68). Here the dead girl offers a substitute for Olmsted's dead mother, a situation his words at the grave further displace in that they assert his belief (echoed by the ballads Howe describes) that death is not in fact permanent.

That Olmsted was a designer of parks, which Olmsted defined as "portion[s] of a forest enclosed" (48), makes him an especially important figure for Howe; his life's work involved the design of physical spaces that she implies both spatialized and displaced his childhood experience of loss. Howe mostly emphasizes the spatial (and more exactly geographical) connections between herself and Olmsted; as Howe notes, she lives, as Olmsted did, in Buffalo, the site of a park Olmsted designed, and Guilford, Connecticut, where he worked as a farmer. Howe emphasizes the significance of this connection, although it is accidental and metonymic. This accidental quality evokes the difficulty of gaining access to the past and the contingency of belatedness, which I have been exploring throughout this book. As Howe reveals, the bonds of memory are fragile and thus easily lost. Because his mother died when he was young, Olmsted claims, "I now only remember that I did . . . remember her" (67). As Howe indicates, this failure of memory also extends to Olmsted, since "now no one living remembers the fall of [his] voice from sound into silence" (48), as well as, elsewhere in the sequence, to Howe herself, who "think[s she] remember[s]" certain childhood scenes that may not in fact have occurred (63).[16] In this way, Howe links herself to Olmsted not through shared experience or loss but through their absence. The implication is that absence can be described only indirectly, by considering what is nearby.

But superficial connections characterized by physical proximity also imply depths and even resemblances that recall the contradictions I noted above in the definitions of postmodern spatialization and metonymy. The volume's photographs visually exemplify such contradictions. They mostly represent books owned by Manning, often with other, unrelated objects juxtaposed with or overlaid onto them in ways that partly or entirely obscure the text beneath and draw attention to the artificiality of their composition.[17] These books were clearly much handled and loved; Howe makes their annotated margins, taped covers, and the like visible. But the photos also render the actual books flat, small, and black and white; we cannot touch or smell them or hear their pages turn. Although Howe does not, as Graham does, dwell on the ways photos distort real preexisting scenes, these photos emphasize the disjunction between the three-dimensional world depicted within the photos and their two-dimensional reproduction on her own pages.

Howe's prose claim that books functioned as "transitional objects" for "my mother's close relations" partly explains this visual tension between the flat and the deep: the books, she asserts, existed "to be held, loved, carried around, meddled with, abandoned, sometimes mutilated" (60). The phrase "transitional objects" evokes Howe's recurrent interest in transitions; books are here tactile "objects" "to be held" rather than texts whose contents should be read and understood. But a transitional object is also a psychological concept closely related to Freudian displacement, one that signals depth and interiority. Donald Winnicott first used the term in the

1950s to refer to often "soft" objects (4)—a term, as I indicated above, that Howe uses later in the sequence (70)—that enable "the infant to weave other-than-me objects into the personal pattern" (3).[18] More specifically, such objects enable the child to create substitutes for his absent mother in ways that distract him from her absence (5).[19]

Substitutes, however, are by definition inadequate replacements for what is gone: the child's stuffed animal is not the same as the absent mother. This sense of inadequacy is evident, as several theorists have noted, in all photos, which both memorialize the past and signal its inaccessibility. On the one hand, by making fleeting, lived moments permanent, they offer an alternative to narrative and mortality. Photos of the dead allow the dead to remain present and thus figuratively alive; they are, according to Roland Barthes, "the living representation of a dead thing" (78). But because such representations suppress movement and change, photos also affirm death's inevitability. In Barthes's terms, "by shifting [the] reality [of what has been alive] to the past ('this-has-been'), the photograph suggests that it is already dead" (79). Photos thus for Barthes, according to one reader, emphasize a "look . . . in which the imperative of displacement seems to reign supreme" (Silverman 183). Howe's photos take this sense of distancing one step further; as representations of photos, books, or arrangements of objects, they are representations of representations.

Photos, according to Barthes, impel the viewer's future death into the present; they reveal an "anterior future" and "death in the future" (Barthes 96). Such terms recall the anticipatory quality of several AIDS elegies, and Howe's photos in some ways evoke the ghosts in AIDS poems. In Mark Doty's "The Wings," a poem I discussed in chapter 3, the pants of a dead man sewn onto a panel of the AIDS quilt reveal the discrepancy between the inanimate, enduring object and the absent, living person; the pants at once reanimate and deanimate the man who wore them. Manning's possessions similarly refer to the two notions of displacement I described above. The books, which Manning once held and read and which survive her death, remain adjacent to her: they belonged to her but cannot replace her. But they also displace her in the sense implied by Winnicott, converting her absence into an always inarticulate mode of presence. Because these objects survive her death, they allow her, at least for a while, to be remembered.

||||||||||||||||

In the extensive sections of the sequence that do not refer to Manning or death, Howe elaborates related tactics of displacement. Such dynamics are especially evident in Howe's references to ghostliness and spectrality in the context of remembered events, which several other readers have noted.[20] Textual ghosts, as I indicated in chapter 3, often blur past with present, the living with the dead, the tactile with the abstract, and what can be retained with what must be released. In the process, they reveal the kinds of boundaries and spaces that interest Howe. Ghosts are also poetically useful for Howe because they offer, as Susan Stewart has argued in general terms, a succinct way to consider poetic lineage and inspiration (*Poetry* 113). Howe indicates in *The Midnight* that she is "skeptical" about her mother's belief that "tables move without contact" (149), but she has elsewhere associated writing with "hearing something" and "receiving orders from somewhere" ("Interview" 33).[21]

The Midnight does not restore the actual dead to life, but what Howe calls specters several times appear in and through books, often in ways that reveal the simultaneity of living, sleep, and death and that evoke "every first scrap of memory" (68).[22] A prose description of exploring an abandoned grain elevator in Buffalo with an out-of-town visitor includes a catalog of the objects Howe found there, items such as "wagons, rusty buckets, tires, . . . newspapers, memos, business records" (139). Then follows this sentence: "When the other half of the dialogue of mind with itself is nothing but a picture, the status of a spectral self resurfaces" (139). Howe seems partly to be reflecting on the "status" of the objects she discovered; we belatedly gain access to previously lost "spectral sel[ves]" (for example, the lives of the people who worked in the elevator) by examining the artifacts they left behind. But Howe's syntax complicates this straightforward meaning. Modifications recur (the word *of* recurs three times), making the sentence nearly impossible to paraphrase and drawing attention to its "status" not (only) as the expression of an extrinsic meaning but as a series of signifiers whose contradictions and self-cancelings draw the reader's attention to their linguistic surface. The "spectral self," it seems, can be accessed only through acts of remembering, but the passage refuses to define this self's "status." And while spectrality is evident within the sentence as semantic slippage, it is impossible to locate or fix, something like the transitional space of the interleaf, which Howe describes as a "spectral scrap."

I have so far been focusing on prose passages that reveal Howe's tendency to juxtapose what she calls distinct "materials" and blocks of text in ways that gesture toward concealed, often remembered events. The sequence's poems also explore the relation between surface and depth. Mostly untitled, unpunctuated, compressed, and short—most are no longer than ten lines— the poems contain multiple punlike slippages that recall but extend the effects of Paul Monette's similarly unpunctuated lines: just as the interleaf impels the reader both forward and "*back*" (73), the meaning of a given word often varies depending on whether it is read in relation to what follows or precedes it. More directly than in the prose sections, the poems present, then destabilize their own surfaces, letting the reader shift, in ways that recall the similar alternation in Graham's *Region*, between what is on the surface and under it.

It is a truism that reading old texts restores their authors (as well as the characters within them) to life. Howe implies as much when she claims that "spirits . . . inhabit" her mother's books (74). One poem in "Bed Hangings I" extends this idea by literalizing it; here, the text's materiality is what enables the ghostly appearance of the dead. Howe's addressee in the poem is probably Charles Sanders Peirce:[23]

> hedged by paper
> you appear to me walking
> across the text to call an
> unconverted soul King James
> lyricism another C minor
> Coeval decades hereafter (25)

Physically located on ("walking / across") the "text" he apparently authored, the addressee reveals that this text is simultaneously a physical terrain and a container for ideas. The verb "hedged" embodies this simultaneity by converting a physical object (a hedge) into a sensation (being hedged in) in ways that conflate protection with imprisonment. Howe's poem does something similar: it allows Peirce to "appear" while also containing him. Doing so enables the past to be made present. The addressee speaks in an archaic "King James / lyricism" that remains "Coeval decades after." Or perhaps the last line's referent is the soul's arrival, the addressee's act of "call[ing] an / unconverted soul," or Howe's act of summoning him. In fact, Howe here seems to include—and thus make "coeval"—all these possibilities.

Reading, Howe here implies, allows surface and depth to coexist, which in turn enables the past to be revived even as it remains remote. To read is thus to participate in a spectral joining of disparate parts. The volume's first two sequences of poems, entitled "Bed Hangings I" and "II," join surface with depth in ways that evoke, though they often do not name, the capacity of specters to cross boundaries. Howe is interested in the hangings' "surface material," their fabric and stitchwork, which she describes in detail and which one poem identifies as "sheer white muslin." But she is also interested in the often evanescent scenes they simultaneously represent, as in the same poem, which depicts "a tree fair hunted Daphne" (17).[24] Moreover, bed hangings create contingent spaces that exist only when the hangings are closed, and Howe's poems, centered and symmetrical on facing pages, visually resemble them. Thus, as the same poem asserts, "non-connection is itself distinct / connection" (17).

An early poem directly links Howe's poetic project to her simultaneous exploration of the surface and what is beneath it by implying that Howe herself engages in techniques similar to those used by weavers.

Go too—my savage pattern
on surface material the line
in ink if you have curtains
and a New English Dictionary

there is nothing to justify a
claim for linen except a late
quotation knap warp is flax
Fathom we without cannot (8)

Like weaving, writing involves both surface and depth, here distinguished as "surface material" and "pattern"; in bed hangings this material seems to be the visible "knap warp [and] flax," while in writing it is "the line / in ink." (Linen links these activities, since it is used both in weaving and paper.) But the poem also refers to other, less apparent materials, including "a New English Dictionary," to which the poet can refer and from which she can quote. (In fact, *The Midnight* includes several sections of dictionary "quotation[s].") At times, the poem's "materials" are harder to classify. Howe's reference to "curtains" evokes the superficial, curtainlike look of her poems on the page. The term *curtains* also evokes similar references throughout the sequence, thematically connecting the poem's different surfaces.

A range of surface materials is thus evident in the poem's finished "savage pattern." But in the doubly negative last line, "Fathom we without cannot," Howe suggests something different: the various juxtapositions, analogies, and slippages that precede this line in fact enable the possibility of depth or fathoming, which itself seems to require multiple and unspecified refusals ("we without cannot"). Perhaps these negations prevent the depths revealed by "fathom[ing]" from occurring here, but the poem also seems to yearn toward the possibility of being able to fathom, a possibility that its fundamentally metaphoric structure also implies; insofar as writing poems is like weaving, Howe here "justif[ies]" her extensive exploration of weaving and fabric throughout the sequence. The earlier reference to "a late / quotation" signals something similar. To quote is to move or displace language from one context to another, a metonymic act, but because the quotation is "late," it also reaches back and down.

Here, as throughout the sequence, Howe acknowledges her belatedness. To create, she makes clear, is to reuse what already existed and thus to remake older texts. Related questions about debt and originality are central to Howe's subsequent prose discussion of textual defacement and recycling.

Jonathan Edwards, Howe claims, was "a paper saver" who "kept old bills and shopping lists, then copied out his sermons on the verso sides and stitched them into handmade notebooks" (58), while Emerson as a young man engaged in a more extreme act: he "cut his dead minister father's sermons in manuscript out of their bindings, then used the bindings to hold his own writing. He mutilated another of Emerson senior's notebooks in order to use the blank pages" (58). (Howe's description of her mother's family's similar "mutilat[ion]" of their own books occurs just a few pages later [60]). Howe's insistence on these acts of revision and remaking recalls Harold Bloom's notion of belatedness, which focuses on the "anxiety" experienced by authors compelled to conceal their debt to the earlier authors from whom they have borrowed or stolen.[25] But the fact that, for Howe, no anxiety is associated with such borrowings is perhaps consistent with Jameson's assertion that anxiety, a recurrent feature of the modern, is absent from the postmodern (14) and with Marjorie Perloff's recent claim that "citation" (*Unoriginal* 4) and "appropriation" (11) are central elements of twenty-first-century poetry.[26] According to Perloff, the mutilation and rearrangement of earlier texts is not concealed in many recent poems; their overt acts of appropriation not only produce new texts but reanimate earlier ones. As Howe asserts in the context of her discussion of textual recycling, "the relational space is the thing that's alive with something from somewhere else" (58).

Howe elsewhere makes a related point in reference to what the poem beginning "Go too—" calls "late / quotation" (8). In a section entitled "*Scare Quotes*" within "Scare Quotes II," Howe cites Emerson's epigraph to his essay "Quotation and Originality": "'Every book is a quotation; . . . and every man is a quotation from all his ancestors'" (116). Howe then cites a published footnote to this comment written later by Emerson's son. The son first notes the thousands of "named references, chiefly to authors" within Emerson's writings, then cites "Dr. Holmes['s]" claim—the original quotation marks are his (and Howe's)—that Emerson "'believed in quotation, and borrowed from everybody and every book. Not in any stealthy or shamefaced way, but proudly, as a king borrows from one of his attendants the coin that bears his own image and superscription'" (116).

This passage wittily enacts Emerson's point about the ubiquity of quotation by elaborating it via a quotation within a quotation. But it also reveals the importance of often invisible, belated acts of rereading. The king must create the coins containing his image before he can borrow one; his act of borrowing thus affirms his prescience. Similarly, Emerson's son's "borrow[ing]" of Holmes's words affirms his belated capacity to redact his father's works. According to this logic, Howe's citation of these and other authors reveals her presence in *The Midnight* even when she is not speaking directly. While her quotations revive the dead precursors she cites, it is Howe who decides what to excerpt and (at times) alter. Her acts of "late / quotation" thus ensure that these antecedent texts remain relevant, although citations from them appear in *The Midnight* in fractured forms. By continuing to reread, amass, and compile them, Howe also reveals her own presence, which is also ghostly insofar as it is concealed, or mostly, behind the words of others.

ııııııııııııı

In a series of poems in *The Midnight*'s final section, "Kidnapped," Howe explores a number of the topics I have been considering throughout this chapter, including maternal loss, restoration, spectrality, and allusion. These poems consider the apparently real inscriptions in Manning's books by giving voice to them; the books, speaking posthumously and prosopopoeically, seem to defy the fact of Manning's death. Yet Howe also disrupts the apparent authenticity of this speech. As they progress, the poems become increasingly cryptic, undermining the fiction of actual speech; several also shift from prosopopoeia to apostrophe, speaking in the end not for but to Manning in ways that, as in similar moments in AIDS elegy, affirm her unresponsiveness. These poems thus reveal not only the efficacy of their strategy of metonymic displacement but also this strategy's limitations, as the poet makes clear by referring several times not to actual proximity but to its performance, thus literalizing a concern recurrent in my earlier chapters.

From the outset, the sequence's first poem confuses intimate with public speech. Here is the entire poem:

Dedication to M enough
to the wood if you have
aconite and poppy she
said "Lie still, sleep well"
Quiet for it is a small
world of covered bone
Come veil the thought of
I shall dress primrose (151)

It is unclear whether the poem's first word announces the poem's genre (as the section's first poem, this is the dedicatory poem) or expresses Howe's personal "dedication to M." The use of the initial "M" similarly evokes both the removed "Mary" and "Manning," the poet's mother's given name, and the intimate "Mother." A related slippage is evident in the poem's narrative structure: early, the poem cites the recalled words of the "she" who "said 'Lie still, sleep well,'" but the last four lines seem to present an address to her, as is implied by the shift to the present tense midway through and the last line's mention of "I." But even if this shift has occurred, the daughter's speech remains too late, as the reference to the "small / world of covered bone" implies; the mother is no longer alive or sentient. Or perhaps the poem recounts a different story, in which not the poet but "she" speaks throughout the poem, implying toward the end sleep's adjacency to death or at least to the bodily reality of "bone."

Such confusions about agency are spatialized in the multiple acts of concealment in the last part of the poem. The references to "cover[ing]" and "veil[ing]" both deny and recall loss even as they evoke a physical act of burial. The fragmentary penultimate line, "Come veil the thought of," for example, seems to imply that the poet is asking the addressee to "veil"— conceal or turn away from—something painful. In promising to "dress primrose," she seems to offer the possibility that she can put on a costume that will conceal or "cover" the body's "bone." Or perhaps M is doing just this. Howe does not give us enough information to locate these references; the poem by the end seems to evoke a private narrative from which the reader is meant to be excluded. The dedications in books are similarly private, meant only for the eyes of their intended recipient. Howe's use of the dedication, like the poem that follows, reminds us that we are trespassing into a space in which we do not belong.

By permitting us to overhear its speech but excluding us from its implications, "Dedication to M" sets us outside the poem's intense and private address. But two poems later, Howe situates herself as the trespasser. The poem begins with an apparently real dedication Mary Manning wrote in a book given not to Howe but to Manning's sister:

> Mary Manning presents this
> book to her Dear Sister as a
> token not to be appreciated
> so must act extreme affection
> Affection take this book Dear
> to every moment she cannot
> Invisible she grows tired
> and beside vast catacomb Thebes (153)

The poem's first two or three lines read like an actual book dedication; but then words are omitted (as in the line "so must act extreme affection"), and syntax is altered (as in the subsequent line "Affection take this book Dear"). The line breaks further displace the poem's initial immediacy. The phrase "Affection take this book Dear," for example, can be read both as an address to the sister and as a description of Manning or her sister (who is "Dear / to every moment").

The poem thus emphasizes obstructions to speech, a topic that becomes explicit in its last three lines. The "tired" "she" may be Manning's sister, who Manning acknowledges cannot receive her posthumous offering. Or it may be Howe acknowledging either her own failure to summon Manning or Manning's subsequent vanishing. The last reference to Thebes also seems to refer both to mourning and its obstruction; the Egyptian city Thebes contains a catacomb, but in the Greek city of the same name, Antigone was prevented from burying her dead father. Howe thus implies that she is both compelled and unable to bury her mother, as the mother's posthumous and increasingly fragmentary speech indicates. The poem's multiple and overlaid displacements of voice reveal both the poet's desire for presence and the futility of this desire: the poet's voice is displaced onto Manning's, Howe as possible addressee becomes Manning's sister, and Manning speaks only through her book's dedication. But if Manning cannot speak to her daughter directly, we also understand that Howe is in fact speaking *for* Manning. We cannot know whether the poem's opening dedication is real or invented; nor can we know whether Howe has "mutilated" an actual "quotation." What we are left with are the poem's disjointed words and phrases, a series of fragments that remain adjacent to one another in a poem that exposes the randomness of its own assemblage.

A later poem in the sequence ("Reader of poetry . . .") further extends this sense of provisionality by refusing the relatively stable personae of the earlier dedication poems in favor of a direct, if fragmentary, depiction of a scene of theatrical performance. This scene recalls a motif central to the volume, especially its prose sections. Not only was Mary Manning an actress—this, her maiden name, was also her professional name—but Howe describes acting in family theatrical productions staged by her mother (64–65). Such literal facts differ from the figurative allusions to theater in the poems I have discussed in previous chapters. Howe also considers the topic of theater in several other poems in the volume, especially a sequence focusing on Noh drama (168–71), and acting may also be implied in the first dedication poem's reference to the speaker who "shall dress primrose." Here is the poem:

Reader of poetry this book
contains all poetry THOOR
BALLYLEE seven notes for
stage presentations May
countryside you reader of
poetry that I am forgotten
Long notes seem necessary

Unworthy players ask for
legend familiar in legend
the arrow king and no king (167)

The identity of the narrator in this poem is even less clear than in the other
poems in the sequence. The speaker may be Manning, as Perloff has suggested (*Unoriginal* 115), or perhaps Yeats (associated with Thoor Ballylee
castle) here addresses the readers of his plays. The line "I am forgotten"
(which recalls Olmsted's failure to "remember" his mother and others' subsequent forgetting of his "voice") reveals a larger problem: because books
endure longer than their authors, their continuing speech does not ensure
their authors eternal life but rather ends up eradicating them.

The poem's addressee is also both unclear and inconsistent. The speaker
twice addresses "you reader of / poetry," although the book described is apparently a collection of plays, since it includes "seven notes for / stage pre-
sentation" and refers to "unworthy players." The speaker thus seems to turn
away from one group of readers (who are "unworthy" and "ask for" something they should not or cannot receive) to another. And while the poem
seems to address us ("you reader of / poetry"), it refuses to allow us to locate
ourselves in relation to its words.

Yeats's poem "King and No King," to which, as Perloff points out, the last
line alludes (*Unoriginal* 115), refers to "the blinding light beyond the grave"
in which what is "lost" can be "f[ou]nd." These assertions evoke Howe's
implication in a late poem that performances function as "cenotaph[s]" or
funerary monuments (159). Her poems, she there implies, are staged utterances that require (as does "Mary Manning presents") multiple displacements of voice. In fact, theatricalism here seems indistinguishable from
poetry. Like her mother, who acted in Yeats's plays, Howe is engaging in
ventriloquism, although we do not know whom she is making speak or
why. This doubt, as Howe reveals in all these poems, inheres both in survivorship and readership; because both she and we are belated, we cannot
separate what is true from its performance. Belatedness thus, more clearly
than in the poems I discussed in earlier chapters, here seems to enable
performance: it impels the poet to speak indirectly, in a different voice,

on a stage constructed specifically for such speech. But belatedness also *is* a performance. Rather than a preexisting staged utterance, it is revealed through and remains inescapable from this utterance. Here, then, through the very force of her insistence on actual, tactile things and the ways they connect, Howe detaches belatedness from the literal in a way that frees it from verisimilitude and history.

Yet it is also worth noting that Howe's sequence can be read quite differently, as the expression of a distinctively postcolonial sensibility evident, for example, in recurrent scenes of geographical exile, including both that of Manning and Robert Louis Stevenson.[27] That this reading—which I do not here elaborate—can coexist with the linguistic, thematic, and psychoanalytic one I have presented evokes among other things the complex relation between postmodernism and the political. Postmodernism is sometimes accused of being apolitical or antipolitical; its emphasis on the play of surfaces often seems to preclude a "real" alternative to virtuality and simulacra. Yet, as I have just implied, Howe's lack of explicit interest in direct or legible processes of memory and history can also be read as a symptom of, or even an indirect elegy for, the ways places and times become lost. In the process, Howe's poetics of formal and aesthetic destabilization can be understood, in ways consistent with critical discussions of postmodernism by Jameson and others, as what Jameson calls "protopolitical" (160) or even political.[28]

||||||||||||||||

The poems I considered in previous chapters, it could be argued, repeatedly struggle with the difficulty of eradicating the distinctions between the literal and the figurative; the tensions that persist in many of these poems may derive from the tenacity of these distinctions. In contrast, the insistently metonymic mode of connection in *The Midnight* seems to derive from a quite different and wholly visual model, one in which the figure is defined in opposition not to the literal but to the ground it occupies. (Howe, as is often observed, was trained as a visual artist.) This change in orientation, it seems, lets Howe avoid much of sadness and helplessness with which other postwar poets tend to imbue belatedness.

While the dedication poems become increasingly fragmented as they progress, implying a failure or diminishment of contact, the volume's final poem elaborates the pleasures that can be created through spatial, metonymic connections. Unsurprisingly, the poem is concerned with an anticipated ending:

I am still moving one wave
twicewashed these are pas-
times voice of evening half
local gold half peregrine red
Where the escaped and their
frolic nobody knows aslant
Style in one stray sitting I
approach sometime in plain
handmade rag wove costume
awry what I long for array (173)

As the speaker awaits night (it is now "evening") and perhaps winter (suggested by "gold" and "red," evoking autumn leaves), she delays and repeats, allowing a single "wave" to be "twicewashed," an image that strongly recalls the twice-breaking wave in Graham's similarly hopeful "Soul Says" (*Region* 125). A similar sense of repetition and delay is also evident in the midword break at the second line's end, which implies that past times remain embedded in the present moment's amusements or "pas- / times." In this context, imagery of unbalance—"aslant," "stray"—reveals the halting quality of the speaker's, and the poem's, forward progress, although the speaker affirms her "approach" to an unspecified goal. This approach involves a "costume" that recalls the speaker's offer to "dress primrose" in "Dedication to M." But here the costume, or the act of putting it on, forestalls disorder, apparently transforming what is "awry" into an "array."

Although it does not directly state that they are analogous, the poem describes world and self using similar imagery. The "costume[d]" and "array[ed]" self recalls the landscape's similar array, "half / local gold half peregrine red." This sense of similarity reverberates beyond the poem: the "gold" and "red" recall Howe's earlier citation of a passage by Aytoun, mentioned by Emerson and written about by his son, of a banner that "mingled / . . . crimson and . . . gold" (47). Howe juxtaposes this citation with Emerson's depiction of God as an upholsterer: "We want design, and do not forgive the bards if they have only the art of enameling. We want an architect, and they bring us an upholsterer" (46–47). This passage is metonymically linked both to Howe's other citations of Emerson and to her own repeated references to woven fabric. The image also anticipates the fabric described in the poem's penultimate line, which refers to a "costume" of "plain / handmade rag wove." The homely quality of this costume may suggest that the world's array is evident in its ordinariness. Howe does not often emphasize desire in *The Midnight*, but the final line's "what I long for" is an exception. In fact, the acknowledgment of "long[ing]" seems to be what permits the speaker to "approach" and then move into and through ending. And so the passage becomes "moving" in a different sense; it hints at the possibility of a culmination and integration that *The Midnight* mostly disavows.

Throughout this chapter, I have been emphasizing what is distinctive about Howe's metonymic poetics. But Howe's implication in this final poem—that surfaces can reveal the past in ways linked to desire—evokes similar concerns in many of the poems I have considered throughout this book: the connection between deflection and longing has recurred in each of my earlier chapters. In this way, *The Midnight* reveals a tendency evident, if less overtly, in the other postwar poems I have examined. All these poets challenge equivalence and certainty, although less systematically (and in less fragmentary ways) than Howe, who considers loss and memory indirectly, by displacing them onto what is visible. But Howe's sequence illuminates a more general pattern of evasion in postwar American poetry. In fact, this impulse to disguise loss and impose it onto something else may, as much as anything else, define the postwar American poetics of belatedness.

"To begin the forgetting"

Belatedness beyond Memory

I finished the reading and looked up
Changed in the familiar ways. Now for a quiet place
To begin the forgetting. The little delays
Between sensations, the audible absence of rain
Take the place of objects. I have some questions
But they can wait. Waiting is the answer
I was looking for. Any subject will do
So long as it recedes.
—Ben Lerner, "Mean Free Path"

I have been focusing throughout this book on the ways postwar poems gesture toward partly occluded past events. Often, the past is not fully accessible, or else the poem defaces it; at times, as in Howe's *The Midnight*, the act of remembering is simply uninteresting. In some poems—several of Graham's, for example, or Rich's—what remain are only memory's figurative manifestations, especially the tendency to assert connections, however inadequate or corrupted. Such remnants often draw attention to the process of poetic making and the ways poems are transmitted to their readers.

To read a poem is to inhabit the space it has created; reading revives what the poem has already brought into existence. Postwar poems often express their awareness of the belatedness inherent in this situation by preemptively staging their own obsolescence, an act that seems partly designed to stave off its actual future occurrence. In the process, these poems often do more than disavow the past. They also gaze forward into a future that is not too late but later. This proleptic gaze recurs throughout the roughly fifty-year period I have been considering, but it seems especially pronounced in recent poems.

This intensification doubtless has several overlapping causes, which almost certainly include the historically and culturally particular. One such cause is undoubtedly that poets, like everyone else, have become increasingly aware of the urgent, humanly created threats to our continued existence on earth, variously evident in the proliferation of weapons of mass destruction, climate change, and the demographic and political changes that have accompanied late capitalism. This increased concern with the future can also be explained chronologically; the turn of the millennium has prompted, unsurprisingly, millennial reflection both about the past and the future. It can also be located in a more particularly literary context, as I intimated briefly in the introduction: American poetry and those who produce it, it seems inarguable, have become increasingly irrelevant to American culture over the last fifty or so years. Several critics have explained this irrelevance in terms of obsolescence—poetry no longer serves the cultural function it once did—which itself implies having stayed too long or, to recall one of the definitions of belatedness that I cited at the start of this book, being "detained beyond the usual time." Graham's prose, for example, implies that poetry is no longer relevant, though it once was, to a culture accustomed to finding not only diversion but inspiration from other media.

But recent and postwar poems do not only look ahead. They also acknowledge the dangers of doing so, often by violating what in chapter 2 I called the poem's frame. When poems speak from a hypothetical future moment that requires them to adopt what several have called the future anterior, their speakers become especially vulnerable.[1] Depicting the future as if it is present reveals the poet's literal inability to predict such a future. In this context, depictions within poems of scenes in which poems are offered to readers or read to audiences are especially transgressive, partly because they so explicitly violate the fiction of completeness that many poems present and thus the frame surrounding poetic utterance. Such scenes gesture proleptically toward a moment of receipt that is always deferred for the poet. Yet this same moment is immediate and present for the (herself belated) reader, who comes to understand the poem in the now of reading.

I wish in this coda to connect two apparently disparate features of postwar poems, both of which extend my discussion of memory and belatedness in the preceding chapters. Trauma theory has at times argued that remembering is the effect of an earlier act of forgetting or "forgetful memory." In one critic's terms, traumatic events can be experienced only through their "inherent forgetting" (Caruth, Introduction 8); in another's, "memory and forgetting are facets of the same phenomenon of understanding" (Bernard-Donals, *Forgetful* 3).[2] But in postwar poems, especially recent ones, something different seems evident: scenes of forgetting, as well as of anticipation, prolepsis, and waiting, alter memory itself. And as memory is changed, belatedness is freed, at least partly, from the weight of the past and allowed to gesture forward, toward a future that by definition remains eternally deferred.

The opening of Ben Lerner's 2010 long poem "Mean Free Path," which I have used as this coda's epigraph, juxtaposes forgetting, waiting, and belatedness.[3] The poem begins in a situation of aftermath. An undefined "reading"—it is not clear whether this term refers to a private, silent act or a public performance—has "finished," and the speaker seems to be casting about for what will happen next. (The poem's later use of the phrase "*déjà lu*" ["already read"] [22], which was its original title, directly asserts this sense of aftermath.) Belatedness here seems tactile, or at least, in ways that recall Graham's recurrent concerns in *Region*, "little delays between sensations" have "taken the place of objects." This scene of delay and lateness creates the precondition for forgetting, which the speaker asserts that he is "now" ready to "begin," at least once he finds the right "quiet place." Yet despite the immediacy of "now," forgetting never occurs in the poem.[4] It is instead one of several things—including the speaker's "questions" which "can wait" and "waiting" itself—that are deferred until later still.

Abstract concepts ("the forgetting," "the little delays," "the absence") recur in these lines, as does an insistence on deferral. Forgetting may in fact remain deferred because, as trauma theory might predict, it is so entangled with remembering. Certainly the speaker describes his present predicament in reference to his past way of being and thinking: while he recognizes that he has "changed," this change is "familiar," and even "waiting" for a *future* event confirms "the answer / I *was* looking for" (italics added). The speaker thus hesitates before, and may even be paralyzed by, the transition from an undefined past way of being to a similarly inchoate future. In this context, lateness, forgetting, and waiting (terms that here seem to some extent interchangeable) create a kind of bridge, offering the speaker a possible escape not only from the past but from linearity and chronology more generally.

By juxtaposing these terms, I do not mean to conflate them; nor will I attempt to define exactly how each functions in postwar poems. Rather, by discussing these differing but—as Lerner's poem demonstrates—connected tendencies, I hope to gesture (at times proleptically) beyond the confines of my earlier chapters and in the process to conclude them. As the poems I discuss here disavow the logic of remembering I have traced in these chapters, they illuminate related refusals. Similar acts of resistance have been evident throughout this book. To cite just two examples, Plath's "Amnesiac" directly celebrates the condition of forgetting, while Rich's "What Kind of Times Are These" insists on the impossibility of explaining past atrocities to contemporary uninterested listeners. In this coda, I return (again) to these and several poems discussed, considering in particular the connection between their assertions of liberation from the past and their invention of proleptic and often artificial or theatrical spaces. I also examine several other poems that systematically explore such tendencies and that attempt to provide an alternative to the (belated and redundant) need to keep retelling what has already been told.

Such spaces are in some ways liberating, they allow the speaker to take on other personae and voices, to harangue or be funny or ironic. Yet, paradoxically, these stage-like spaces also reveal the difficulty of escaping the logic of temporality insofar as they reveal, often poignantly, that the poem is a similarly framed and artificial space designed for just this kind of performance, one that, as I implied above, seems increasingly irrelevant in contemporary American society. I began this coda by suggesting that postwar poems often gesture forward in time, and I will end by considering the implications of proleptic and often indirect references to scenes of poetic receipt or reception. Such scenes clearly serve a function for the poet, but they also have implications for the reader, whose belated act of reading signals the movement of the poem's figurative performance outward into what is often called the "real world."

||||||||||||||||

Insofar as they are written for readers who postdate the time of writing, poems always look forward. More exactly, they proleptically create a future moment from which the past can be surveyed in ways that refer, at least indirectly, to processes of memory even as they reveal memory's artificiality. Anticipation and prolepsis recur in the poems I have discussed, and I have often considered these features as disruptions of linear chronology. But prolepsis signals more than the difficulty of remembering; it also gestures toward an actual, literally unknown and unknowable future. According to Judith Butler, this human capacity to construct a future moment from which to look back at one's life reveals the distinctively precarious nature of life itself.

> The future anterior, "a life has been lived," is presupposed at the beginning of a life that has only begun to be lived. In other words, "this will be a life that will have been lived" is the presupposition of a grievable life, which means that this will be a life that can be regarded as a life, and be sustained by that regard. (*Frames* 15)

The worth of human life is defined, Butler asserts, by our capacity, at life's "beginning," to anticipate its end, partly by understanding one life in the context of others that have already been lived and grieved. This distinctively human consciousness of the fragility of our own existence and that of others makes life "grievable": to live, that is, is to anticipate *future* grief and also to experience anticipatory grief at what will later occur. Determining that life has value thus requires detachment, even spectatorship; observing "an infant" who has "come . . . into the world," we anticipate its death by projecting ourselves forward into the position of its future grieving survivors (15).

Yet we are not in fact certain that we will survive to grieve that death, and so anticipating the newborn's death also impels us to anticipate our own.

Grief is thus the "presupposition" of grievability; we can anticipate future grief because we already know what grief is. In my earlier chapters, I made a related point: prolepsis in postwar poems is bound to loss, but it defers past losses by considering them from an often provisional future time. Grievability thus functions in a different way in the real-life situations described by Butler from in poems, where it defends against the history of grief even as it confirms grief's inescapability.

In several of the poems I examined in earlier chapters, prolepsis is a direct response to loss; depictions of future grievability displace and therefore help manage actual grief. This double impulse seems to explain the certainty expressed by the speaker of Rich's "In Those Years" (*Dark* 4) about a future moment when the present will rendered comprehensible. As I argued in chapter 2, the poem's speaker omnisciently describes a future moment when an undefined group of "people will say" currently unsayable things. This prolepsis lets her describe what exists now, an apparently present-day "los[s]" of the "meaning of *we*, of *you*" that, insofar as it will be remembered in the future, is probably the state of affairs now. In the process, the poem constructs a kind of viewing platform that permits access to events that seemingly cannot be spoken of in the ordinary present tense. The rhetoric of grievability thus lets the poet indirectly express her grief at current events, by looking forward and then back. This proleptic rhetoric also lets her warn her readers, also indirectly, to change their behavior before it is truly too late.

While Rich's use of the future tense allows her speaker to disguise grief as grievability, prolepsis in the excerpt from Bidart's "The Second Hour of the Night" (*Desire* 58), with which I began chapter 3, lets the poem's speaker avoid acknowledging grief at all. Instead of expressing grief for the dead addressee, the speaker presents a doubled scene of waiting—first for the addressee to appear and then, by implication, for his own lent-out body's subsequent "return." Waiting here occupies the speaker, displacing not only grief but the need to acknowledge a future moment of grievability. But we are also meant to understand that the friend's appearance is artificial and staged. In fact, this artificiality reveals the fragile and provisional quality of the speaker's impulse to disavow the grief that might otherwise overwhelm him.

In these poems, then, prolepsis displaces grief, but anticipation also affirms grief's inevitability and thus what Butler calls life's precarity. Other poems go further, refusing even the stability offered by a future moment from which the past or present can be surveyed and instead insisting on the uncertainty involved in waiting for what has not yet occurred. It is perhaps unsurprising that such acts are often depicted in ambivalent terms, reflecting a conundrum that has less to do with mortality (as prolepsis may) than with closure: to continue, the poem must keep deferring the endpoint that it also anxiously awaits.

Jorie Graham tends, as I indicated, to connect lateness with waiting. In "Act III, Sc. 2" (*Region* 66), which I discussed in both the introduction and chapter 4, she directly considers the relation between these elements, implying that lateness both creates and is antithetical to waiting. At first, the poem seems overwhelmed by lateness. The question "And is it // too late?" is answerable only through references to "*after*effects and whatnot recalled the morning *after*" (italics added). But later in the poem, this condition of aftermath becomes, crucially, a precondition for waiting, as in the poem's final description of its undefined addressee: "Then the you, whoever you are, peering down to see if it's done yet").[5] The speaker's scrutiny of the condition of waiting here deflects her attention from lateness by enabling her to put things off, even as she complains about having to do so. And waiting for the end itself seems an "aftereffect" of this poem's need to defer.

The detached tone of "Act III" resembles that of several of John Ashbery's poems, including "Soonest Mended," part of which I used as an epigraph for the introduction. Here, too, the poem insists on the inevitability of deferral by exploring both waiting and lateness through the eyes of a powerless protagonist. As in many of Ashbery's poems, "Soonest Mended" enacts an acute and awkward sense of belatedness. New events repeat earlier ones in ways that prevent change: "we were always having to be rescued / . . . . / Before it was time to start all over again"; the plural protagonists are "always coming back / To the mooring of starting out, that day so long ago." At the same time, though, time moves forward, threatening to leave the protagonists behind: "the summer's energy wanes quickly, / A moment and it is gone. And no longer / May we make the necessary arrangements."

Within this situation of belated powerlessness, Ashbery's protagonists await a future that is unlikely to differ much from what has already repeatedly occurred, although they retain hope that "Tomorrow would alter the sense of what had already been learned." In this context, as in Lerner's "Mean Free Path," which reprises a number of Ashbery's recurrent concerns, forgetting seems to offer the only viable escape. More specifically, "Angelica, in the Ingres painting" looks "as though" she is "wondering whether forgetting / The whole thing might not, in the end, be the only solution." As in "Act III," Angelica's thoughts concern "the end" yet defer its arrival. This ending involves forgetting, but Ashbery also emphasizes the limitations of forgetting as a solution by presenting it as highly provisional, what an imaginary character may be wondering about. In fact, as in "Mean Free Path," forgetting offers not an actual answer to the problems of belatedness and waiting but rather the fantasy of such an answer. Like Graham's "Act III," this poem takes place in a context in which the condition of belatedness has already made memory impossible, along with agency and forward progress.

|||||||||||||||

The condition of waiting in poems, I claimed above, evokes their status as poems; we are meant to understand this condition partly as an expression of the poet's wish to defer the poem's ending and thus his falling into silence. Certainly both Graham and Ashbery link waiting to performance. Graham's speaker is, as the poem's title indicates, watching a theatrical production in which she may also be a participant. In "Soonest Mended," Angelica's thoughts are in fact the speakers', projected onto a painted image. Elsewhere in the poem, references to theater and invention are more direct: Ashbery's speakers ask whether they are "acting this out / For someone else's benefit," then assert their "shock" at understanding "for the first time" that others "were the players, and we . . . / Were merely spectators." Such scenes of performance reveal the contingency of the position both poems establish between a past that cannot be recovered and a future defined by ending. In the process, both draw attention to their artifice as poems.

A more sustained exploration of such issues is central to James Merrill's "Farewell Performance" (*Collected* 581–82) Here, as I indicated in chapter 3, the title punningly conflates the final performance of a dance troupe witnessed by the poem's speaker with the dance-like "last jeté on / ghostly—wait, ah!—point" performed by the ashes of the dead addressee as they are released into the sea. These two acts of leave-taking or "farewell" blur recollection and deferral; like Bidart's "The Second Hour," the poem pretends to anticipate what has already occurred. These two performances are also asynchronous: the dance performance postdates the addressee's death ("How you would have loved it," the speaker affirms), but the addressee seems to remain alive during and even after the dance performance, having "caught like a cold [the dancers'] airy / lust for essence."

These contradictions expose the third sense of the poem's title; the poem is itself a farewell performance, a virtuoso, belated linguistic attempt both to delay a now-past moment of vanishing and proleptically to anticipate the poet's similar vanishing, as well as ours. That Merrill was HIV-positive when he wrote the poem only makes the poem's attempt at denying this future more personal: in mourning Kalstone's death from AIDS, he is anticipating his own. At the end of the poem, the audience keeps summoning the dancers back onstage in an attempt to defer the inevitable final leave-taking. Yet Merrill also makes it clear that both the dancers and the audience are aware of the future moment in which they too will "join the troupe" of the dead. The implication is that because all of us will die, we are complicit in the poem's acts of denial. We can all, that is, see forward to our own death, although we may try not to; the moment of grievability is here both ensured by and superimposed over the poem's explicit acts of grieving. Merrill enables this connection by evoking the constructed and artificial space of a performance hall, which itself (belatedly) reveals a way to read the moments of theatricalization I have noted in previous chapters. That is, the artificial space of the poem itself allows the poet to consider the poem's effect, not only now but later. Merrill associates the vulnerability of the theatrical space—its confinement and artifice—with both loss and recuperation, which here coexist, affirming not only grief but precarity, which, as Butler claims, makes our life valuable.

To write, Maurice Blanchot has argued in terms that recall Butler's description of the future anterior, is "to know that death has taken place even though it has not been experienced," a knowledge that Blanchot claims contains "the forgetfulness that [death] leaves" (66). "Farewell Performance" does not refer directly to forgetting, but it depicts, as elegy always does, a death that "has not been experienced" firsthand by the poet. All poems according to this logic are farewell performances. Their proliferating words and figures pretend to defer what has already occurred even as they affirm that "it's over" or will be soon.

||||||||||||||||

Because both Lerner and Ashbery project forgetting into the future, they never need to explain exactly what it involves. But Robert Pinsky's 2007 "The Forgetting" (*Gulf* 14–15), published in the same volume as "The Anniversary," which I discussed in the introduction, describes an immediate and ongoing process of forgetting linked to an actual public performance of poetry. Poetic performances, and by implication poems themselves, Pinsky insists, are distinct from actual or literal past events and thus cannot represent them. On the contrary, such performances enable the forgetting of these events. But rather than lamenting this situation, the speaker celebrates it, perhaps because he recognizes that as a poet he too participates in this process of obliteration.

Lerner and Ashbery juxtapose forgetting with remembering, but Pinsky lays out the connection directly. The poem begins by asserting that "The forgetting I notice most as I get older is really a form of memory." Forgetting here affirms chronology (the inevitable process of "get[ting] older" over time); it is "a form of memory" because it evokes earlier "forgettings." Forgetting, the speaker implies, is an effect of the excessive number of things that need to be remembered. But this situation does not impel the speaker toward nostalgia. Instead, he anticipates a future time of comeuppance for the currently oblivious young: "You'll see, you little young jerks: your favorite music and your political / Furors, too, will need to get sorted in dusty electronic corridors."

This proleptic assertion, like Rich's in "In Those Years," is expressed with certainty, but this confidence is belied later in the poem when the speaker first anticipates, then, in the last lines of the poem, describes a reading of an "anti-Semitic" poem. (The poem is probably Amiri Baraka's controversial "Somebody Blew Up America," read by Baraka at the 2002 Dodge Poetry Festival, in which Pinsky also participated.[6]) Pinsky's focus is not on the poem's accuracy or inaccuracy at conveying the motivations behind the 9/11 attacks. Instead, "The Forgetting" considers the performed poem's reception, in the process diverging from at least one account of the actual reading:[7]

> The crowd was applauding and screaming, they were happy—it isn't
> That they were anti-Semitic, or anything. They just weren't listening. Or
>
> No, they were listening, but that certain way. In it comes, you hear it and
> That selfsame second you swallow it or expel it: an ecstasy of
> forgetting.

Whereas Graham's "Act III" and Merrill's "Farewell Performance" depict their speakers as audience members, Pinsky's speaker separates himself from "the crowd" he describes even as (like the speaker of "Act III") he generalizes this crowd's reaction by using "you." His correction of his initial claim that "they just weren't listening" reveals his capacity for reflection, a response that further distinguishes him from the members of the audience, who "swallow . . . or expel" the poem the "selfsame second" that they "hear it."

In contrast to "The Anniversary," which emphasizes the difficulty of understanding the attacks and their aftermath, in "The Forgetting" the 9/11 attacks have no existence outside the poem about them. Nor does Pinsky condemn the audience's forgetting; instead, he depicts it as "an ecstasy" that offers an alternative to the need to remember or possibly, as in his first line, an alternative "form of memory." Forgetting here is not, as it seems to be earlier in the poem, merely an ordinary effect of aging. Instead, it is engendered by the public, collective, and also anonymous experience of receiving art.

In fact, Pinsky likely witnessed Baraka's performance before or after reading his own poems at the same festival. Although he does not refer to this situation, "The Forgetting," like "Farewell Performance" and perhaps all poems, is clearly a performance. Certainly it raises questions about its speaker; we must determine whether his celebration of forgetting is meant to be read straightforwardly, ironically, or in some other way.[8] Moreover, the poem presents a doubled and, to recall the term I used in chapter 2, asymmetrical scene of performance; the poet onstage performs before a crowd whose oblivious members may or may not be the "young jerks" the speaker earlier addresses.

As with the reader address in Rich's poems, this doubled scene of performance and reception implies a third, also asymmetrical scene in which "The Forgetting" is received by us, Pinsky's actual readers. Such a scene is only indirectly evident, in a way that recalls Merrill's implication that "Farewell Performance" is both an elegy and an anticipatory self-elegy, both a description of a performance and a performance itself. Such scenes are in both cases indirectly and proleptically conveyed, a situation that may explain the instabilities of tone in "The Forgetting"; Pinsky, like Rich in "In Those Years," clearly wishes for us to respond to his poem differently from the audience *in* the poem. Yet the logic of Pinsky's poem makes such a response unlikely, and in any case, he reveals the utility of failed memory by arguing that amnesia can become, through the mediation of art, a mode of "ecstasy."

||||||||||||||||

"The Forgetting" embraces a collective mode of response seemingly at odds with its status as a lyric poem. As such, it raises questions I have been considering throughout this book about both aesthetics and ethics. Pinsky here implicitly asks whether poems should facilitate forgetting or attempt to record and memorialize past events. Is their capacity to elicit "ecsta[tic]" reactions in their readers more important than the truth or accuracy of their claims? What ethical and political obligations, if any, do poems have? For and to whom should they speak? And what obligations, if any, do readers have toward the poems they read?

In essence, all these questions concern whether poems can convey real-life events, as well as whether they should. Similar questions are also central to Butler's argument about precarity and grievability. Butler makes it clear that her claims are political; she notes that some lives (for example, those of Israeli troops killed in the 2008–2009 attack on Gaza) are defined as more grievable and thus more valuable than others (for example, those of the local women and children who were also killed) (*Frames* xx–xxv). The capacity to recognize that all lives, rather than simply some, are precarious constitutes, Butler claims, a necessary component of "living socially"; this mode of living requires that we recognize our "obligations toward others, most of whom we cannot name and do not know." Furthermore, the capacity to speak collectively, using "we," even if that term is "riven from the start, interrupted by alterity" (14), offers one way to move toward and acknowledge these obligations.

Butler has elsewhere more directly considered the ways that "the structure of address" implies an "obligation" to "respond" (*Precarious* 129), and she is clearly interested in scenes of reception and audience.[9] Scenes of address, hearing, and mishearing recur in "The Forgetting," as well as in other poems I have considered in this coda and throughout this book. Such scenes for Pinsky seem to involve misunderstanding and hostility, but they also affirm our connection to one another and may in fact raise questions about our "obligation" to "respond" to experiences like the reading of Baraka's poem. As Butler implies, even though we may distance ourselves from the addressees of the poems we read, we are at least partly implicated in their acts of address. "The Forgetting" affirms multiple modes of contact—between speaker and young jerks, between poet and audience, and among the strangers who compose the audience. Such scenes mitigate Pinsky's defensive tone in the poem, which we recognize partly as a distancing strategy. His anger, that is, deflects the possibility of grief at, for example, the actual deaths that resulted from the 9/11 attacks. Yet the poem's scene of poetic reception is also proleptic; as Merrill's performance of grief indirectly evokes the possibility that others will grieve at his own death, Pinsky here evokes a scene he can only anticipate, the future moment when "The Forgetting" is itself read and judged by its actual readers. But because our response can occur only after the poem's composition, we are compelled neither to respond identically to nor differently from the enthralled, uncritical audience within the poem. In fact, no matter how we respond, our response exceeds the poet's capacity to predict it. This situation, one shared by all poems, puts our response under "pressure," to recall Jacqueline Rose's description of the influence of "linguistic figuration" on the Holocaust (207). Pinsky's poem thus implicitly asks whether it is possible to respond to poems with a consciousness of what Butler calls our "obligations toward others." To do so seems to require not only our affirmation of the truth of what occurred— or perhaps the impossibility of extracting a single truth from "real" events— but also poetry's value, which lies partly in its capacity to ask just these questions.

Asking and attempting to answer such questions involves multiple risks. The poetics of belatedness in particular seems often to lead to repetitiveness, inconsistency, stridency, solipsism, or an embrace of incoherence for its own sake. All the poets I have considered in this book reveal some of these tendencies, and all have been faulted for at least one of them. Yet despite or because of these aesthetic problems, these poems reveal that belatedness is also hopeful. Like all poems, these become relevant only when, after the events they convey and the time of their publication, they are read. And so they keep speaking to us, if only to convince themselves proleptically, as Rich claims, that we are "still listen[ing]" (*Dark* 3). Repeating and overlaying scenes of performance and address, these poems also reach beyond their frames toward those about whom they may feel most suspicious. This act of approach is essential, as Butler affirms, to an ethical life. We may, and indeed perhaps must, sometimes feel skeptical about or critical of these poems or tired of their ambivalence toward the past, present, and future. Yet we are also belatedly and repeatedly invited, partly by means of their hostility and stridency, not only to judge but also to receive them.

Notes

Introduction

1. Bahti notes "the difficulty of distinguishing and relating these . . . terms [*trope, figure,* and *scheme*], or of giving a principled definition of any one of them." Trope is generally seen, in Bahti's terms, as "a delimited form of the more expansively conceived f[igure]," focusing on "the meanings of words" rather than "changes in the words and meanings of larger units of discourse." Both *trope* and *figure* refer to "nonliteral, altered, or improper uses of lang[uage]'s words and meanings."

2. For example, in a discussion of AIDS rhetoric, Lee Edelman asserts that a "defensive appeal to literality" can instead "produce the literal *as a figure*" (313). I will return to this idea in chapter 3.

3. Here I am building on the critical tendency to see metonymy in terms of an adherence to "the literal plane," so that the projection of "emotion and perception" onto this "outer reality" leads to a "displace[ment]" (Martin, "Metonymy"). By depicting a part of what is in fact whole, synecdoche arguably offers a still more fragmented version of a preexisting literal reality.

4. Berger's focus is on the ways what he calls "a secular apocalyptic moment" can "defin[e] the horizon . . . of contemporary culture" ("There's No" 52).

5. I am referring to splits between the "raw" and the "cooked" and between the straightforward and the highly crafted that are often ascribed to postwar poetry. Another, partly overlapping distinction is that between the experiential, autobiographical, or "confessional" on the one hand and the "experimental" on the other. This latter mode is often linked to Language poetry and tends to be defined in terms of its concerns with destabilizing the lyric subject and challenging claims to authenticity and lived experience.

6. De Man's focus is on the ways that literary texts are concerned with and elaborate their own figurativeness, although Neil Hertz has convincingly linked de Man's discussions of linguistic figuration with actual scenes of disfigurement, dismemberment, mutilation, and violence ("Lurid" and "More Lurid").

7. Bloom asserts that the process of becoming a "strong poet" requires that "the

poet-reader begin . . . with a trope or defense that *is* a misreading. . . . A poet inter-preting his precursor . . . must *falsify* by his reading" (*Map* 69). These views have been much contested, especially by feminist readers, who point out that this model privileges the competition between male poets and their poetic forefathers while ignoring the possibility of a different model based on maternal relations.

8. Spargo derives ethics in poetry from the perception by "anti-elegiac mourn-ers" of "a lateness that comes after grief," which leads to "a point where they no longer trust themselves to grieve as others have" (*Ethics* 135). "Literary mourners confess their anti-elegiac resentment as they profess their belatedness" (136). In a brief discussion of the role of witness, Kalaidjian cites Judith Butler's claim that "newness . . . has within it a sense of belatedness, of coming after, and of being thus fundamentally determined by a past that continues to inform it" (qtd. on 11). He also acknowledges the importance of belatedness in several poems, including those of Rachel Blau DuPlessis (88–96 passim).

9. Kalaidjian refers to "what Freud defined as deferred action (*nachträglichkeit*)" (9). Rose associates "'*Nachtraglichkeit*' [*sic*] or after-effect" with several lines in Plath's "Daddy," arguing that they assert "a wholly other order of time" in which "narrative [becomes] repetition" (224).

10. Cameron argues that poets seek to "shelter themselves" (24) from such anxieties through a range of strategies, including a "recoil from temporality," an embrace of "the trespass of proleptic utterances," and an exploration of "the grief of the . . . relationship between language, temporality, and loss" (24). For explicit lyric avowals of lateness, see the "no more" of John Milton's "Lycidas," the "never-more" of Edgar Allen Poe's "The Raven," and the archetypally modern sense of being "neither living nor dead" in T. S. Eliot's *The Waste Land*.

11. While lyric is famously difficult to define, it is generally seen as both non-narrative and nondramatic, a tendency that goes back to the Greek term "*mele*," which described works "intended to be sung to musical accompaniment" (John-son). Helen Vendler has claimed that lyric "depends on gaps," which "the reader" must "fill in" (*Poems*, xliii).

12. Hardy's poems, in very general terms, often emphasize scenes in which characters from the past (in particular a figure associated with Hardy's dead wife) return to haunt the present-day speaker, while Eliot's *The Waste Land* depicts a past broken into sometimes spectral "fragments" (as when the protagonist glimpses the dead crossing London Bridge) that cannot be reassembled into a coherent whole.

13. For general discussions of the reliance of postwar poetry on modernist poetry, see, for example, Longenbach, *Modern Poetry*; Perloff, *21st-Century*; and Keller, *Re-Making*.

14. Modernism's formal innovations, that is, have often been read as expressions

of the impossibility of devising an accurate history of already-fragmented events, especially those related to World War I. Jameson, it is important to note, also resists the idea of periodization (4–5).

15. Jameson, for example, defines postmodernism in terms of a more radical "breakdown of temporality" that "releases th[e] present of time" (27) in ways that effectively annihilate even fractured traces of the past as past (xiii), replacing it with "spatial logic" (25). Such a shift is mostly evident through what he repeatedly calls a "waning of affect" (11, 15, 16) that marks the replacement of the modern "alienation of the subject" with a postmodern "fragmentation" (14). Yet Jameson also associates postmodernism with "a well-nigh Freudian *Nachträglichkeit*, or retroactivity" (xix).

16. While the influential two-volume *Norton Anthology of Modern and Contemporary Poetry* does not use these terms, it distinguishes "modern" from "contemporary" using the year 1945 (Ramazani et al.).

17. For example, Jean Baudrillard defines the fourth and final of his "phases of the image" as one that "bears no relation to any reality whatever: it is its own pure simulacrum" (*Selected* 173).

18. The term has been belatedly applied to the Turkish massacre of the Armenians in the 1910s and, more recently, to events in Rwanda and Darfur, among others.

19. Such questions often have explicitly political repercussions. For example, should the U.S. make reparations for its killing of Native Americans? Was the phrase *War on Terror* intended to conceal what was in fact a preemptive war against anyone the U.S. government designated an enemy? If recent events in Darfur or Syria constituted genocide, what actions were therefore required by developed nations?

20. In reference to an assertion by Theodor Adorno beginning with the phrase "After Auschwitz" (qtd. on 87), Lyotard claims "Adorno counts time (but which time?) from 'Auschwitz.' Is this name the name of a chronological origin? What era begins with this event?" (88).

21. Young explores in detail the Jewish tradition of reading events "archetypally and figuratively" (95) as well as the Nazi equation of Jews with vermin, which Young claims undermined "the distinction between figurative and literal language" in a way that allowed a "literalization of metaphor . . . [that] may have destroyed the possibility of innocent figuration thereafter" (93).

22. See Huyssen for a detailed discussion of the "memory boom," which he claims began in about 1960 (16–21 passim).

23. Elie Wiesel is best known for his repeated insistence on the danger of forgetting the Holocaust: "If we forget, we are guilty, we are accomplices. . . . Salvation,

like redemption, can be found only in memory" (118). James Young has discussed the paradox by which the Holocaust's uniqueness can only be understood in relation to "other calamities," including the earlier Armenian Genocide; to represent the Holocaust is thus always to "grasp [this event] in relation to other events; even in their unlikeness, they are thus contextualized and understood in opposition to prevailing figures, but thus figured nonetheless" (*Writing* 88).

24. Blanchot's claim is that "When . . . disaster comes upon us, it does not come. The disaster is its imminence, but . . . there is no future for the disaster, just as there is no time or space for its accomplishment" (1–2).

25. Trauma theory arose in response to the increase in discussion and formal study of the Holocaust in the 1980s as well as to the 1980 recognition of the term "post-traumatic stress disorder" by the American Psychiatric Association (Caruth, Introduction 3) In Cathy Caruth's terms, traumatic experience undermines literal ways of seeing: "repetitions" of traumatic events create a "relation to the [traumatic] event that *extends beyond what can simply be seen or what can be known*" (*Unclaimed* 92, italics added). These repetitions are "inextricably tied up with . . . belatedness and incomprehensibility" (92).

26. Lacan's term was *après coup*; see Evans 209.

27. LaCapra makes a similar claim: "especially for victims, trauma brings about a lapse or rupture in memory that breaks continuity with the past. . . . The traumatic event is repressed or denied and registers only belatedly (*nachträglich*) after the passage of a period of latency" (9).

28. However, Caruth specifies that it is not possible definitively to pin down the relation of the instigating event to the response: "the pathology cannot be defined . . . by the event itself . . . [;] nor can it be defined in terms of a *distortion* of the event. . . .The pathology consists, rather, solely in the *structure of its experience or reception*" (Introduction 4).

29. Such debates extend back to Freud's still-controversial abandonment of the seduction theory: Freud repudiated his earlier notion that hysterics had suffered abuse in favor of the idea that this abuse was a fantasy. More recently Dori Laub has asserted that factual errors in the memories of Auschwitz survivors are less important than "the fact of the occurrence" (Felman and Laub 60).

30. Kalaidjian, for example, asserts that "poetry . . . provides a formal medium for giving testimony to trauma across the generations" (9). Harriet Davidson has argued that "the literature of testimony . . . is central to much contemporary poetry, which presents a self wishing to express a seemingly unspeakable situation, and through an intersubjective contract, make it speakable, real, and political (166).

31. Young claims that because the members of this generation "remember not actual events but the countless histories, novels, and poems of the Holocaust they

have read, the photographs, movies, and video testimonies they have seen over the years," they do not "attempt to represent events [they] never knew" (1).

32. This cultural marginality has been evident in many contexts, including the mid-2000s controversy following the Poetry Foundation's decision to focus its funds on obtaining a larger readership for poetry (see Goodyear). It has also recurred in academic discussions of poetry. For example, several of the contributors to a 2008 special segment of *PMLA* devoted to poetry (including Virginia Jackson and Jonathan Culler) began by claiming that poetry risked irrelevance in contemporary American culture.

33. For a more extended discussion of the relevance of Lowell's phrase to twenty-first-century poetry, see Keniston and Gray.

34. Brogan's focus is on the ways "ghosts in contemporary American ethnic literature . . . recreate ethnic identity through an imaginative recuperation of the past" (4).

35. In modernist poems, ghosts often signal the speaker's lack of control and the uncanny and threatening inability of the dead to stay dead. For example, the grotesque corpse "planted last year in your garden" that threatens to "sprout" and "bloom" in part 1 of T. S. Eliot's *The Waste Land* is terrifying to the speaker, who has not invited it; its liminal status also reverberates against an earlier speaker's sensation of being "neither / Living nor dead."

36. Insofar as the poet herself is the creator of the ghosts in poems, their presence reveals a more radical temporal disjunction, which resembles what Bloom has called *apophrades* or "the return of the dead," a situation in which "it seem[s]. . . as though the later poet himself had written the precursor's characteristic work" (*Anxiety* 16). Although Bloom's focus on a wholly literary belatedness is quite different from what I am describing, Bloom too insists on a radical defiance of chronology. Postwar poetic ghosts also recall what Susan Stewart has called lyric possession, the also artificial analogy between haunting, poetic inspiration, and possession by the muse ("Lyric" 115–16).

37. Slavoj Žižek, for example, has asserted that comparing the attacks to the Holocaust is a "blasphemy" (136), implying that such an analogy has in fact been proposed.

38. See, for example, Jean Baudrillard's claim that "we dreamt of this event" (*Spirit* 5), representing it before it occurred through "countless disaster movies" (7). Such a claim undermines the attacks' uniqueness and even their "real[ity]"; rather, they revealed that "reality is everywhere infiltrated by images, virtuality and fiction" (27–28).

39. For a more detailed discussion of belatedness in this and other post-9/11 American poems, see my "Not Needed."

40. The poem was originally published in the *Washington Post*. A revised version published in *Best American Poetry 2003* (ed. Yusef Komunyakaa) was entitled "Anniversary," and the final version, entitled "The Anniversary," was published in Pinsky's 2007 collection *Gulf Music*.

41. Pinsky in an earlier essay associated "the great work of memory itself" with being human and claimed that "deciding to remember, and what to remember, is how we decide who we are." He further claims that "the alleged absence of memory is an illusion; cultural artifacts, high or low, successful or failed, shining or dismal, draw on recollection" ("Poetry").

42. The poem also specifies that Will Rogers was "a Cherokee" and so devises a single lineage from individuals of different ethnic origins.

43. This sense of omission and replacement is clearest in the passage about the firefighters' act of self-marking, which in some ways recalls the identification numbers tattooed on the arms of concentration camp victims by the Nazis before they were killed, although Pinsky does not make this analogy explicit.

44. Bidart's note is ambiguous: it does not specify whether the poem addresses those who performed the attacks, who died, or those who planned them, who survived. Related ambiguities are for David Simpson fundamental to the rhetoric of revenge, which always involves the substitution of "those now being punished" for "the original aggressors" (4).

45. For example, the line following the passage I cited above, "May what you have made descend upon you," compresses and reiterates rather than develops earlier lines.

46. In J. L. Austin's terms, "to utter the sentence . . . is to do" what it describes (6).

47. In this way, the poem resembles Bidart's earlier dramatic monologs, including "The War of Vaslav Nijinsky" (*In the Western* 21–49), "Ellen West" (109–21), and "Herbert White" (127–31).

48. I am thinking in particular of Thomas Gardner's *Regions of Unlikeness*, a study of the ways a range of contemporary poets consider "the limits of language" (1) and "the limits of knowledge" (4).

49. Among the features that critics have associated with what some have called the rise of the "post-postmodern" in the twenty-first century are "intensification" (Nealon 40), "remixed hybridity" (Irvine), and "authenticity" (Docx).

Chapter One

1. Throughout this chapter, references to Plath's poems are to *Ariel: The Restored Edition* (*Ariel Restored*) unless otherwise indicated. Among the earlier readers who have dealt with this topic are Irving Howe, George Steiner, Jahan Ramazani (*Poetry*), Jacqueline Rose, James Young (*Writing*), Susan Gubar, and Al Strangeways.

2. Rose comments extensively on readings that "treat [Plath's] texts as the person" (4) in the context of a more general argument that Plath "haunts and is haunted by the culture" (8). Several other critics have noted the ways that criticism on Plath and debates within that criticism replicate and exaggerate features of Plath's writing.

3. Rose, for example, notes that Plath's claim that she has killed an already dead Daddy in "Daddy" locates the poem in "the time of 'Nachtraglichkeit' [sic] or after-effect" and locates this moment in a larger pattern in which "narrative" is represented "as repetition" (224).

4. Throughout this chapter, I am relying on the dates of composition provided by editor Ted Hughes in Plath's *The Collected Poems*.

5. An especially vivid example is Sandra Gilbert's essay "'A Fine, White Flying Myth': Confessions of a Plath Addict," in which she describes Plath's posthumously published poems as having "their heads in ovens" (587).

6. As is well known, Plath and Ted Hughes were separated during the months before her death.

7. A list of the contents of Plath's *Ariel* was first made public in the notes section of Hughes's 1981 edition of *The Collected Poems* (295); Marjorie Perloff (in "The Two Ariels") was the first to identify the importance of Plath's ordering of the volume.

8. The foreword argues that the Plath's version of *Ariel* is neither definitive nor particularly authentic; rather, it is, Hughes claims, marred by its bond to Plath's life in that the volume reveals its author "caught" in a particular "moment" (*Ariel Restored* xxi), that of "revenge" (xx) against Ted Hughes.

9. The foreword includes in the space of twelve pages a wide range of approaches and perspectives, including the following: objective biographical information (xi–xii passim); analysis of Plath's style (xii) and process (xiii; "the *Ariel* voice . . . had been waiting, practicing itself, and had found a subject on which it could really get a grip" [xiv]; another poem, despite its apparently recent subject matter, "is also tangled with the grievous loss of [Plath's] father" [xv]); Frieda Hughes's opinions about the poems (xv) and her "imagin[ings]" of why her mother wrote certain things (xv); omniscient accounts of Ted Hughes's feelings and wishes (xv–xvi) as well as his "profound respect for [her] mother's work" (xvii); discussion of what the original *Ariel* "symboli[zed]" for Frieda ("it was as if the clay from her poetic energy was taken up and versions of my mother made out of it, invented to reflect only the inventors" [xvii]); excoriations of the "cruel" and inaccurate things written about the "quiet . . . and loving . . ." Ted (xvii) and affirmations of Ted's posthumous dedication to Plath (xviii); and Frieda Hughes's opinions about how to memorialize Plath (xviii–xix).

10. Among the only critical discussions of *Ariel: The Restored Edition* is Tracy

Brain's, which focuses on the textual indeterminacies that remain in this edition, especially in relation to the manuscripts of the poems.

11. Art Spiegelman's graphic novels *Maus I* and *II* are perhaps the works that have been most fully integrated into and praised by readers of Holocaust writing; the depiction of the Jews as mice and the Nazis as cats is seen as a masterful and distinctively postmodern way of depicting the dynamics of the Holocaust itself while ironically alluding to Nazi propaganda equating Jews with vermin. The controversy surrounding Binjamin Wilkomirski's fictitious Holocaust memoir *Fragments: Memories of a Wartime Childhood* has similarly enabled readings that interrogate the notion of facticity in Holocaust accounts of the Holocaust.

12. These readers include Irving Howe, George Steiner, and Seamus Heaney.

13. Among influential feminist readings is that of Sandra Gilbert and Susan Gubar; more recent political readings include those of Robin Peel and Deborah Nelson.

14. Young claims that Plath's representation is characterized by "metaphors" but ones that break down the distinction between the public and the private in ways that reveal the "reciprocal exchange between private and historical realms" and that expose the "atrocity" that already informs "a public pool of language" (121–2).

15. These claims are elaborated in Butler's 1990 *Gender Trouble*. Van Dyne views "Lady Lazarus" as a "highly theatricalized performance of the feminine victim" (5), an argument elaborated by Christina Britzolakis and, more recently, Matthew Boswell.

16. Rose's interest is generally in "the way fantasy operates inside historical processes" (7). In this context, she claims that "Plath is a fantasy," a notion she sees being enacted in both "Plath's writing, and responses to her writing" (5).

17. Boswell goes on to bind Plath's postmodernism to "a more modernistic (even pre-modernistic) understanding of events," identifying Plath in this way as "on the cusp" of a new way of understanding Nazism (58).

18. These passages are generally read as expressing Plath's views about the relation of the public to the private.

19. Young asserts that by equating Jews with vermin who had to be exterminated, the Nazis removed metaphor from "innocen[ce]" (*Writing* 93).

20. This situation echoes the belated awareness of the Holocaust in postwar culture more generally. The term "Holocaust" in relation to the German atrocities became prevalent only in the late 1950s ("What Is the Origin") and interest in this event was fostered by Eichmann's trial.

21. The first, holograph draft of the poem described Daddy as possessing a "Hitler moustache" and referred to "my Nazi" and, a few lines later, "a . . . Nazi look." ("Daddy").

22. In a passage excerpted from the introduction to *The Collected Poems*, Ted

Hughes notes Plath's refusal to "scrap . . . any of her poetic efforts" and her capacity to bring "every *piece* she worked on to some final form acceptable to her" (italics added). An excerpt from Frieda Hughes's foreword to *Ariel: The Restored Edition* notes Plath's ability to "use . . . every emotional experience as if were a scrap of material that could be *pieced* together to make a wonderful dress; she wasted nothing of what she felt" (xix–xx, italics added).

23. According to Anne Stevenson's biography, Plath "read 'Daddy' aloud in a spooky, comical voice" to Clarissa Roche (277).

24. Plath underlined the following definitions of "charge" in her dictionary: "5. An <u>accusation of a wrong</u> or offence; allegation. . . . 7. <u>A person or thing entrusted to</u> the care of another. 8. <u>Pecuniary burden; expense</u>." Other pertinent definitions in the dictionary include "3. A duty or task laid upon a person; responsibility; obligation. 4. An order; a command. . . . 9. The price demanded for a thing or service" (*Webster's*).

25. Plath's first draft contains still more shifts in address; the holograph of the poem includes an address to a particular "lady" along with "yessir, yessir" ("Lady Lazarus").

26. Frederick Buell, for example, argues that the striptease scene "allow[s] the reader less room to distance himself from identification with the mob, those who search confessional poetry for the 'word or a touch / Or a bit of blood'" (150–1); Howe more forthrightly claims that here the "writer speaks *to* the reader (12, italics in original).

27. For a useful discussion of Plath's prosopopoeia as an attempt to "reanimate[e] . . . the dead," see Gubar, "Prosopopoeia" (192).

28. Gosmann argues that Plath's poems, especially in *The Colossus,* reveal that "personal" memory is always involved with "collective memory": "Plath practices poetic memory by revealing the pervasive influences of collective memory and by finding methods to subvert it" (48).

29. The poem's speaker is involved in an attempt to "get across" Russia as part of "some war or other" in a scene filled with wounded men, severed limbs, and unending cries that fracture "the men" into pieces ("what is left of the men").

30. The speaker describes the poppies, which are still blooming in autumn, as "late."

31. In the *Restored Ariel*, the poems "The Detective" (31), "Fever 103°" (78), and "The Bee Meeting" (82) refer to smoke; "Purdah" (63), "The Moon and the Yew Tree"(65), "A Birthday Present" (66), "The Bee Meeting" (81)," and "The Arrival of the Bee Box" (85) refer to veils; and "Morning Song" (5), "The Couriers" (6), "The Courage of Shutting Up" (46), "Purdah" (62), and "A Birthday Present" (67) refer to mirrors.

32. Poems like "A Birthday Present" (66–68) and "The Rival" (73) contain references to ordinary events but refuse to clarify their situation; in others, including "The Couriers" (6), the context or lived situation is omitted entirely. These opaque poems reveal Plath's interest in the effects of such excisions.

33. In the latter poem, the "shut mouth" is "pink," but contains a "tongue" that is "dangerous."

34. This poem was added to Plath's typed contents list but crossed out by her and published only in the American version of Hughes's *Ariel*.

35. See, for example, Perloff's "Two *Ariels*."

36. The amnesiac replaces an untouchable "sister" with one whom he apparently will not resist and imagines their "travel[s]."

37. "Getting There" (*Ariel Restored* 57–59), for example, ends with its speaker "stepping from this skin / Of old bandages, boredoms, old faces // . . . from the black car of Lethe, / Pure as a baby." The word "sweet" recurs in several of the bee poems (85, 86, 87); "Ariel" (33–34) claims, "White / Godiva, I unpeel—."

Chapter Two

1. Steiner asks in the context of a discussion of Plath's late poems whether such a "larceny" more generally is the result of evoking "the echoes and trappings of Auschwitz . . . [for one's] own private design?" (301).

2. According to Michael Bernard-Donals, "testimony is always . . . cast forward" (Review 342); it requires "a secondhand witness" (the one receiving the testimony) distinct from the survivor (341). Froma Zeitlin argues that testimony is often "vicarious" as well as belated; for example, the testimony of survivors' children "reflects an inevitable awareness of their own belatedness," which leads these non-survivors to "become . . . witness[es] to what they did not see at first hand" (6). Dominick LaCapra distinguishes "primary memory" or "that of a person who has lived through events" (20) from "secondary memory," which may be expressed by the survivor but "more typically, by an analyst, observer, or secondary witness such as the historian" (21). Michael Levine's focus is on the belatedness inherent in "the role played by the listener, interviewer, or reader in the testimonial act" (7). In this "supplementary witness" (7), the listener takes "co-responsibility" for the testimony (9).

3. Bernard-Donals and Richard Glezjer define witness as "seeing an event" and testimony as "telling the event"; these two acts are "radically incommensurable" (xv).

4. Forché defines *aftermath* as "a temporal debris field, where historical remains are strewn" and "where that-which-has-happened remains present" ("Reading").

5. Forché also asserts that "the saying of the witness . . . is not a translation of

experience into poetry but is itself experience. . . ." In an interview published at the same time as these comments, Forché responds tentatively to a question about the importance of personal experience in poetry about adversity, saying that "great poetry might in part depend on engagement with the extremity of existence" ("Lost"). She adds that while such experience characterized the poems in *Against Forgetting*, "not all experience is of this kind."

6. Harriet Davidson has recently claimed that the poetry of witness "combines a sense of historical and personal urgency (about more than yourself but about yourself) with a performative mode" (166).

7. Several readers have identified Rich's poetic project with the poetry of witness. Cynthia Hogue argues that Rich's poems "transport the reader into the testimonial position from which the poem speaks" (413–14), creating for the reader "an active, indeed ecstatic, identification with otherness" (422), while Jane Hedley claims that for Rich, the poet's "power . . . in the world . . . includes the prerogative of bearing witness for others" (49). Kendall Smith associates Rich's poems with a "postmodern poetics of witness."

Rich has indicated her concern with the question of "how to bear witness to a reality from which the public—and maybe part of the poet—wants to turn away" (*What* 115) and has sympathetically defined the poetry of witness as "poetry of dissent, poetry that is the voice of those and on behalf of those who are generally unheard" (Rothschild).

8. Rich made this statement in response to an interviewer's comment that "you almost seem to ask yourself whether writing poetry of witness is adequate to the task at hand, or even a good use of your time" (Rothschild).

9. The addressee in Rich's poems may be singular or plural, male or female, specific or general; the "you" may be a character in the poem, the reader, or an aspect of the poet's self.

10. The poem ends with an image of "A mirror handed to one . . . just released / from the locked ward from solitary from preventive detention" who "sees in her hair . . . / whole populations." In contrast, a recently discharged war veteran stares into "the looking-glass of home" at "his own eye."

11. Late in the poem, the speaker proffers a hypothetical "ethical flower . . ." to the comrade "with love."

12. Celan claims that "a poem, as a manifestation of language and thus essentially dialogue, can be a message in a bottle, sent out in the—not always greatly hopeful—belief that it may somewhere and sometime wash up on land . . . perhaps" (qtd. in Levine 3).

13. Rich was not a Holocaust survivor; the daughter of a gentile mother and an assimilated Jewish father, she was, like Plath, an American child during the

Holocaust. Unlike Celan, who was a survivor, and Plath, who was not, Rich meticulously refuses to write in *Dark Fields* from the position of a Holocaust survivor or a survivor of any kind.

14. Jane Hedley claims that Rich's poems "engage . . . with the politics of the personal pronouns 'I,' 'we,' and 'you'" (15), as well as "the 'difficulty of saying "we"'" (146). Hedley refers to poems written throughout Rich's career but emphasizes those written in the 1970s.

15. Rich entitled a 2001 collection of her selected and new poems *The Fact of a Doorframe*; in "Frame," included in this volume, she several times situates her narrator "just outside the frame / . . . trying to see."

16. Helen Vendler has argued that the lyric poem is "a script for performance by its reader" (*Poems*, xl) and "wants us to be its speaker" (185). More often, critics of lyric have associated the reader with the "you."

17. The essay was published in book form in 1993, and the poems of *Dark Fields* were composed, the subtitle indicates, between 1991 and 1995.

18. This situation, she goes on, affirms Arturo's claim that "there is no death, only dying" (27).

19. I am, I should make clear, making more systematic a distinction at which Rich's essay only hints. The passage I cited from the essay is followed by an amplification in which Rich seems to espouse something like identification, a situation in which "our own 'questions' meet . . . the world's 'questions,' [and] recognize how we are in the world and the world is in us—" (26).

20. Performative speech, in Austin's terms, equates "utter[ing] the sentence" with "do[ing]" what it says (6). It "make[s] a bet" (6) on what it defines as true. While Austin's terms do not correspond directly to Rich's statement, which refers to Arturo rather than to herself, it resembles what Austin terms a perlocutionary act, one that involves "what we bring about or achieve *by* saying something" (109).

21. The title, according to Rich's note, comes from Bertolt Brecht (75); the original text, Hedley notes, also refers to the difficulty of talking about trees (62).

22. In the note on the poem, Rich's attribution of the phrase "revolution in permanence" to Karl Marx confirms something like this second reading, emphasizing the persistence of the "future in the present" (77).

23. Two earlier poems, "Eastern War Time" (*Atlas* 35–44) and "1948: Jews" (*Atlas* 52), emphasize the contrast between someone resembling Rich herself—a part-Jewish girl living in the United States during World War II—and the events of the Holocaust. The juxtaposition of time and place reveals the discontinuity between the two situations, but the processes of memory are unhindered in these earlier poems; the scenes described seem real. Each of the sections of "Then or Now," in contrast, describes a chronologically and geographically distinct scene.

24. "Deportations," the only poem in the sequence directly to compare us with them and now with then, does so within a space explicitly characterized as dreamed.

25. William Logan accuses *Dark Fields* of both faults, calling the volume "a jeremiad" filled with "sketchy, angry poems" and an "icy tundra of abstraction."

Chapter Three

1. One part of the poem recounts a historical event—Berlioz's experience of his mother's death—while the other is mythological: the poem retells Ovid's myth of Cinyras's incestuous relationship with his daughter Myrrha, which Myrrha escapes by metamorphosing into a myrrh tree. For earlier poems on sexual violence, see the dramatic monolog "Herbert White" (*In the Western* 127–31); virtually all Bidart's early volumes contain poems dealing with extreme states of often suppressed suffering and guilt.

2. "In Memory of Joe Brainard," for example, refers directly to "the plague that full swift runs by" and "took you, broke you" (13). Brainard died of complications from AIDS.

3. Here it is unclear whether the description is of an actual dream or a state of grace that resembles a dream.

4. Other volumes that emphasize ghosts in relation to AIDS include Marie Howe's *What the Living Do* and Rafael Campo's *Diva*, several of whose poems are narrated by "the ghost of epidemiology."

5. Spargo has recently argued that "anti-elegy" characterizes modern elegy ("Contemporary"). Poetry is anti-elegiac, he claims, when it "deflat[es] poetry's value" and "empties poetry of its inherited cultural status" ("Contemporary" 414), partly by considering and then turning away from "elegiac convention" (416).

6. Gubar defines the term more specifically as "the impersonation of an absent speaker or a personification" (178), a definition consistent with the *Princeton Encyclopedia*, which defines it as "the speech of an imaginary person," in some cases "the dead" (Brogan and Halsall).

7. Gubar links Plath's poems' prosopopoeia with their rhetoric of death and suicide, claiming that "prosopopoeia in the Holocaust context shapes [her] unsettling, disturbing poetry" (*Poetry* 179). Simone Weil, according to Susan Sontag's gloss, asserts that "violence turns anyone subjected to it into a thing" (12).

8. John Vincent, for example, asserts that "queer lyrics do not simply record lives" and feelings but "at their best, . . . offer performances, or demonstrations, of living and feeling" (xiii).

9. The AIDS poems I discuss were composed at approximately the same time as Rich's *Dark Fields*.

10. Here Bidart describes "the plague you have *thus far* survived" but "they didn't," then acknowledges that the pronoun *you* is partly a stand-in for "I" (*Metaphysical* 82, italics added).

11. The activist camp was split between attempts to appeal to mainstream Americans through sympathetic identification and attempts to convey the true horrors of the disease.

12. Paula Treichler calls AIDS not "an invented label . . . for a clear-cut disease entity caused by a virus" but rather "constructed through language" (31); it is "a story" that must be read (42).

13. Stewart discusses the situation in which "one cannot intend to be possessed" in relation to several dialogues of Plato ("Lyric" 36).

14. Maslan claims that "Whitman's poetry claims literary and political authority by identifying itself as the product not of a sovereign individual but rather of a possessed one" (1); it insists that "people are or can be involuntary agents of a will greater than their own" (157). Moon asserts that Whitman "fuses . . . the invasive, automatic nature of the poetic impulse . . . with the involuntary nature of the sexual drive" (4) in a way that "sexualiz[es] . . . poetic inspiration" (7) and authenticates "the oldest form of cultural authority in the Western tradition: inspiration" (142).

15. The "New Poems" included in Doty's 2008 *Fire to Fire: Selected Poems* are grouped under the title "Theories and Apparitions" and include four poems entitled "Apparition" (9, 15, 21, 39), mostly concerning visions of long-dead poets.

16. Deborah Landau has also provided readings of both these poems, emphasizing Doty's general capacity to "envision . . . sustaining moments despite great suffering" (205), partly through "an ability to perceive animation in . . . a dying world" (207).

17. This "defensive appeal to literality," though, "produce[s] the literal *as a figure*" (313) and thus paradoxically undermines the possibility of "immunity" (312).

18. Simile and metaphor are, Doty argues, "not simply decorative devices"; rather, "metaphor [is] a kind of arguing, a 'thinking through' of what's implied in a relation between things apparently unlike" ("Speaking").

19. Several of the volume's poems, including "Long Point Light" (44–48) and "Nocturne in Black and Gold" (94–98) end by personifying the entities described (in these cases, respectively, a lighthouse and the bay) and allowing them to speak, often in the poem's last words.

20. Berger claims that because angels "do not come back from the dead," they indicate that the past can be "let go" (*After* 53). In contrast, ghosts are "a symptom of historical trauma" (52).

21. The late reference to "time" also disrupts the poem's refusal to acknowledge

the loss implicit in time's actual passage. And while the final "casual embraces" recall those shared by the poem's protagonists, they also refer to the ways that time itself embraces not the "us" of Paul and Rog but all who have survived.

22. Powell is the author of two subsequent collections that consider AIDS, *Lunch* and *Cocktails*; the topic of illness also recurs, but more obliquely in the 2009 *Chronic*.

23. The volume does, though, contain endnotes (68–71), which gloss many of these references.

24. Powell's introduction insists that his poems resist the idea that "'AIDS [is] a metaphor for a consumptive relationship'" (xii); "I do not understand 'metaphor.' I have the sort of mind that lumps together odd events, that enjoys the simultaneity of experience" (xii). Instead, he claims, "AIDS moves through the text, just as other forces, events and characters move through it" (xii).

25. The references to "us[ing] my teeth" and "burn[ing] him with my whiskers" may describe antipathy or love.

26. Powell received an HIV-positive diagnosis after *Tea* was completed (Burt 93 n.1); because of the availability of new drugs, this diagnosis was not, as it was for Monette, an automatic death sentence.

27. Powell has claimed in an interview that the poems of *Tea* are not elegies; while elegy speaks "for the community," his poems "sidestep speaking for any-one but myself" ("Between" 275), although he also acknowledges that "the elegiac mode does sweep in at the darndest times" (275).

28. The other is "Investiture at Cecconi's" (*Collected* 580).

Chapter Four

1. It is often noted that Graham's poems have moved from more to less con-tained forms and topics; more recent volumes tend to forego the possibility of unity in favor of more radically undefined and shifting surfaces. Graham's poems also reveal a recurrent concern with what Thomas Gardner identifies, citing Graham herself, as "*the now, the present, the invisible, or the eternal*" (Introduction, 8). Cal-vin Bedient notes that such concerns pertain to "the historical . . . burden of the present" and comments that Graham's poems in general focus on "the moment when . . . history [has] become unbearable" (282).

2. For references to waiting in more recent poems, see, for example, "The Er-rancy" (*Errancy* 4–6), "The Scanning" (*Errancy* 7–10), "Lapse" (*Place* 71–74), and "Employment" (*Place* 32–33). See also "End" (*Place* 23–25) and *The End of Beauty*, which includes the poem "What the End Is For" (26–29).

3. Roman Jakobson claimed in 1956 that metaphor involves relations of similar-ity, while metonymy emphasizes contiguity (129).

4. Helen Vendler focuses on Graham's poetics of lateness in one essay ("Fin" 249), and Thomas Gardner discusses her rhetoric of waiting (*Regions* 192–96), but neither associates these concerns with Graham's consideration of likeness, although Gardner elsewhere considers this element of the poems (190–91). Vendler describes Graham's references to history and lateness in terms of a particular historical moment, associating these references with "fin de siècle poetry," which she links to Graham's preoccupation with "ends" ("Fin" 244), including "the end of history" (245). In contrast to Vendler's historicism, Gardner associates Graham's recurrent references to waiting with larger philosophical questions pertaining to what he calls "what one does in that charged, temporarily immobile place where language's drives to master and sort and go on have been checked," a place in which "we examine and take responsibility for our lives in language" (*Regions* 192). Several critics have also argued that Graham's volume, in Vendler's terms elsewhere, "connect[s] things widely disparate in time and space by means of metaphor and simile" ("Mapping" 231), relying on what Bonnie Costello has called "allegor[y]" (39). Vendler has also noted the ways Graham "spatializes her own life" ("Fin" 246); Longenbach contrasts *Region*'s "spatial poems" with earlier poems of "negative argument" and later "linear" ones ("Jorie Graham's" 93).

5. Vendler, for example, describes the poems of *Region* as "autobiographical," focusing on "continuous narrative memory" ("Indigo" 173), although she has elsewhere argued that the volume combines three elements, "the autobiographical, the historical, and the mythical" ("Mapping" 227).

6. Graham has called her "belief that creating a restored sensibility is a way of affecting the consciousness of the race so that we might not destroy ourselves" "probably a delusion I create for myself in order to get myself off the hook" (Gardner, Interview 223).

7. For images of the panels, see Sullivan ("Orvieto Cathedral: The Low Reliefs").

8. The mosaics at Orvieto depict several scenes including the coronation and the assumption of the virgin. See Sullivan ("Orvieto Cathedral").

9. This poem, in which the speaker bathes a baby in a hotel room while a demonstration passes by, includes several references to an apparently actual "fire" in the streets below.

10. The reversal was based on new evidence. Demjanjuk was subsequently found guilty in Germany but deemed too frail to serve prison time; even after his 2012 death, it remained unclear whether or not he was Ivan (McFadden).

11. Costello concurs, asserting that "From the New World" implies that "all of this history really serves only as a trope" (38); Vendler emphasizes a "parallel" between its various scenes, especially (and problematically) the helpless "girl in the camp" and the similarly helpless grandmother ("Mapping" 229). In contrast,

Susan Gubar emphasizes the poem's "attention to the contradictions between the Shoah—an event defying all analogies—and literature itself" (*Poetry* 98).

12. Moreover, this look may be literal (it involves physically being looked at) or figurative (involving the capacity to "see" what is not readily apparent).

13. Costello, for example, calls Graham's "effort to cut . . . images [of contemporary violence] loose from sensational journalism . . . a little facile," associating the poems with a "display [of] a politically engaged and righteous sensibility" that lacks "much historical scrutiny or political reflection"; the poems "swerve" away from the "implications" of the narratives she invokes (38).

14. I cited above Graham's assertions both that readers are deeply distracted and that poems can "coax" them into action. Elsewhere, she acknowledges that while her poems express "those currents I see outside me that have potentially destroyed the world (and that are potentially unstoppable)" ("Conversation" 17), there remains hope that "we [can] each act" so that "we might, as a species, evolve out of the mess we've gotten into" (18). Her poems, Graham thus here implies, are attempts to intervene in and alter the outcome of what she sees as wrong in contemporary culture.

Chapter Five

1. Howe's writings are often associated with the disjunctive poetic practices of the Language poets. Perloff notes that Howe's poems have been "included in every anthology of 'Language poetry' to date," although Perloff also interrogates that category ("Language Poetry"). One reviewer of a critical study of Howe's writing calls Howe's poems "required reading for anyone interested in postmodern poetry and poetics" (Mossin 179).

2. This treatise's full title is, Howe indicates, *Bed Hangings: A Treatise on Fabrics and Styles in the Curtaining of Beds 1650–1850* (43).

3. The first *Bed Hangings* volume, for example, included illustrations by Susan Bee; sections of "Scare Quotes" were included in the essay "Ether Either," although this text focused not, as does *The Midnight*, on Stevenson's *The Master of Ballantrae* but on Bram Stoker's *Dracula*.

4. Elizabeth Joyce's study of this topic, which does not consider *The Midnight*, focuses on Howe's references to "framing and mapping," arguing that Howe "reshapes cultural configurations of space through her drive to infiltrate interstitial areas of 'third' spaces: the silences of history, the margins of the page, the placeless migrants, and the uncharted lands" (15). Joyce also emphasizes the ways that Howe blurs the spatial with the temporal (16–17).

5. Rather than looking back and forth through the interleaf at the frontispiece and title page, the two opening photos offer two views of the same page, something

possible only by reversing the photographic negative. Howe's double-sided discussion contains no page numbers.

6. Howe describes the man hesitating at "each line of transition between pavement slabs" and implies that his back-and-forth movement resembles "a chiasmus," in which "the second half of a sentence repeats the first; but with the order of the two main elements inverted" (115).

7. Laplanche and Pontalis define *displacement* as the "detach[ment]" of "an idea's emphasis, interest, or intensity" from that idea and its reattachment to "other ideas, which were originally of little intensity" (121). They also associate the concept with Freud's definition of obsessional neurosis, which they characterize as "the formation of a substitute by means of displacement" (122). For Freud, displacement is most evident in dreams.

8. Jakobson associates these modes with literary styles (metaphor is associated with romanticism, metonymy with realism [130]) and genres (poetry is primarily metaphoric while prose is metonymic [132–33]).

9. Later in his career, Jakobson asserted that both metaphor and metonymy "can result from substitution of one word for another (on the paradigmatic axis) or from combination (the succession of words on the syntagmatic axis)" (Martin, "Metonymy").

10. Craig Owens cites de Man's discussion of a case in which the "'necessary link' of [a] metaphor has been metonymized" (232) and argues more generally that "allegory is . . . the projection of the metaphoric axis of language onto its metonymic dimension" (208).

11. Graham has mostly been read as what Bonnie Costello calls an "heir to modernism" (qtd. in Karagueuzian 7), but Catherine Sona Karagueuzian calls her recent work "similar to late-Twentieth Century, Post-Modern poetry such as that of the Language Poets" (9).

12. In "allegorical structure," Owens claims, "one text is *read through another*, however fragmentary, intermittent, or chaotic their relationship may be" (204), and he associates this mode with the palimpsest (205), a term sometimes used in relation to Howe's poetic practices. Postmodern allegory, he continues, "finds its most comprehensive expression in the ruin" (206).

13. Megan Simpson argues that Howe's poems are fundamentally "paratactic" in that they "arrange . . . phrases, words, and lines of poetry . . . side by side rather than in . . . causal hypotactic relationships" (185). In contrast, Susan Vanderborg claims they exemplify a "postmodern palimpsest[ic]" aesthetic that "juxtaposes" different elements but also recombines them into a "visual collage" (62) that includes overlay and concealment. Michael Davidson's description of them as

"palimtexts" evokes both these tendencies. Including "a still-visible record of its responses to . . . earlier writings," palimtexts according to Davidson exemplify "a kind of ruin that emerges in an era when ruins no longer signify lost plenitude" (68). In Howe's work, earlier versions or texts are continually "displace[d]," a process spatially evident "as a kind of overwriting" (92).

14. Sacks's view that elegy moves from "loss to consolation" has been countered by a number of readers, especially readers of modern and contemporary elegy. For example, Jahan Ramazani has claimed that modern elegy refuses the "substitut[ion]" central to elegy in favor of an "immersion" in loss (*Poetry* 4).

15. Howe exemplifies this failure of expressivity by describing the gap between an actual object and assertions about its "exist[ence]": "If at the heart of language lies what language can't express, can it be false to say that the golden mountain which exists exists?" (70).

16. She claims, for example, that "I am told I played Titania," in a family production of *A Midsummer Night's Dream*, then wonders why she "know[s] only the Fairy's first speech by heart" (64).

17. For example, one photo, which serves as the cover illustration, depicts a book page, part of an interleaf, and behind that an image of a costumed woman.

18. Howe notes there the tendency of those aware of "what language can't express" to attempt to "capture for our world some soft object, a fuzzy conditional" (70).

19. According to one gloss, transitional objects help children "make the necessary shift from the earliest oral relationship with the mother to genuine object relationships" (Scheimberg).

20. Finkelstein and Bruns are among these readers.

21. In an interview, Howe asserts that when she writes she does not "hear voices" ("Interview" 33). Yet in response to a question about an earlier claim that "as a poet you feel you're taking dictation" (33)—the reference may be to Howe's claim in her 1993 critical study *The Birth-Mark* that her "writing has been haunted and inspired by a series of texts" (45)—Howe demurs: "No, no. I don't hear voices. . . . You don't hear voices, but yes, you're hearing something. You're hearing something you see. . . . Your hand is receiving orders from somewhere" (33).

22. Among these references are Howe's citation of Valdemar's request in Edgar Allen Poe's story "The Facts in the Case of M. Valdemar" to be both "put . . . to sleep" and "waken[ed]" because he is "dead" (*The Midnight* 144). Her citation of Henry James's reference to his still-living "correspondent" Robert Louis Stevenson as "a kind of unnatural uncomfortable unburied mort" (57) involves a similar slippage between living and death.

23. Peirce was the founder of American pragmatism. The poem, like the one

following, refers both to "Pragmatism" and to "Pragmaticism," a term later adopted by Peirce. Howe elsewhere cites and discusses Peirce's 1889 definition of nominalism (48–49, underlining in original).

24. Howe begins the poem by describing "numerous surviving / fair trees," and only afterward explains that these trees have been "wrought with a needle." Then she shifts back to a discussion of what is represented; the earlier "fair trees" become a singular but mutating "tree fair hunted Daphne."

25. Bloom has recently described his early work as an argument that influence is "*achieved* in a literary work, whether or not its author ever felt it" (*Anatomy* 6). His later definition of influence is "*literary love, tempered by defense*" (8), although he also maintains, as he did earlier in his career, that "strong or severe poets" attempt to "unname the precursor while earning [their] own name" (10).

26. Perloff elaborates this general claim in relation to a number of poems and sequences, including Howe's *The Midnight* (*Unoriginal* 99–122).

27. Manning left Ireland for America (119); the Scottish Stevenson lived in later life in the South Pacific, where he composed *The Master of Ballantrae*. I am grateful to Jahan Ramazani for suggesting this alternate reading (Respondent).

28. Jameson counters the notion that postmodernism is wholly "antipolitical" (158) by suggesting that a "Utopian" strain in postmodern art (159) and the "theoretical, nonfigurative" nature of this art (164–65) gesture toward political critique.

Coda

1. In the context of a discussion of trauma's "ruptures [of] the historical sense of time as such," Kalaidjian claims that "the special vantage point of the future anterior—conceiving a future in terms of what will have been—offers a salutary departure from history as a totalizing regime of the same" (10). Roland Barthes also uses this term, as I mentioned in chapter 5 (96), as does Judith Butler, in ways that I will discuss in more detail (*Frames* 15).

2. Bernard-Donals defines "forgetful memory" as a situation in which "the making present of what is irretrievably past acknowledges [the] absence" of coherence and of memory itself (14).

3. The poem is one of two with this title in Lerner's volume, which also has the same title.

4. Later, the speaker more directly commands, "Wake up, it's time to begin / The forgetting" (12).

5. The trajectory is not linear; the poem first chronicles the protagonist's capacity to "hear the actions / rushing past," which are followed by "the silence, / or whatever it is that follows," which itself contains a "buzzing."

6. Both Baraka and Pinsky were featured readers at this biannual festival in

Waterloo Village, New Jersey ("Geraldine"). The controversy about the poem derived largely from its assertion that "Israeli workers" knew ahead of time about the 9/11 attacks.

7. In contrast to Pinsky's description, one source describes the reading quite differently; it was met not by applause but instead "the crowd reacted with stunned silence, and several people booed" (Erickson).

8. The poem offers a self-consciously complex performance of voice that evokes Pinsky's views on the subject of persona and disguise, although Pinsky has expressed his discomfort with the convention of referring to the poetic "I" as "the speaker" ("A Poet"). In the context of this poem, Pinsky notes (in personal correspondence) his "longstanding resistance to a too-blanket use of the term 'the speaker,'" noting that "very early on, it was liberating for me to feel that sometimes the poet can speak with no more mask or dramatic character than any other kind of writer. Or speaker. I respect, sometimes even revere the dramatic. But in my own work I think more in terms of vocal inflection, ironic tones of voice, a whole gestural-vocal-idiomatic vocabulary that is as much 'me' or 'mine'" ("Message").

9. Butler's *Frames of War* considers, among other things, the ways that texts and photographs circulate within and outside the structures that attempt to frame them (9–11 passim).

Works Cited

Adorno, Theodor W. "Cultural Criticism and Society." *Prisms*. Trans. Shierry
  Weber Nicholsen and Samuel Weber. Cambridge: MIT P, 1983. 17–34. Print.
Altieri, Charles. "Contemporary American Poetry and Its Public Worlds." Poetry
  and the Public Sphere: The Conference on Contemporary Poetry. Rutgers
  University, New Brunswick, NJ. 24–27 Apr. 1997. Address. *Dept. of English,
  Rutgers University*. Web. June 2012.
Altman, Lawrence K. "New Homosexual Disorder Worries Health Officials."
  New York Times. New York Times, 11 May 1982. Web. 3 July 2012.
Ashbery, John. "Soonest Mended." *The Double Dream of Spring*. Boston: Dutton,
  1975. 17–20. Print.
Auden, W. H. "In Memory of W. B. Yeats." *Selected Poems*. Ed. Edward Mendel-
  son. New York: Random, 1989. 80–83. Print.
Austin, J. L. *How to Do Things with Words*. Cambridge: Harvard UP, 1975. Print.
Bahti, Timothy. "Figure, Scheme, Trope." Preminger and Brogan.
Baraka, Amiri. "Somebody Blew Up America." *Counterpunch*. Ed. Alexander
  Cockburn and Jeffrey St. Clair. Counterpunch, 3 Oct. 2002. Web. 13 Nov.
  2012.
Barthes, Roland. *Camera Lucida: Reflections on Photography*. Trans. Richard How-
  ard. New York: Hill and Wang, 1981. Print.
Baudrillard, Jean. *Selected Writings*. Ed. Mark Poster. 2nd ed. Stanford: Stanford
  UP, 2001. Print.
———. *The Spirit of Terrorism and Other Essays*. New York: Verso, 2003. Print.
Bedient, Calvin. "Toward a Jorie Graham Lexicon." Gardner, *Jorie Graham*
  275–91.
Benjamin, Walter. *Illuminations*. Ed. Hannah Arendt. New York: Harcourt, 1955.
  Print
"Belatedness." *Oxford English Dictionary Online*. Oxford UP, 2012. Web. 10 June
  2012.
Berger, James. *After the End: Representations of Post-Apocalypse*. Minneapolis:
  U of Minnesota P, 1999. Print.
———. "There's No Backhand to This." Greenberg 52–59.

Bernard-Donals, Michael. *Forgetful Memory: Representation and Remembrance in the Wake of the Holocaust.* Albany: State U of New York P, 2009. Print.

———. Rev. of *The Belated Witness: Literature, Testimony, and the Question of Holocaust Survival,* by Michael G. Levine, and *Testimony after Catastrophe: Narrating Traumas of Political Violence,* by Stevan Weine. *Comparative Literature Studies* 44.3 (2007): 340–45. *Ebscohost.* Web. 16 June 2012.

Bernard-Donals, Michael, and Richard Glejzer. *Between Witness and Testimony: The Holocaust and the Limits of Representation.* Albany: State U of New York P, 2001. Print.

Berryman, John. "Dream Song 29" ("There sat down, once"). *The Dream Songs.* New York: Farrar, 2007. 33. Print.

Bidart, Frank. *Desire.* New York: Farrar, 1997. Print.

———. *In the Western Night: Collected Poems, 1965–90.* New York: Farrar, 1990. Print.

———. *Metaphysical Dog: Poems.* New York: Farrar, 2013. Print.

———. *Star Dust.* New York: Farrar, 2005. Print.

Blanchot, Maurice. *The Writing of the Disaster.* Trans. Ann Smock. Lincoln: U of Nebraska P, 1995. Print.

Blasing, Mutlu Konuk. *Politics and Form in Postmodern Poetry: O'Hara, Bishop, Ashbery, and Merrill.* New York: Cambridge UP, 1995. Print.

Bloom, Harold. *The Anatomy of Influence: Literature as a Way of Life.* New Haven: Yale UP, 2011. Print.

———. *The Anxiety of Influence: A Theory of Poetry.* 2nd ed. New York: Oxford UP, 1997. Print.

———. *A Map of Misreading.* New York: Oxford UP, 2003. Print.

Boswell, Matthew. "'Black Phones': Postmodern Poetics in the Holocaust Poetry of Sylvia Plath." *Critical Survey* 20.2 (2008): 53–64. *Academic Search Premier.* Web. 17 May 2012.

Brain, Tracy. "Unstable Manuscripts: The Indeterminacy of the Plath Canon." *The Unraveling Archive: Essays on Sylvia Plath.* Ed. Anita Helle. Ann Arbor: U of Michigan P, 2007. 17–38. Print.

Britzolakis, Christina. *Sylvia Plath and the Theatre of Mourning.* New York: Oxford, 2000. Print.

Brogan, Kathleen. *Cultural Haunting: Ghosts and Ethnicity in Recent American Literature.* Charlottesville: UP of Virginia, 1998. Print.

Brogan, T. V. F., and Albert W. Halsall. "Prosopopoeia." Preminger and Brogan.

Brontë, Emily. *Wuthering Heights.* Ed. U. C. Knoepflmacher. New York: Cambridge UP, 1989. Print.

Brophy, Sarah. *Witnessing AIDS: Writing, Testimony, and the Work of Mourning.* Toronto: U of Toronto P, 2004. Print.

Bruns, Gerald L. "Voices of Construction: On Susan Howe's Poetry and Poetics (A Citational Ghost Story)." *Contemporary Literature* 50.1 (2009): 28–53. *Project MUSE.* Web. 6 Sept. 2012.

Buell, Frederick. "Sylvia Plath's Traditionalism." *Critical Essays on Sylvia Plath.* Ed. Linda W. Wagner. Boston: Hall, 1984. 140–53. Print.

Burt, Stephen. "Here Is the Door Marked *Heaven*: D. A. Powell." *American Poets in the 21st Century: The New Poetics.* Ed. Claudia Rankine and Lisa Sewell. Middletown: Wesleyan UP, 2007. 83–96. Print.

Butler, Judith. *Frames of War: When Is Life Grievable?* New York: Verso, 2010. Print.

———. *Gender Trouble: Feminism and the Subversion of Identity.* New York: Routledge, 1990. Print.

———. *Precarious Life: The Powers of Mourning and Violence.* New York: Verso, 2004. Print.

Cameron, Sharon. *Lyric Time: Dickinson and the Limits of Genre.* Baltimore: Johns Hopkins UP, 1979. Print.

Campo, Rafael. *Diva.* Durham: Duke UP, 1999. Print.

Caruth, Cathy. Introduction. *Trauma: Explorations in Memory.* Ed. Caruth. Baltimore: Johns Hopkins UP, 1995. 3–12. Print.

———. *Unclaimed Experience: Trauma, Narrative, and History.* Baltimore: Johns Hopkins UP, 1996. Print.

Chambers, Ross. *Untimely Interventions: AIDS Writing, Testimonial, and the Rhetoric of Haunting.* Ann Arbor: U of Michigan P, 2004. Print.

Costello, Bonnie. "The Big Hunger: *Region of Unlikeness* by Jorie Graham." *New Republic* 27 (Jan. 1992): 36–39. *Ebscohost.* Web. 27 July 2012.

Culler, Jonathan. "Why Lyric?" *PMLA* 123.1 (2008): 201–06. Print.

Davidson, Harriet. "Poetry, Witness, Feminism." *Witness and Memory: The Discourse of Trauma.* Ed. Ana Douglass and Thomas A. Vogler. New York: Routledge, 2003. 153–72. Print.

Davidson, Michael. *Ghostlier Demarcations: Modern Poetry and the Material Word.* Berkeley: U of California P, 1997. Print.

de Man, Paul. *Allegories of Reading: Figural Language in Rousseau, Nietzsche, Rilke, and Proust.* New Haven: Yale UP, 1979. Print.

———. "Semiology and Rhetoric." *Diacritics* 3.3 (1973): 27–33. *JSTOR.* Web. 6 Sept. 2012.

"Displacement." *Oxford English Dictionary Online.* Oxford UP, 2012. Web. 2 June 2012.

Docx, Edward. "Postmodernism Is Dead." *Prospect Magazine*. Prospect, 20 July 2011. Web. 20 Sept. 2013.

Donne, John. "A Valediction: Forbidding Mourning." *The Collected Poems of John Donne*. Roy Booth. Ware: Wordsworth Poetry Library, 1994. 33. Print.

Doty, Mark. *Atlantis: Poems*. New York: Harper, 1995. Print.

———. *Fire to Fire: New and Selected Poems*. New York: Harper, 2008. Print.

———. *Heaven's Coast: A Memoir*. New York: Harper, 1997. Print.

———. *My Alexandria: Poems*. Urbana: U of Illinois P, 1993. Print.

———. "Speaking in Figures." *Poets.org*. Academy of American Poets, n.d. Web. 3 July 2012.

———. "Souls on Ice ('A Display of Mackerel')." *Introspections: American Poets on One of Their Own Poems*. Ed. Robert Pack and Jay Parini. Middlebury: Middlebury College P, 1997. 70–77. Print.

Drayton, Michael. "Since There's No Help." *Elizabethan Sonnet-Cycles: Michael Drayton, Bartholomew Griffin, and William Smith*. Martha Foote Crowe. Charleston: BiblioBazaar, 2009. 70. Print.

Edelman, Lee. "The Plague of Discourse: Politics, Literary Theory, and AIDS." *South Atlantic Quarterly* 88.1 (1989): 301–17. Print.

Edkins, Jenny. *Trauma and the Memory of Politics*. New York: Cambridge UP, 2003. Print.

Eliot, T. S. *The Wasteland*. *T. S. Eliot: Collected Poems, 1909–1962*. Orlando: Harcourt, 1991. 51–76. Print.

Erickson, Ceilidh. "In Newark, Amiri Baraka Recites Infamous Poem Again, This Time to Applause." *Capital: This Is How New York Works*. Capital, 11 Oct. 2010. Web. 13 Nov. 2012.

Evans, Dylan. "Retroaction." *An Introductory Dictionary of Lacanian Psychoanalysis*. New York: Routledge, 1996. Print.

Felman, Shoshana. "Education and Crisis, or the Vicissitudes of Teaching." Felman and Laub 1–56.

Felman, Shoshana, and Dori Laub. *Testimony: Crises of Witnessing in Literature, Psychoanalysis, and History*. New York: Routledge, 1992. Print.

Finkelstein, Norman. "'Making the Ghost Walk About Again and Again': History as Séance in the Work of Susan Howe." *Literature Interpretation Theory* 20.3 (2009): 215–40. *Taylor & Francis Online*. Web. 6 Sept. 2012.

Forché, Carolyn. Introduction. *Against Forgetting: Twentieth-Century Poetry of Witness*. Ed. Forché. New York: Norton, 1993. 29–47. Print.

———. "The Lost and Unlost: Poetry and the Irrevocable Past." Interview with the Editors of *Poetry* Magazine. *Poetry Foundation.* Poetry, 2 May 2011. Web. 20 Sept. 2013.

———. "Reading the Living Archives: The Witness of Literary Art." *Poetry Foundation.* Poetry, 2 May 2011. Web. 20 Sept 2013.

Freud, Sigmund. "On Transience." *Standard* 14: 305–07.

———. "Remembering, Repeating, and Working-Through." Freud, *Standard* 12: 145–56.

———. "Screen Memories." Freud, *Standard* 3: 301–22.

———. *The Standard Edition of the Complete Psychological Works of Sigmund Freud.* Ed. James Strachey, et al. 24 vols. London: Hogarth, 1953–74. Print.

Fuss, Diana. "Corpse Poem." *Critical Inquiry* 30.1 (2003): 1–30. JSTOR. Web. 3 July 2012.

Gardner, Thomas. "An Interview with Jorie Graham." Gardner, *Regions* 214–237.

———, ed. *Jorie Graham: Essays on the Poetry.* Madison: U of Wisconsin P, 2005. Print.

———. Introduction. Gardner, *Jorie Graham* 3–12.

———. *Regions of Unlikeness: Explaining Contemporary Poetry.* Lincoln: U of Nebraska P, 1999. Print.

Geraldine R. Dodge Poetry Program. "2002." *Geraldine R. Dodge Poetry Program.* Geraldine R. Dodge Foundation, n.d. Web. 13 Nov. 2012.

Gilbert, Sandra M. "'A Fine, White Flying Myth': Confessions of a Plath Addict." *Massachusetts Review* 19.3 (1978): 585–603. JSTOR. Web. 17 May 2012.

Gilbert, Sandra M., and Susan Gubar. *No Man's Land: The Place of the Woman Writer in the Twentieth Century.* Vol. 3. New Haven: Yale UP, 1994. 266–318. Print.

Glück, Louise. *Averno.* New York: Farrar, 2006. Print.

Glück, Louise, and James Longenbach. *Lannan.* Lannan Foundation. Lensic Performing Arts Center, Santa Fe. 16 Feb. 2005. Reading and Conversation. Web. 10 June 2012.

Goodyear, Dana. "The Moneyed Muse." *New Yorker.* New Yorker, 19 Feb. 2007. Web. 20 Sept. 2013.

Gosmann, Uta. *Poetic Memory: The Forgotten Self in Plath, Howe, Hinsey, and Glück.* Lanham: Fairleigh Dickinson UP, 2011. Print.

Graham, Jorie. "A Conversation about *Materialism*." *Seneca Review* 24.2 (1994): 5–19. Print.

———. *The End of Beauty.* New York: Ecco, 1999. Print

———. *The Errancy.* New York: Ecco, 1998. Print.

———. Introduction. *The Best American Poetry, 1990.* Ed. Graham and David Lehman. New York: Collier, 1990. xv–xxxi. Print.

———. *Materialism*. New York: Ecco, 1993. Print.

———. *Place*. New York: Ecco, 2012. Print.

———. *Region of Unlikeness*. New York: Ecco, 1991. Print.

Greenberg, Judith, ed. *Trauma at Home: After 9/11*. Lincoln: U of Nebraska P, 2003. Print.

Gubar, Susan. *Poetry after Auschwitz: Remembering What One Never Knew*. Bloomington: Indiana UP, 2003. Print.

———. "Prosopopoeia and Holocaust Poetry in English: The Case of Sylvia Plath." *Yale Journal of Criticism* 14.1 (2001): 191–215. Print.

Gunn, Thom. *The Man with Night Sweats: Poems*. New York. Farrar, 2007. Print.

Hardy, Thomas. *Unexpected Elegies: "Poems of 1912–13" and Other Poems about Emma*. Ed. Claire Tomalin. New York: Persea Books, 2010. Print.

Heaney, Seamus. "The Indefatigable Hoof-Taps: Sylvia Plath." *The Government of the Tongue: Selected Prose 1978–1987*. New York: Farrar, 1990. 148–70. Print.

Hedley, Jane. *I Made You to Find Me: The Coming of Age of the Woman Poet and the Politics of Poetic Address*. Columbus: Ohio State UP, 2009. Print.

Helle, Anita. "Lessons from the Archive: Sylvia Plath and the Politics of Memory." *Feminist Studies* 31.3 (2005): 631–52. Print.

Hertz, Neil. "Lurid Figures." *Reading de Man Reading*. Ed. Lindsay Waters and Wlad Godzich. Minneapolis: U of Minnesota P, 1989. 82–104. Print.

———. "More Lurid Figures." *Diacritics* 20.3 (1990): 2–27. *JSTOR*. Web. 17 May 2012.

Hirsch, Marianne. "Marked by Memory: Feminist Reflections on Trauma and Transmission." *Extremities: Trauma, Testimony, and Community*. Ed. Nancy K. Miller and Jason Tougaw. Urbana: U of Illinois P, 2002. 71–91. Print.

Hogue, Cynthia. "Adrienne Rich's Political, Ecstatic Subject." *Women's Studies* 27.4 (1998): 413–29. *Ebscohost*. Web. 16 June 2012.

Howe, Irving. "The Plath Celebration: A Partial Dissent." 1972. *Sylvia Plath: Modern Critical Views*. Ed. Harold Bloom. New York: Chelsea, 1989. 5–16. Print.

Howe, Marie. *What the Living Do: Poems*. New York: Norton, 1999. Print.

Howe, Susan. *Bed Hangings*. Illus. Susan Bee. New York: Granary, 2001. Print.

———. *The Birth-Mark: Unsettling the Wilderness in American Literary History*. Hanover: UP of New England, 1993. Print.

———. "Ether Either." *Close Listening: Poetry and the Performed Word*. Ed. Charles Bernstein. New York: Oxford UP, 1998. 111–27. Print.

———. *Frame Structures: Early Poems 1974–1979*. New York: New Directions, 1996. Print.

———. "An Interview with Susan Howe." By Lynn Keller. *Contemporary Literature* 36.1 (1995): 1–34. *JSTOR*. Web. 6 Sept. 2012.

———. *The Midnight*. New York: New Directions, 2003. Print.

———. *That This*. New York: New Directions, 2010. Print.

Hughes, Frieda. Foreword. Plath, *Ariel Restored* xi–xxi.

Hughes, Ted. *Birthday Letters*. New York: Farrar, 1998. Print.

———. Introduction. Plath, *The Collected Poems*. 13–19.

Huyssen, Andreas. *Present Pasts: Urban Palimpsests and the Politics of Memory*. Palo Alto: Stanford UP, 2003. Print.

Irvine, Martin. "'The Postmodern,' 'Postmodernism,' 'Postmodernity': Approaches to Po-Mo." *Georgetown University*. 9 Sept. 2013. Web. 20 Sept. 2013.

Jackson, Virginia. "Who Reads Poetry?" *PMLA* 123.1 (2008): 181–87. Print.

Jakobson, Roman. "Two Aspects of Language and Two Types of Aphasic Disturbances." *On Language*. Ed. Linda R. Waugh and Monique Monville-Burston. Cambridge: Harvard UP, 1990. 115–133. Print.

Jameson, Fredric. *Postmodernism, or, The Cultural Logic of Late Capitalism*. Durham: Duke UP, 1991. Print.

Johnson, James William. "Lyric." Preminger and Brogan.

Joyce, Elisabeth W. *"The Small Space of a Pause": Susan Howe's Poetry and the Spaces Between*. Cranbury: Rosemont, 2010. Print.

Kalaidjian, Walter B. *The Edge of Modernism: American Poetry and the Traumatic Past*. Baltimore: Johns Hopkins UP, 2006. Print.

Karagueuzian, Catherine Sona. *"No Image There and the Gaze Remains": The Visual in the Work of Jorie Graham*. New York: Routledge, 2005. Print.

Keller, Lynn. *Re-Making It New: Contemporary American Poetry and the Modernist Tradition*. Cambridge: Cambridge UP, 1987. Print.

Keniston, Ann. "'Not Needed, Except as Meaning': Belatedness in Post-9/11 American Poetry." *Contemporary Literature* 54.4 (2011): 658–83. Print.

———. *Overheard Voices: Address and Subjectivity in Postmodern American Poetry*. New York: Routledge, 2006. Print.

Keniston, Ann, and Jeanne Follansbee Quinn. "Representing 9/11: Literature and Resistance." Introduction. *Literature after 9/11*. Ed. Keniston and Follansbee Quinn. New York: Routledge, 2008. 1–15. Print.

Keniston, Ann, and Jeffrey Gray. "Saying What Happened in the 21st Century." Introduction. *The New American Poetry of Engagement: A 21st Century Anthology*. Ed. Keniston and Gray. Jefferson: McFarland, 2012. 1–15. Print.

Kermode, Lloyd E. "Using Up Words in Paul Monette's AIDS Elegy." *Canadian Review of Comparative Literature* 30.1 (2003): 217–47. Web. 3 July 2012.

Kinzie, Mary. *A Poet's Guide to Poetry*. Chicago: U of Chicago P, 1999. Print.

Komunyakaa, Yusef, ed. *The Best American Poetry 2003*. New York: Scribner's, 2003. Print.

Lacan, Jacques. "The Mirror Stage as Formative of the *I* Function, as Revealed in Psychoanalytic Experience." *Écrits: A Selection*. Trans. Bruce Fink, Héloïse Fink, and Russell Grigg. New York: Norton, 2002. 3–9. Print.

LaCapra, Dominick. *History and Memory after Auschwitz*. Ithaca: Cornell UP, 1998. Print.

Landau, Deborah. "'How to Live, What to Do': The Poetics and Politics of AIDS." *American Literature* 68.1 (1996): 193–225. *JSTOR*. Web. 3 July 2012.

Langdell, Cheri Colby. *Adrienne Rich: The Moment of Change*. Westport: Praeger, 2004. Print.

Laplanche, Jean, and J.-B. Pontalis. *The Language of Psycho-Analysis*. New York: Norton, 1974. Print.

Laub, Dori. "An Event without a Witness: Truth, Testimony and Survival." Felman and Laub 75–92.

Lerner, Ben. *Angle of Yaw*. Port Townsend, WA: Copper Canyon, 2006. Print.

———. "From *déjà lu*." *New American Writing* 25. Ed. Paul Hoover and Maxine Chernoff. Mill Valley: Oink!, 2007. Web. 13 Nov. 2012.

———. *Mean Free Path*. Port Townsend: Copper Canyon, 2010. Print.

Levine, Michael G. *The Belated Witness: Literature, Testimony, and the Question of Holocaust Survival*. Stanford: Stanford UP, 2006. Print.

Leys, Ruth. *Trauma: A Genealogy*. Chicago: U of Chicago P, 2000. Print.

Logan, William. "Martyrs to Language: On *Can You Hear Bird* by John Ashbery; *Dark Fields of the Republic: Poems 1991–1995* by Adrienne Rich; *Red Sauce, Whiskey, and Snow* by August Kleinzahler; *The Art of Drowning* by Billy Collins; *Mother Love* by Rita Dove; *Passing Through: The Later Poems, New and Selected* by Stanley Kunitz; and *Worldling* by Elizabeth Spires." *New Criterion* (Dec. 1995): n. pag. *New Criterion*. Web. June 2012.

Longenbach, James. "Jorie Graham's Big Hunger." Gardner, *Jorie Graham* 82–101.

———. *Modern Poetry after Modernism*. Oxford: Oxford UP, 1997. Print.

Lowell, Robert. "Epilogue." *Day by Day*. New York: Farrar, 1977. 127. Print.

Lyotard, Jean-François. *The Differend: Phrases in Dispute*. Trans. Georges Van Den Abbeele. Minneapolis: U of Minnesota P, 1988. Print.

MacLeish, Archibald. "Ars Poetica." *Collected Poems 1917–1982*. Boston: Mariner, 1985. 106. Print.

Martin, Wallace. "Metaphor." Preminger and Brogan.

———. "Metonymy." Preminger and Brogan.

Maslan, Mark. *Whitman Possessed: Poetry, Sexuality, and Popular Authority*. Baltimore: Johns Hopkins UP, 2001. Print.

McFadden, Robert D. "John Demjanjuk, 91, Dogged by Charges of Atrocities as Nazi Camp Guard, Dies." *New York Times*. 17 Mar. 2012. Web. 27 July 2012.

Merrill, James. *The Changing Light at Sandover*. New York: Atheneum, 1982. Print.

———. "Farewell Performance." *Collected Poems*. New York: Knopf, 2001. 581–82. Print.

———. *A Scattering of Salts: Poems*. New York: Knopf, 1995. Print.

Milton, John. "Lycidas." *The Complete Poetry and Essential Prose of John Milton*. Ed. William Kerrigan, John Rumrich, and Stephen M. Fallon. New York: Modern Library, 2007. 99–109. Print.

Monette, Paul. *Borrowed Time: An AIDS Memoir*. New York: Harcourt, 1988. Print.

———. *Love Alone: Eighteen Elegies for Rog*. Boston: St. Martin's, 1988. Print.

Moon, Michael. *Disseminating Whitman: Revision and Corporeality in* Leaves of Grass. Cambridge: Harvard UP, 1993. Print.

Moore, Marianne. *The Poems of Marianne Moore*. Ed. Grace Schulman. Penguin Classics Reprint Ed. New York: Penguin, 2009. Print.

Mossin, Andrew. Rev. of *Led by Language: The Poetry and Poetics of Susan Howe* by Rachel Tzvia Back. *Partial Answers: Journal of Literature and the History of Ideas* 1.2 (2003): 173–83. Web. 20 Sept. 2013.

Nealon, Jeffrey. *Post-Postmodernism: or, the Cultural Logic of Just-in-Time Capitalism*. Palo Alto: Stanford UP, 2013. Print.

Nelson, Deborah. "Plath, History, and Politics." *The Cambridge Companion to Sylvia Plath*. Ed. Jo Gill. New York: Cambridge UP, 2006. 21–35. Print.

Orr, Peter, ed. *The Poet Speaks: Interviews with Contemporary Poets*. London: Routledge, 1966. Print.

Owens, Craig. "The Allegorical Impulse: Toward a Theory of Postmodernism." *Art after Modernism: Rethinking Representation*. Ed. Brian Wallis. Boston: Godine, 1984. 203–38. Print.

Peel, Robin. *Writing Back: Sylvia Plath and Cold War Politics*. Madison: Fairleigh Dickinson UP. 2002. Print.

Perloff, Marjorie. "Language Poetry and the Lyric Subject: Ron Silliman's Albany, Susan Howe's Buffalo." *Critical Inquiry* 25.3 (1999): 405–34. *Electronic Poetry Center*. Web. 6 Sept. 2012.

———. "The Two *Ariels*: The (Re)Making of the Sylvia Plath Canon." *American Poetry Review* (Nov./Dec. 1984): 10–18. *JSTOR*. Web. June 2012.

———. *Unoriginal Genius: Poetry by Other Means in the New Century*. Chicago: U of Chicago P, 2010. Print.

———. *21st-Century Modernism: The "New" Poetics.* Oxford: Wiley-Blackwell, 2002. Print.

Pinsky, Robert. "9/11." *Washington Post*, 8 Sept. 2002. Web. 16 May 2012.

———. "Anniversary." Komunyakaa 140–42.

———. "Commencement Speech." Stanford University. Stanford University, Palo Alto. 13 June 1999. Address. *Modern American Poetry.* Web. 16 May 2012.

———. *Gulf Music.* New York: Farrar, 2007. Print.

———. Message to the author. 2 July 2012. E-mail.

———. "A Poet by Any Other Name: Who Is 'The Speaker' and Does It Matter?" *Slate Magazine.* 17 July 2012. Web. 20 Sept. 2013.

———. "Poetry and American Memory." *Atlantic Monthly*, Oct. 1999: n. pag. *Modern American Poetry.* Web. 16 May 2012.

Plath, Sylvia. *Ariel.* New York: Perennial, 1965. Print.

———. *Ariel: The Restored Edition: A Facsimile of Plath's Manuscript, Reinstating Her Original Selection and Arrangement.* New York: Harper, 2004. Print.

———. *The Collected Poems.* Ed. Ted Hughes. New York: Harper, 1998. Print.

———. "Context." *Johnny Panic and the Bible of Dreams: Short Stories, Prose, and Diary Excerpts.* New York: Harper, 1962. 64–65. Print.

———. "Daddy." MS. Sylvia Plath Collection. William Allan Neilson Lib., Smith College, Northampton.

———. "Lady Lazarus." MS. Sylvia Plath Collection. William Allan Neilson Lib., Smith College, Northampton.

Poe, Edgar Allan. "The Raven." *Complete Stories and Poems of Edgar Allan Poe.* New York: Doubleday, 1984. 754–55. Print.

Pound, Ezra. *ABC of Reading.* New York: New Directions, 2010. Print.

Powell, D. A. "Between the Brackets: An Interview with D. A. Powell." By Matthew Cooperman. *A Centenary Portfolio on Louis Zukofsky.* Spec. issue of *Chicago Review* 50 (2004): 265–81. *JSTOR.* Web. 3 July 2012.

———. *Chronic.* Port Townsend: Graywolf Press, 2009. Print.

———. *Cocktails.* Port Townsend: Graywolf Press, 2004. Print.

———. *Lunch.* Middletown: Wesleyan UP, 2000. Print.

———. *Tea.* Middletown, CT: Wesleyan UP, 1998. Print.

Preminger, Alex, and T. V. F. Brogan, eds. *The New Princeton Encyclopedia of Poetry and Poetics.* Princeton: Princeton UP, 1993. *Literature Online.* Web. 6 Sept. 2012.

Ramazani, Jahan. *Poetry of Mourning: The Modern Elegy from Hardy to Heaney.* Chicago: U of Chicago P, 1994. Print.

———. Respondent. "New Approaches to Elegy." Modern Language Association Convention. Washington, D.C. 2005.

Ramazani, Jahan, Richard Ellmann, and Robert O'Clair, eds. *Norton Anthology of Modern and Contemporary Poetry*. 2 vols. New York: Norton, 1993. Print.

Redfield, Marc. "Virtual Trauma: The Idiom of 9/11." *Diacritics* 37.1 (2007): 55–80. *Project MUSE*. Web. 10 Oct. 2013.

Rich, Adrienne. *An Atlas of the Difficult World: Poems 1988–1991*. New York: Norton, 1991. Print.

———. *Dark Fields of the Republic: Poems 1991–1995*. New York: Norton, 1995. Print.

———. "Dearest Arturo." Rich, *What Is Found There* 22–27.

———. *The Fact of a Doorframe: Poems 1950–2001*. New ed. New York: Norton, 2002. Print.

———. "Frame." Rich, *The Fact of a Doorframe* 187–92.

———. *Midnight Salvage: Poems 1995–1998*. New York: Norton, 1999. Print.

———. "Someone Is Writing a Poem." 12 May 2010. *Poetry Foundation*. Web. 11 Feb. 2013.

———. *What Is Found There: Notebooks on Poetry and Politics*. New York: Norton, 1993. Print.

Ricoeur, Paul. "Word, Polysemy, Metaphor: Creativity in Language." *A Ricoeur Reader: Reflection and Imagination*. Ed. Mario J. Valdés. Buffalo: U of Toronto P, 1991. 65–85. Print.

Rose, Jacqueline. *The Haunting of Sylvia Plath*. Cambridge: Harvard UP, 1993. Print.

Rothschild, Matthew. "Adrienne Rich: 'I Happen to Think Poetry Makes a Huge Difference.'" *Progressive*, Jan. 1994: n. pag. *Modern American Poetry*. Web. 20 Dec. 2012.

Sacks, Peter M. *The English Elegy: Studies in the Genre from Spenser to Yeats*. Baltimore: Johns Hopkins UP, 1985. Print.

Scheimberg, Nora. "Transitional Object." *International Dictionary of Psychoanalysis*. 2005. *Encyclopedia.com*. Web. 6 Sept. 2012.

Shakespeare, William. *The Tempest*. Ed. Stephen Orgel. Oxford World Classics Reprint Ed. Oxford: Oxford UP, 2008.

Silverman, Kaja. *The Threshold of the Visible World*. New York: Routledge, 1996. Print.

Simpson, David. *9/11: The Culture of Commemoration*. Chicago: U of Chicago P, 2006. Print.

Simpson, Megan. *Poetic Epistemologies: Gender and Knowing in Women's Language-Oriented Writing*. Albany: State U of New York P, 2000. Print.

Smith, Kendall Marie. *A Postmodern Poetics of Witness in the Poetry of Elizabeth Bishop, Adrienne Rich, and Lorna Dee Cervantes*. Riverside: U of California P, 2009. Print.

Sontag, Susan. *Regarding the Pain of Others*. New York: Farrar, 2003. Print.

Spargo, R. Clifton. *The Ethics of Mourning: Grief and Responsibility in Elegiac Literature*. Baltimore: Johns Hopkins UP, 2004. Print.

———. "The Contemporary Anti-Elegy." *The Oxford Handbook of the Elegy*. Ed. Karen Weisman. New York: Oxford UP, 2010. 413–29. Print.

Spiegelman, Art. *Maus I*. New York: Pantheon, 1986. Print.

———. *Maus II*. New York: Pantheon, 1991. Print.

Steiner, George. *Language and Silence: Essays on Language, Literature, and the Inhuman*. New York: Atheneum, 1967. Print.

Stevenson, Anne. *Bitter Fame: A Life of Sylvia Plath*. Boston: Houghton, 1989. Print.

Stewart, Susan. "Lyric Possession." *Critical Inquiry* 22.1 (1995): 34–63. JSTOR. Web. 3 July 2012.

———. *Poetry and the Fate of the Senses*. Chicago: U of Chicago P, 2002. Print.

Strangeways, Al. "'The Boot in the Face': The Problem of the Holocaust in the Poetry of Sylvia Plath." *Contemporary Literature* 37.3 (1996): 370–90. Print.

Sturken, Marita. *Tangled Memories: The Vietnam War, the AIDS Epidemic, and the Politics of Remembering*. Berkeley: U of California P, 1997. Print.

"Substitution." *Oxford English Dictionary Online*. Oxford UP, 2012. Web. June 2012.

Sullivan, Mary Ann. "Orvieto Cathedral." *Digital Imaging Project*. Bluffton University, n.d. Web. 27 July 2012.

———. "Orvieto Cathedral: The Low Reliefs." *Digital Imaging Project*. Bluffton University, n.d. Web. 27 July 2012.

Treichler, Paula A. "AIDS, Homophobia, and Biomedical Discourse: An Epidemic of Signification." *AIDS: Cultural Analysis, Cultural Activism*. Ed. Douglas Crimp. Cambridge: MIT Press, 1988. 31–70. Print.

Vanderborg, Susan. *Paratextual Communities: American Avant-Garde Poetry since 1950*. Carbondale: Southern Illinois UP, 2001. Print.

Van Dyne, Susan. *Revising Life: Sylvia Plath's Ariel Poems*. Chapel Hill: U of North Carolina P, 1993. Print.

Vendler, Helen. "Fin-de-Siècle Poetry: Jorie Graham." Vendler, *Soul Says* 244–56.

———. "Indigo, Cyanine, Beryl: Review of *Never* (2003)." Gardner, *Jorie Graham* 170–84.

———. "Mapping the Air: Adrienne Rich and Jorie Graham." Vendler, *Soul Says* 212–34.

———. *Poems, Poets, Poetry: An Introduction and Anthology*. 3rd ed. Boston: Bedford/St. Martin's, 2009. Print.

————. *Soul Says: On Recent Poetry.* Cambridge: Harvard UP, 1995. Print.

Vincent, John. *Queer Lyrics: Difficulty and Closure in American Poetry.* New York: Palgrave, 2002. Print.

Webster's New Collegiate Dictionary. 2nd ed. Springfield: G & C Merriam, 1949. Sylvia Plath Collection. William Allan Neilson Library, Smith College, Northampton.

Weeks, Jeffrey. "Post-Modern AIDS?" *Ecstatic Antibodies: Resisting the AIDS Mythology.* Ed. Sunil Gupta and Tessa Boffin. London: Rivers Oram, 1990. 133–41. Print.

"What Is the Origin of the Word 'Holocaust'?" *United States Holocaust Memorial Museum.* United States Holocaust Memorial Museum, 2008. Web. 17 May 2012.

White, Edmund, ed. *Loss within Loss: Artists in the Age of AIDS.* Madison: U of Wisconsin P, 2001. Print.

Whitehead, Anne. *Trauma Fiction.* Edinburgh: Edinburgh UP, 2004. Print.

Whitman, Walt. "Song of Myself." *Whitman: Complete Poetry and Selected Prose.* Ed. Justin Kaplan. New York: Library of America, 1982. Print.

Wiesel, Elie. "Nobel Peace Prize Acceptance Speech Delivered by Elie Wiesel in Oslo on December 10, 1986." *Night.* Trans. Marion Wiesel. New York: Hill and Wang, 2006. 117–20. Print.

Wilkomirski, Binjamin. *Fragments: Memories of a Wartime Childhood.* New York: Schocken, 1997. Print.

Williams, William Carlos. *Collected Poems.* Ed. A. Walton Litz and Christopher J. MacGowan. 2 vols. New York: New Directions, 1986. Print.

Winnicott, Donald W. "Transitional Objects and Transitional Phenomena." *Playing and Reality.* New York: Routledge, 1999. 1–25. Print.

"Witness." *Oxford English Dictionary Online.* Oxford UP, 2012. Web. 3 June 2012.

Wordsworth, William. Preface to *Lyrical Ballads.* 1802. *University of Pennsylvania, Department of English.* Web. 12 Feb 2012.

Yeats, William Butler. "King and No King." *The Collected Poems of W. B. Yeats.* Ed. Richard J. Finneran. 2nd rev. ed. New York: Scribner's, 1996. 91. Print.

Young, James E. *At Memory's Edge: After-Images of the Holocaust in Contemporary Art and Architecture.* New Haven: Yale UP, 2002. Print.

————. *Writing and Rewriting the Holocaust: Narrative and the Consequences of Interpretation.* Bloomington: Indiana UP, 1988. Print.

Zeiger, Melissa F. *Beyond Consolation: Death, Sexuality, and the Changing Shapes of Elegy.* Ithaca: Cornell UP, 1997. Print.

Zeitlin, Froma I. "The Vicarious Witness: Belated Memory and Authorial Presence in Recent Holocaust Literature." *History and Memory* 10.2 (1998): 5–42. *Ebscohost*. Web. 16 June 2012.

Žižek, Slavoj. *Welcome to the Desert of the Real!: Five Essays on September 11 and Related Dates*. New York: Verso, 2002. Print.

Index

Abu Ghraib, 70

"Act III, Sc. 2" (Graham), 1, 2, 146, 187, 191

Address: and belatedness, 67, 108; and Bidart, 18, 91–93, 186, 189, 200n44; Butler on, 88, 193; in Celan, 68–69; and disruption, 69; and Doty, 102–10; Felman on, 68–69; and Graham, 2, 148, 187; and Gunn, 116–21; and Howe, 162, 168–69, 173–76; and Merrill, 116–21, 189; and Pinsky, 192; and Plath, 27–28, 37, 41, 47, 51–53, 57, 61–66, 203n25; and Rich, 27, 61–91, 96, 124, 142, 192–94, 205n9; Stewart on, 68; and trauma theory, 67–69. *See also* Apostrophe; Reader address

Adorno, Theodor, 11, 197n20

AIDS: as condition, 96, 97, 107, 116; figurative meaning of, 97, 209n24; personification of, 104; and politics, 98, 105; rhetoric of, 97, 104, 111, 195n2, 208n12, 209n24; test, 102, 104, 115; and trauma, 94. *See also* AIDS poetry; Elegy

AIDS poetry: ash in, 116–20; and Bidart, 91–94, 96–97, 100; and Doty, 98, 99–106; as elegy, 95, 108, 160–62, 166, 172; general features of, 27–29, 94–97, 151; ghosts in,

94–96, 107, 109, 112–13, 115, 121; and Gunn, 116–18; and Merrill, 102, 116, 118–22; and Monette, 106–11; and Powell, 111–16. *See also* AIDS; Elegy; Immunity as poetics; Infection as poetics; Prosopopoeia

Allegory, 158, 210n4, 212n10, 212n12, 214n28

Altieri, Charles, 86

American culture, 182–84, 199n32, 211n14

"Amnesiac" (Plath), 57–59, 184

"And eventually I would take him back" (Powell), 114, 127

"And Now" (Rich), 82–84

Animation: and Doty, 102–8, 115–19, 208n16; and Graham, 125, 145–48; and "Lady Lazarus" (Plath), 52–54; and "The Second Hour" (Bidart), 93. *See also* Prosopopoeia

Anti-elegy, 95, 106, 196n8, 207n5. *See also* Elegy

Apostrophe: and AIDS poetry, 95–96; and elegy, 47; and Howe, 172; and Monette, 110; and Plath, 27, 37, 47, 50–51; and Rich, 61, 65, 68–71. *See also* Address

Appropriation, 10, 85, 136, 171. *See also* Quotation

"Little Fugue" (Plath), 55
Logan, William, 207n25
Longenbach, James, 143–44, 210n4
Love Alone (Monette). *See* Monette,
    Paul; *specific poems*
Lowell, Robert, 16, 199n33
Lyotard, Jean-François, 10–11, 197n20

MacLeish, Archibald, 74
"Magi" (Plath), 53, 55
The Man with Night Sweats (Gunn). *See*
    Gunn, Thom; *specific poems*
Manning, Mary, 160–66, 172–77
"Mary Manning presents this book"
    (Howe), 174–75
"Mary's Song" (Plath), 55
Maslan, Mark, 208n14
"Mean Free Path" (Lerner), 183–84,
    188
Memory: and American culture, 11;
    Bernard-Donals on, 183, 214n2; and
    Gosmann, 203n28; and the Holo-
    caust, 57; and Howe, 160–67, 177–
    79; LaCapra on, 198n27, 204n2; and
    Pinsky, 20–22, 190–92, 200n41;
    and postmodernism, 158; and post-
    war poems, 183; Wiesel on, 197n23
Merrill, James: "Farewell Perfor-
    mance," 116–18, 189–91; and ghost-
    liness, 103; "An Upward Look,"
    120–21
Metaphor: in AIDS rhetoric, 97–98,
    104; de Man on, 157; and Doty, 98,
    102–4, 107, 112–13, 153, 208n18;
    Edelman on, 104; and elegy, 161;
    and ghosts, 17; and Graham,
    124–29, 133–43, 148, 153, 158; and
    Howe, 159–61, 170; Jakobson on,
    157, 209n3, 212n8; and metonymy,

158; and Plath, 28, 32–36, 41–45, 49,
    54, 124, 153, and postmodernism,
    158; and Powell, 113, 209n24; and
    Rich, 74, 79, 81, 95; and Ricoeur, 36;
    Vendler on, 210n4; Young on, 35,
    197n21, 202n14, 202n19
Metonymy: characteristics of, 195n3;
    definition of, 156, 159; and Graham,
    29, 125–27, 135, 140; and Howe,
    29, 153–79; Jakobson on, 209n3,
    212nn8–9; and MacLeish, 74; and
    metaphor, 158; and Plath, 32, 36,
    43–49, 124; as poetics, 160–62,
    177–78. *See also* Spatialization
The Midnight (Howe). *See* Howe,
    Susan; *specific poems*
Miller, D. A, 113
Modernism, 8, 9, 196n14, 199n35
Monette, Paul: and AIDS poetry, 98–
    99, 106–7; and ghostliness, 112–16;
    "The House on King's Road," 107–8;
    "No Goodbyes," 110–11; "Three
    Rings," 110

Narrative, 67, 129–32, 145
Nelson, Deborah, 202n13
"No Goodbyes" (Monette), 110
"Nocturne in Black and Gold" (Doty),
    105
Nonwitness, 15, 62. *See also* Witness

Olmsted, Frederick Law, 164–65, 176
Owens, Craig, 158, 212n10

Parody, 51
Peel, Robin, 35, 202n13
Performance: and AIDS poetry, 96; and
    American culture, 184–85; and Ash-
    bery, 188; and belatedness, 15, 29;

and Bidart, 23, 189; and Graham, 127–29, 145–49, 152, 188; and Gunn, 96, 118; and Howe, 172–77; and Lerner, 183; and Merrill, 118, 119–20, 189–93; and Pinsky, 29, 190–92, 215n8; and Plath, 35, 38, 41, 46, 48, 51–59, 96, 202n15; and postwar poetry, 184–85; in queer lyrics, 207n8; and Rich, 72, 96, 194; theatrical, 2, 175; Vendler on, 206n16

Performative speech, 72, 206n20. *See also* Austin, J. L.

Perloff, Marjorie, 171, 176, 204n35, 211n1

Personification, 102–4, 125, 144, 207n6, 208n19. *See also* Prosopopoeia

Pinsky, Robert: "The Anniversary," 7–8, 20–22, 53, 191, 200n40; "The Forgetting," 29, 190, 192–94; and September 11, 2001, 191–94, 214n6

Plath, Sylvia: "Amnesiac," 57–58, 184; "Ariel," 54; "The Bee Meeting," 54; *The Colossus*, 203n28; "The Couriers," 203n31, 204n32; critical approaches to, 33–35, 42, 53, 62–63, 201n9, 202n22; "Cut," 54; "Daddy," 27, 35–50, 53–58, 196n9, 201n3, 202n21, 203n23; "The Detective," 53; dictionary underlining, 45, 50; "Elm," 54, 55; "Fever 103°," 54; "Getting There," 53, 204n37; "Gulliver," 53; and haunting, 201n2; and Holocaust, 31, 59; and Hughes, 201n6; and Jewishness, 43; "Lady Lazarus," 35–42, 47–58, 61–64, 96, 202n15; "Little Fugue," 55; "Magi," 53, 55; "Mary's Song," 55; and metaphor, 34–35, 202n14; and performance,

46; "Poppies in October," 53; "Purdah," 53, 55; "Sheep in Fog," 56; "Stings," 54; and suicide, 32–33, 42, 52, 56, 59; "The Swarm," 55; "Thalidomide," 54; "Totem," 56; and witness, 61, 64; "Years," 56. See also *Ariel*

Poetic reception, 185, 193

Poetics: belatedness as, 7, 24, 32, 129; of immunity, 28, 98–99, 102–4; of infection, 27–28, 98–99, 111, 115–16

Pontalis, J.-B., 12, 212n7

"Poppies in October" (Plath), 53

Possession: and AIDS poetry, 99, 101, 105, 107, 113; in Bidart, 93, 100; as trope, 98

Posthumousness: and AIDS poetry, 95, 108–11; and anti-elegy, 115; and Howe, 172; and Merrill, 122; and performance, 96; and Plath, 33, 36, 56

Postmemory, 15

Postmodernism: characteristics of, 26, 35, 154, 157–58, 171, 197n15; and Plath, 202n17; and poetry, 9, 211n1; and politics, 177; Žižek on, 19

Post-postmodernism, 200n49

Postwar period, 9, 10, 15–16, 24, 59, 157

Postwar poetry, 127, 153, 179, 195n5, 196n13, 199n36

Pound, Ezra, 15

Powell, D. A.: and AIDS poetry, 110–16, 209n22, 209n24; and anti-elegy, 95; "Dead boys make the sweetest lovers," 112; "And eventually I would take him back," 112, 114, 127; and poetics of infection, 98–99; "Sleek mechanical dart," 114–15

and Plath, 50–52; poetry of, 14, 63–66, 80, 85–88, 100, 205nn6–7; and Rich, 27, 70, 76, 87
"Words for Some Ash" (Gunn), 116–18
Wordsworth, William, 8
Wuthering Heights (Brontë), 162

"Years" (Plath), 56
Yeats, William Butler, 176

Young, James: and the Holocaust, 11, 15, 197n21, 198n23, 198n31, 202n19; on Plath, 35–36, 202n14

Zeiger, Melissa, 94
Zeitlin, Froma, 204n2
Žižek, Slavoj, 199n37

Contemporary North American Poetry Series

Paracritical Hinge:
Essays, Talks, Notes, Interviews
By Nathaniel Mackey
University of Wisconsin Press, 2004

Behind the Lines: War Resistance
Poetry on the American Homefront
By Philip Metres

Hold-Outs: The Los Angeles Poetry
Renaissance, 1948–1992
By Bill Mohr

In Visible Movement:
Nuyorican Poetry from the
Sixties to Slam
By Urayoán Noel

Frank O'Hara:
The Poetics of Coterie
By Lytle Shaw

Renegade Poetics: Black Aesthetics
and Formal Innovation in African
American Poetry
By Evie Shockley

Radical Vernacular:
Lorine Niedecker and the
Poetics of Place
Edited by Elizabeth Willis